MIMESIS
INTERNATIONAL

PHILOSOPHY
n. 37

ANNA ICHINO

THE IMAGINATIVE MIND

Imagination's Role in Human Cognition and Culture

MIMESIS
INTERNATIONAL

© 2020 – MIMESIS INTERNATIONAL
www.mimesisinternational.com
e-mail: info@mimesisinternational.com

Isbn: 9788869772993
Book series: *Philosophy,* n. 37

© MIM Edizioni Srl
P.I. C.F. 02419370305

CONTENTS

To Pietro and Lapo,
Whose imagination inspires much thinking

ACKNOWLEDGEMENTS

This book draws on my doctoral dissertation, which was successfully defended at the University of Nottingham in June 2015, being approved without corrections.

I owe big thanks to my PhD supervisors – Greg Currie, Stefano Predelli and Paolo Spinicci. Among many other things, I am especially grateful to Greg for all that I learnt from our co-writing, and for some of the best philosophical discussions I ever had in my life; to Stefano, for all his careful, subtle, and fun comments on earlier drafts of this material; and to Paolo, for the invaluable support and inspiration that he has been giving me since I first met him many years ago as an undergraduate student – it is thanks to his courses that I first felt in love with the philosophy of imagination, and thanks to his continuous encouragements that I kept pursuing my research on these themes, and, indeed, that finally I decided to publish this book.

I am also grateful to my PhD examiners Tim Bayne, Clotilde Calabi, Mark Jago, and Stefano Velotti – who also encouraged me to get this material published, providing insightful feedback on it which has informed my thinking on these themes ever since.

Precious feedback on different parts of this work at different stages of its elaboration came from many other people as well. Among them, I wish to thank in particular James Andow, Marianna Bergamaschi Ganapini, Lisa Bortolotti, Alon Chasid, Paul L. Harris, Jules Holroyd, Dimitria Gatzia, Alex Geddes, David Ingram, Ben McGorrigan, Komarine Romdenh-Romluc, Shen-y Liao, Kengo Myazono, Aaron Meskin, Bence Nanay, Neil Sinhababu, Ema Sullivan-Bissett, Lu Teng, and Alberto Voltolini.

Last but not least, I wish to thank my family and friends for their unconditional love and support. I hope they know how much they mean to me and how deep is my gratitude.

Milan, 24th January 2020

INTRODUCTION

This book offers an account of the imagination which is to some extent revisionary but not so revisionary that we have left the folk conception of the imagination entirely behind. I argue that the imagination to which we so often appeal in ordinary thought and talk has some surprising features, including a capacity to inform behaviour in ways normally understood to be the province of belief alone.

In Chapter 1 I address some methodological issues that the project faces. What is it that makes one account of such things as imagination, belief, desire, emotion, etc. better than another? I identify three basic dimensions along which we can measure the success of such an account: (1) closeness to folk-psychological assumptions; (2) explanatory power concerning various aspects of our experience/behaviours; and (3) integration with the best scientific theories of cognition.

Chapter 2 starts from the examination of paradigmatic cases of human behaviour that we confidently assign to imagination, and those we confidently assign to belief. For example, in daydreaming, engagement with fictions, pretence games, or thought experiments, it is widely accepted that subjects imagine, rather than believe, the contents of the relevant daydreams, fictions, pretences, and thought experiments. I argue, as others have, that imaginings are not distinguished from beliefs by their contents, but rather by their functional roles. Though I observe that also at the functional level there are remarkable similarities. Both imaginings and beliefs 'regard their contents as true', in a phenomenological as well as in a cognitive sense – which I seek to clarify.

It then remains to be explained how imagination and belief differ. In Chapter 3 I introduce the Standard Answer to this question. In the paradigmatic cases just mentioned, imagination and belief seem to differ in two key respects. First, beliefs are formed in response to real-world evidence, while imaginings are formed in response to the will, or to other evidence-insensitive factors. Second, believing that p motivates actions that would promote the satisfaction of one's desires if p were true, while imagining that p does not motivate actions in this way. However, I claim that only the first of these provides a reliable criterion to distinguish imagination from belief, since motivational differences between imaginings and beliefs are actually merely apparent. I bring some initial support to this claim on the basis of an analysis of pretence actions. My central argument for this claim is then developed in the following two chapters.

In Chapter 4 I consider a range of actions very pervasive in our lives: what I call 'superstitious' and 'magical' actions (broadly construed). I argue that in all these cases we are moved to act by representational states that are not sensitive to real-world evidence, nor integrated in our whole system of beliefs. I argue that sensitivity to evidence and inferential integration are necessary features of belief. Hence, the cognitive states that motivate superstitious and magical actions in conjunction with subjects' desires cannot be beliefs. Imagination is the best alternative candidate.

In Chapter 5, developing a suggestion by J. David Velleman, I argue that if it is true that such cases are explained in terms imaginings, then we should recognize that imagination has the same motivating power of belief. Imaginings and beliefs dispose us to act in the same ways, and do that under the same conditions; they may contingently differ with respect to the satisfaction of such conditions, but their dispositional connection to action is precisely the same.

In Chapter 6 I conclude by considering some implications of my view for our understanding of religious cognition. I argue that so-called religious beliefs are, in many cases, not beliefs. Lacking such crucial features of belief as responsiveness to evidence and holistic coherence, they display many typical features of imaginings (notably, subjection to the will). I make my case on the basis of two sorts of arguments: empirical arguments drawing on recent anthropological and psychological studies of religion; and arguments suggesting conceptual reasons why religious propositions are more apt to be imagined than to be believed.

Insofar as my arguments in this book are successful, many cognitions that are standardly classified as beliefs – including superstitious, ideological and religious 'beliefs' – turn out to be better understood as imaginings. And imagination turns out to have a larger role in our thought and action than it is commonly taken to have. It does not just allow us to 'escape' from reality into fictional worlds, but plays a key, direct role in our representation of – and practical engagement with – the real world itself.

1.
ACCOUNTS OF FOLK-PSYCHOLOGICAL STATES

In order for the arguments I am going to present in favour of my account of imagination to be properly assessed, I should first of all say something on what I take the measures of success for such an account to be. In this chapter I consider this question at a quite general level – a level at which it can be asked about any other folk-psychological mental state: what is it that makes an account of such things as imagination, belief, desire, emotion, etc. good, or (at least) better than other rival accounts? I identify and discuss three features that seem important for a good account, having to do, respectively, with: closeness with folk-psychological assumptions (§1), explanatory power (§2), and integration with the best scientific cognitive theories (§3).

1. *Matching folk-psychological assumptions*

Since the notions here in question are folk-psychological notions originally featuring in the view that ordinary people have about how the mind works, I take it that a good account of these notions should match, at least to some extent, such commonsensical view. That is, it should match, at least to some extent, the basic assumptions which underlie our understanding, ascribing, predicting, and manipulating our own and other people's mental states and overt behaviours. The specification 'at least to some extents' is important: matching our folk-psychological view is a more difficult task than it might initially seem to be, and there are limits to the extent to which an account *can* be – and also, I will argue, *ought* to be – committed to such task.

A first difficulty here arises from the fact that the folk-psychological assumptions which inform our view of the mind are seldom explicit in our thoughts and talk. Of course, this doesn't mean that we seldom seek to understand ourselves and others in mentalistic terms. On the contrary, we do that all the time. We ascribe to each other mental states such as beliefs, desires, emotions, and interpret/predict reactions and behaviours in the light of those ascriptions. Practices like these reveal various general ideas about how the mind works, i.e. about how the environment affects our mental states, how different mental states interact to affect behaviours, 'what it is like' to be in a certain state, and so on. But the point is that these general ideas, typically, are not fully articulated in our discourse; they are rather tacitly assumed. And making them explicit might not be straightforward, also because our ordinary linguistic uses in this respect can be misleading. On the one hand, we happen to use the same expression to name states which are in fact different, and which we treat in different ways (compare, e.g. "I *imagine* I can fly" with "As I *imagine* you all know..." – where the latter seems rather a way to say 'As I *believe* you all know...'). On the other hand, our rich mentalistic vocabulary often provides us with different expressions to refer to one and the same state (like with "to think", "to take it", "to have it", "to hold", "to reckon", all meant as ways to express a belief). Working out what our mentalistic explanations precisely are, and what kinds of assumptions underlie them, will then require careful empirical observations of our verbal and behavioural practices.[1]

---

1   A point is worth clarifying here, concerning two different senses in which we can talk of folk-psychological assumptions 'underlying' our mental states ascriptions: one sense having to do with the *underlying mechanisms* which are causally responsible for such ascriptions; another having to do with the *underlying principles* which seem to be (implicitly) presupposed by such ascriptions. It is this latter sense of 'underlying' that I am appealing to. What I am interested in are the folk-psychological assumptions that explain *why* we make the mentalistic ascriptions we make. The question of *how* we are able to make such ascriptions – and whether our folk-psychological assumptions play any role in that – is a much debated empirical question, which I am not going to address here (for a review of the debate between *theory-theorists* and *simulation theorists* concerning such question, see Stich and Nichols 2003). So, the folk-psychological assumptions I discuss should not be understood as internally represented assumptions which actually drive our ascriptions of mental states. They should rather be understood as the assumptions which inform our folk-psychological view of the mind in the sense that they are part of what we mean when we ascribe mental states to each other (and that we take others to mean when they use mentalistic predicates). The distinction I just made between two senses of 'underlying folk-psychological assumptions' closely parallels the distinction that Stich and Ravenscroft (1995) make between *internal* vs. *external* accounts of folk psychology. *External accounts* of folk psychology are concerned with the sets of general principles that can be used to explain and systematize our understanding of the mind and mentalistic ascriptions; but are not (necessarily) internally represented and causally responsible for such ascriptions (we can imagine them to be used by an external observer in order to explain and predict our ascriptions). Here I will offer an external account of this sort.

This arguably constitutes the first important step for any good account of folk-psychological states.

But note that developing such an account is not just a matter of making our folk-psychological assumptions explicit and gathering them all together (see Lewis 1994: 416 – *pace* Lewis 1972). One obvious reason why that is not enough, is that our folk-psychological assumptions might not naturally form an orderly and coherent system: indeed, they often happen to be vague and, notably, inconsistent with each other.

A way to deal with the inconsistencies that we might discover within the set of our folk-psychological assumptions, is to include in our account only those assumptions that are 'commonly shared' among us in the sense that (almost) everyone makes such assumptions, (almost) everyone assumes that (almost) everyone else makes them, and so on (see Lewis 1972: 256).[2] To do that, we should focus on uncontroversial cases where our ascriptions of mental states and predictions of future behaviours are almost unanimously agreed upon, and work out the set of general assumptions that they seem to reveal.

Consider, for example, a driver who stops in front of a red traffic light. Almost everyone will agree that the driver behaves in that way because she sees the red light, she forms the related belief that there is a red light in front of her, she also has a prior belief that traffic norms require cars to stop and wait in front of red lights, and she desires to conform to those norms. From the analysis of a case like this we could then extrapolate such common assumptions as: 'visual perceptions are caused by such-and-such physical stimuli, and generate beliefs with corresponding contents'; 'different beliefs relate to one another in such-and-such ways'; 'beliefs and desires are likely to bring about actions in such-and-such ways'... And/or any other assumptions that can plausibly explain the mentalistic ascriptions in question.

Focusing on similar examples that reveal commonly shared folk-psychological assumptions, though, might still not be enough to avoid inconsistencies: sometimes unacknowledged inconsistencies occur also within the set of our commonly shared assumptions.

To take a classic example, our explicit talk, thoughts and behaviours seem to reveal both the common assumption that we do have genuine emotions towards fictional characters (including those that we do not believe exist in reality), and the common assumption that it is not possible to have genuine

---

2   Lewis talks in terms of 'common knowledge' of folk-psychological platitudes. I prefer to avoid this expression because, as I shall argue, some of such common assumptions may be false – while knowledge implies truth. Perhaps 'mutual belief' is more appropriate.

emotions towards someone we believe not to exist. These two assumptions are obviously in tension. To resolve such tension, a good account of the folk-psychological states involved here – i.e. emotion, imagination, belief – will have to drop at least one of them, thereby departing, at least in some respect, from folk-psychological intuitions.[3]

The suggestion so far, then, is that a good account of mental states such as imagination, belief, desire, etc., should try to match common folk-psychological assumptions concerning those states, even though there are a variety of limitations and complications in the extent to which this match can be achieved. Achieving it is not just a matter of forming a big conjunction of common folk-psychological assumptions which are readily available in our discourses, because: (i) the assumptions in question are generally tacit – so they must first of all be made explicit; and (ii) they can at times be inconsistent with each other – so some of them might have to be dropped.

2. *Explanatory power*

Matching common folk-psychological assumptions is not the only concern that a good account of folk-psychological states should have: the sort of account I am interested in should do more than that. Indeed, folk-psychological assumptions might be wrong: there might well be discrepancies between the ways in which folks take the mind to work, and the ways in which the mind actually works. And a good account of folk-psychological mental states should deal also with that – in the ways I am going to suggest.

2.1. *'Accounts of folk-psychological states' vs. 'Folk-psychological accounts'*

It is important to note the difference between 'accounts of folk-psychological mental states' and 'folk-psychological accounts of mental states'. These are to some extent stipulative labels; so, let me briefly clarify what I mean with them.

---

3   Though note that a good account will not simply renounce one of the inconsistent assumptions, but will also have to justify such move by explaining why that assumption is commonly made, and why it should be dropped in favour of the other that contradicts it.

With 'folk-psychological account of mental states', I mean an account which simply reflects the view that ordinary folks have of such states. This is not (necessarily) the sort of account I wish to offer.

What I wish to offer is an 'account of folk-psychological states' – which, in my sense here, is an account concerned with those mental states that feature in our folk-psychological view; but *need not* necessarily be a 'folk-psychological account'. I'd say even more: if it wants to be a good account, it *cannot* be 'folk-psychological in principle'. That is, it cannot uncritically begin with the assumption that the view that ordinary folks have of mental states is correct. What it should do, is rather to asses that view critically, with the best available methods (such as, I shall argue, those of scientific psychology), and consider what reasons there are to take it to be correct, accepting the existence of (something like) the mental states featuring in it. Of course, in order to do that, our account will first need to spell out precisely what such a folk-psychological view is like; this is why that account must be concerned with folk-psychological assumptions in the way discussed above (§1). Matching (to some extents) those assumptions is necessary for any account to be an account *of folk-psychological states*, rather than an account *of something else* (of some different, 'non-folk', psychological states). But this will be just a first step. Once this first step is made, a good account of folk-psychological states will have to weigh up the reasons (if any) that there might be to think that similar states actually exist.

2.2. *How good are folk-psychological explanations?*

Arguably, the basic reason we have to think that beliefs, desires and the other folksy states exist is that they allow us to *explain* a number of phenomena: to make rational sense of important aspects of our own and other people's experience, to predict our own and other people's behaviours. A crucial question to address, therefore, is whether folk-psychological explanations are good explanations; and, notably, whether there are better explanations available. Depending on how we answer this question, we might have different kinds of *accounts of folk-psychological states*. Let's then consider three possible answers to this question, and the kinds of accounts to which they would respectively lead.

2.2.1. *Conservative accounts*

At one end of the spectrum, we have answers that are extremely positive about the explanatory power of folk-psychological explanations. After careful examination, we might conclude that our folk-psychological view *as it is* reasonably approximates the best account we can aim to for how the mind works: assuming the existence of things with the properties commonly associated to beliefs, desires, imaginings and all the other folk-psychological states, allows us to explain almost every aspects of our behaviour and experience that seem to deserve a mentalistic interpretation – i.e. any aspects of our behaviour and experience that we might want to *rationalize* in some way. Behaviours and experiences that are not explainable in these terms are indeed unintelligible: lacking a folk-psychological explanation is tantamount to lacking any rational mentalistic explanations at all. Our folk-psychological characterizations of mental states might need some minor revisions, but they are basically correct; and commonly recognized folk-psychological states taken all together exhaust the taxonomy of causally distinctive mental states. A good account of folk-psychological mental states, then, will remain very close to our folk-psychological account of them.

2.2.2. *Revisionist accounts*

Less positive views of folk psychology's explanatory power will lead to more revisionist accounts of folk-psychological states. Note that 'less positive' does not necessarily mean 'negative'. We might for example think that mental states with the properties commonly associated to beliefs, desires, etc. provide satisfactory explanations for many, or even most, relevant aspects of our experience; *but* there still remain a number of phenomena which cannot be explained in those folk-psychological terms, hence require us to postulate some additional, non-folk-psychological mental states.

Similar additions will necessarily have some impacts also on our account of folk-psychological mental states: our common view of such states will have to be updated, at least with respect to their relations with the newly introduced (non-folksy) states. Other more substantial revisions might also turn out to be necessary. Insofar as we'll find out that mental states with some, but not all, the properties commonly associated with belief, desires, etc. would explain our behaviour/experience better than mental states with precisely the same properties commonly associated with belief, desires, etc., we will have to change our folksy characterizations accordingly. That is, we will have to recognize that beliefs, desires, etc. are not precisely as we commonly take them to be. A good account of such folk-psychological mental states will then be a (more or less) revisionist account.[4]

Here of course the question arises of how much we can change our folksy characterizations for it to still make sense to keep talking in terms of 'beliefs', 'desires', etc. I shall say something more on this question shortly. For the moment, let's just assume that there must be a limit beyond which it no longer makes sense.

2.2.3. *Eliminativist accounts*

Beyond that limit, rather than arguing that, say, beliefs are somewhat different from how we commonly take them to be, we will have to conclude that nothing like the state we use to call 'belief' (i.e. nothing which is enough similar to it to deserve the same name) actually exists. What we use to explain in terms of belief, is better explained by appealing to a different mental state that doesn't belong to our folk-psychological picture of the mind. We should then embrace an 'eliminativist' account of belief.[5]

---

4   In sum, the suggestion here is that we can have two possible kinds of revisions to our folk-psychological view: (i) additions of new states, (ii) substantial changes to the characterizations of familiar folk-psychological states (i.e. changes that do not have to do *just* with the added relationships to the new states). These two kinds of revisions are not alternative to each other. An example of revision of the first kind, is Tamar Gendler's suggestion that we need to recognize the existence of *aliefs* (see Gendler 2008, 2008a, 2010; I shall discuss this suggestion in Chapter 4: §4). An example of revision of the second kind, is the account of belief defended by Eric Schwitzgebel (see Schwitzgebel 2000, 2002, 2009, 2013; I shall say something more on it in Chapter 4: § 2).

5   Note that this would be a much less radical form of eliminativism than the one famously defended (among others) by Paul Churchland (1981). In the scenario I described, the basic conceptual framework of folk psychology would be retained: the category of belief would disappear, but its explanatory job would be done by another mental state of a similar kind – an intentional state with causal powers, semantically evaluable. In Churchland's view, instead, all folk-psychological notions would be eliminated and "our mutual understanding and even our introspection may then be reconstituted within the conceptual framework of completed neuroscience" (Churchland 1981: 67). My hope is that good 'accounts of folk-psychological notions' of the sort I am describing, differently from simple 'folk-psychological accounts', can stand up to Churchland's radical eliminative challenge. In this respect, my project here is very much in line with the view defended by Fodor 1987 (see in particular Chapter 1).

These are, in short, the ways in which our account of a given mental state M will end up being more conservative, more revisionist, or utterly eliminativist, depending on our view about the explanatory power of M.

2.3. *Assessing explanatory power: more (or less) controversial cases*

In order to assess folk psychology's explanatory power at best, we should not consider only the uncontroversial, paradigmatic cases of mental states' ascriptions discussed above. There are a variety of more controversial cases which also deserve our attention.

These include cases where we struggle to understand other people or our own experiences/behaviours, as well as cases where we do think we have some understanding of other people or our own experiences/behaviours, but it is not a fully clear understanding (and, notably, it is not based on folk-psychological assumptions that are commonly shared in the above mentioned way).

Take, for example, phenomena such as mental illness, creativity, or dreams. How do we explain the behaviour and experience of a deluded subject who claims with conviction that she is dead, while acting and reacting in a number of ways obviously inconsistent with that claim? What mental states drive the creative actions of an artist when she paints her canvasses? Can we predict when and how such creative actions will occur? What mental states are we in when we dream?

Many ordinary folks may not have a clear answer to such questions; and even when answers are given, they are not universally accepted.[6]

Something similar happens with familiar phenomena such as self-deception – e.g. a husband who obstinately denies that his wife is cheating on him, though seemingly 'knowing' that she does, and indeed being very jealous; or absent-minded behaviours – e.g. an Italian tourist in Great Britain who seems to know (and indeed claims with conviction) that there is left-hand drive there, yet keeps looking in the wrong direction before crossing the roads.

Here we do not find the subjects' actions and reactions so puzzling, and indeed we often expect them to occur precisely as they do. Yet, we might struggle to tell a fully coherent story about them – notably, a story that accounts both for what subjects *do* and for what they *say*.

---

6   So for example both delusions and dreams are taken by some to be beliefs, and by others to be kinds of imaginings. The fact that folk psychology doesn't provide clear explanations for phenomena like dreams and creativity is one of the reasons that Churchland gives to reject folk psychology altogether (see again Churchland 1981).

Moreover, our explanations and the assumptions that underlie these phenomena tend to vary across individuals. In the Italian tourist case, for example, some of us might think that she behaves like that because she keeps forgetting British driving rules and mistakenly *believes* that in Britain there is right-hand drive like in the rest of Europe (on the tacit assumption that behaviour always reveals beliefs); while others might think that she behaves like that just out of *habit*, while obviously believing that in Britain there is left-hand drive (on the tacit assumption that not all behaviour reveals belief).

Cases like the ones just considered, where our folk-psychological explanations are confused, discordant with each other, or altogether lacking, occur relatively often in our experience (absent-mindedness or self-deceived behaviours happen all the time; many of us dream every night…). In assessing the explanatory power of our folk-psychological view, we cannot treat them as rare exceptions.

Of course, it might well turn out that such cases cannot be convincingly explained by appealing to folk-psychological states, and require us to postulate *new mental states* instead. Or it might even turn out that they *cannot be explained at all* – in the sense that there isn't really a way to rationalize similar behaviours and experiences. Although we cannot rule out in principle either of these conclusions, however, there are reasons to be hesitant about embracing them.

As for the irrationality conclusion, in many cases it simply doesn't sound right. Many of the cases in question, even if somehow puzzling, do not look just absurd and unintelligible: we seem to understand and predict them pretty well (think again of the absent-minded tourist example). And before concluding that such understanding presupposes the existence of downright new mental states, we should – for reasons of economy and simplicity – consider carefully whether the states we are already familiar with can do the job and, if so, *how we should characterize them so that they can do that at best*.

Indeed, the consideration of problematic cases like those exemplified above might influence our account of folk-psychological states in significant ways. For instance, we might realize that some properties that we are used to attribute to one of these states – say, to belief – make it particularly suited to explain some otherwise problematic cases, while other properties commonly associated to it do not help or, worse, make such cases even more mysterious. This would give us reasons to think that some of our common assumptions about belief are more crucial to characterizing it properly; while others are inessential/mistaken, and therefore can/should be abandoned. The analysis of controversial cases like those just mentioned might then lead us to adopt a revisionist account of (at least some) folk-psychological states.

Here we come back to our earlier question: how much can an account of a given mental state M depart from our folk-psychological assumptions about M, for it to still make sense to consider it as a *revisionist* account of M, rather than as an *eliminativist* account according to which nothing like M actually exists (but something else does)?

This is a difficult question. It is not clear whether there is any principled criterion to answer it. According to Ramsey, Stich, and Garon (1990), there isn't any such criterion – and that this is a general problem which affects any theoretical inquiry when it comes to distinguish between 'ontologically conservative changes' (i.e. changes where the entities posited by a theory to explain a given phenomenon are conserved, though with differences in their characterization, into a new theory about the same phenomenon) and 'ontologically radical changes' (i.e. changes where the posits of an old theory cannot be similarly conserved in a new one). How to distinguish ontologically conservative from ontologically radical theory changes, Ramsey, Stich, and Garon suggest,

> is *a question that is easier to ask than to answer.* There is, in the philosophy-of-science literature, nothing that even comes close to a plausible and fully general account of when theory change sustains an eliminativist conclusion and when it does not. In the absence of a principled way of deciding when ontological elimination is in order, the best we can do is to look at the posits of the old theory – the ones that are at risk of elimination – and ask whether there is anything in the new theory that they might be identified with or reduced to. If the posits of the new theory strike us as deeply and fundamentally different from those of the old theory (...) then it will be plausible to conclude that the theory change has been a radical one and that an eliminativist conclusion is in order. But *since there is not easy measure of how 'deeply and fundamentally different' a pair of posits are, the conclusion we reach is bound to be a judgement call.* (Ramsey, Stich, and Garon 1990: 502-503, emphasis mine)[7]

I agree on the intrinsic difficulty – perhaps even impossibility – of answering the ontological question about theory changes that these authors raise. This shouldn't be too much of a worry for my discussion here, though.

After all, my ultimate interest is to advance our understanding of how the mind works – of the mental capacities that are responsible for our actions, reactions, and behaviours. I think that our folk-psychological view is a

---

7   For similar considerations concerning the problems that arise with intertheoretic identifications, see also Stich (1991); and Stich (1996): Chapter 1.

good starting point to address these issues (even if we should then be ready to depart from it in many ways); and this is why my discussion stems from the question of what is a good account of *folk-psychological* mental states. I also think that what I am going to say will do enough justice to our folk-psychological intuitions, and especially to those concerning imagination and belief, to justify continuing talking in those terms; even if it will turn out that our commonsensical views about such things as imagination and belief are in some respects imprecise and incomplete. So, I take the account of imagination I'm going to defend to be in some respects revisionist, but only mildly revisionist – definitely closer to the conservative rather than to the eliminativist end of the spectrum I sketched above.

I see that this is debatable, though. Ultimately, I will have to leave the question open. What matters more to me here is to demonstrate that we need to recognize the existence of a mental state with the features that I ascribe to the imagination. The decision whether such state does indeed deserve to be called 'imagination' is bound to be, as Ramsey, Stich, and Garon suggest, *a judgement call.* Eventually, I shall leave it up to the reader.

3. *Folk psychology and scientific psychology (and other cognitive sciences)*

One at this point might note that, if what I am interested in is the best possible account of how our mind works, then the place to look is scientific psychology, which addresses this question on the basis of rigorous empirical methods, rather than folk psychology, which is indeed nothing more than commonsensical.

I do agree with that; though I don't think there is really an alternative here. Scientific psychologists in the last century have worked a lot with folk-psychological categories, making a variety of empirical discoveries/ claims about the mental states originally featuring in our folk-psychological picture of the mind. The account I wish to offer, as I said, is not a folk-psychological account, but a scientifically informed account of folk-psychological notions: an account which considers seriously the entities posited by our folk-psychological view of the mind, and tries to determine whether anything like them is likely to exist – also (and importantly) on the basis of what the best scientific theories of the mind can tell us about them.

Such an account would fit in the category that Ravenscroft calls 'scientific folk psychology':

> folk psychology quantifies over a range of mental states including perceptions, sensations, emotions, and – importantly – propositional attitudes like beliefs and desires. (...) Many theories in scientific psychology quantify over a similar range of states. (...) It will be helpful to have a label for those scientific psychological theories which quantify over states originally posited by folk psychology. For want of a better term (...) I will use the term 'scientific folk psychology' for any such theory. (Ravenscroft 2005: 69; see also Fodor 1987)

Here note that scientific psychology, as any proper science (and arguably even more than others, since it is fairly young and still in a phase of methodological consolidation), is in continuous change; and few, if any, of its theories/principles are universally accepted. Therefore, matching scientific psychological assumptions is likely to be at least as complicated as we have seen matching folk-psychological assumptions to be. Yet, a good account of folk-psychological states will have to match the claims of scientific psychology as much as possible.

More in general, I would say that a good account should aim to be in line with the best available theories in different cognitive sciences: from neurology and psychiatry to anthropology, from genetics to linguistics... And so on. This means that it should aim to be well integrated in a network of connections with those theories – gaining support from them (and supporting them) to the extents and in the ways in which that is possible.

What these connections precisely amount to, how rich they can be, and how they can be tested, will vary a lot depending on the different disciplines. In some cases, it may be quite difficult to establish that, and we might not be in the position to do that (yet). But this does not undermine the claim that at least some degree of theoretical integration with theories in different cognitive sciences is something a good account should aim at.[8]

Conclusion

In this chapter I have described the sort of account of the imagination that I will offer. I have identified some important dimensions along which we can measure the success of such an account: (1) closeness to folk-psychological assumptions, (2) explanatory power concerning various aspects of our experience/behaviour, and (3) integration with the best scientific cognitive theories.

---

8   I will address this problem more closely in the next chapters, as it will emerge in relation to particular cases.

Requirements concerning (1) should be met in order for my account to be considered as an account of the imagination – rather than of something else. Requirements concerning (2) and (3) should be met in order for my account to provide a plausible representation of how the mind actually works – or, at least, a representation which approximates to that.

Since understanding how the mind actually works is my ultimate interest here, (2) and (3) are more important for me than (1). I think, however, that the account I am going to offer meets also (1). Insofar as my arguments in the next chapters will be successful, they will provide us with a better understanding of what the imagination is, of how it works, and of what roles it plays in our cognitive lives.

2.
IMAGINATION AND BELIEF: SIMILARITIES

Up to this point, I have been taking a holistic approach to the analysis of mental states, talking most of the time of a general account of belief, desire, perception, imagination etc..., rather than of specific accounts of these different states. In a sense, such a holistic approach is unavoidable: even if we didn't subscribe unconditionally to the functionalist view that mental states are essentially constituted by their causal relations to one another (and to external inputs/outputs), it seems reasonable to hold that a good account of a mental state M should at least clarify what is distinctive about M that sets it apart from other mental states, and how, if at all, M interacts with such states to produce behaviour.

Therefore, while my focus here is on imagination, what I am going to say will involve a number of assumptions about other mental states, and will, in turn, have implications for our accounts of them.

The most interesting and controversial implications, arguably, will be those concerning our account of belief. This is not surprising. The kind of imagination that I am going to be mostly concerned with is propositional imagination, which is similar to belief in several respects. One of the main challenges that an account of this kind of imagination faces is to clarify what precisely such similarities amount to and, perhaps most importantly, in what respects they break down – i.e. in what respects propositional imagination differs from belief.

This challenge was originally raised by David Hume – and it is often referred to as 'Hume's Problem' (see e.g. Armstrong 1973: 70; Price 1969: 160; Van Leeuwen 2009: 223):

> The imagination (...) can feign a train of events, with all the appearance of reality, ascribe to them a particular time and place, conceive them as existent, and paint them out to itself with every circumstance, that belongs to any historical fact, which it believes with the greatest certainty. *Wherein, therefore,*

consists the difference between such a fiction and belief? (Hume 1777: Part II,
Section V)[1]

Hume's problem, which is still very much debated, is one of my central
concerns in this book. Indeed, this book as a whole may be seen as an
attempt to provide a satisfactory solution to Hume's Problem.

In this chapter I seek clarify how the problem arises in the first place.
I shall introduce paradigmatic cases of imaginings and beliefs (§1), and
point out some striking similarities between them, both at the level of the
content (§2) and of the attitude (§§3-5) – similarities which explain the
difficulty to distinguish the ones from the others.

Before getting to the heart of these matters, though, an important
clarification is in order. Imagination does not only come in propositional
forms, but can also come in perceptual forms. And propositional forms
themselves might be of different kinds: as we shall see, according to some
there exist 'desire-like' as well as 'belief-like' kinds of propositional
imaginings. Unless otherwise specified, with 'imagination' here I will refer
to *propositional imaginings that are belief-like*. I will at times also refer to
them in terms of 'make-believe' or of 'belief-like imaginings', especially
when I will need to differentiate them from other kinds of propositional
imaginings (such as 'make-desires' or 'desire-like imaginings').[2]

1. Paradigmatic examples

In line with the methodology suggested in Chapter 1, let's start by
considering some paradigmatic cases that we are all happy to explain in
terms of imagination or, vice versa, of belief. Here is a classic case of
daydreaming. I am sitting at my desk, writing on my computer, and it
occurs to me that it would be good to read a recent paper in the *Journal
of Philosophy*. I go on the Internet to download it, but in so doing I start
hanging around on on-line newspapers. Today, they are all for the Royal

---

1   Another passage in the *Treatise on Human Nature* raises the related problem of
     how to distinguish believing a proposition from 'merely entertaining' it (see
     Hume 1739: Book I, Part III, Section 7).
2   As far as I know, the term 'make-believe' to indicate belief-like forms of
     imagination was first used by Walton (1990) and Currie (1990). The term 'make-
     desire', too, is originally due to Currie (1990). Later on, Currie will use the terms
     'belief-like imaginings' and 'desire-like imaginings' (see e.g. Currie 2002, Currie
     and Ravenscroft 2002). Doggett and Egan (2007) and Van Leeuwen (2011) talk in
     terms of 'i-beliefs' and 'i-desires', instead.

Wedding. Some photos of Meghan Markle make me figuring myself dressed in white like her: for a moment 'I become the Duchess of Sussex'. *Wow, tonight I'm going to leave for a honeymoon in tropical islands, I should pack my stuff! Or actually no, I shouldn't: someone will certainly do that for me while I enjoy the wedding party! Yes, I enjoy that, but: what a nightmare to be followed by thousands of eyes wherever I go...* These are some of my thoughts when I get carried away representing myself as the Duchess of Sussex. These thoughts are soon interrupted by the clock that strikes 7pm, reminding me that it's late and I must go back to work: *I'm not the Duchess of Sussex, but an academic philosopher – and one who is very behind with her work – so I should stop wasting my time in silly ways!*

I assume that everyone who knows me would be happy, in this circumstance, to describe my 'academic thoughts' as beliefs, and my 'Royal Wedding thoughts' as imaginings. I believe that I am an academic philosopher, sat in front of my computer, writing my book; while I just imagine, for a moment, that I am the Duchess of Sussex, on the day of my wedding, almost leaving to honeymoon.

Other paradigmatic cases where the belief/imagination distinction looks so clear are our engagement with fictions and with pretence games.[3] I take it that most of us would agree that readers of Harry Potter's stories imagine many things about the adventures of an eleven-year-old child who discovers to be a wizard, without actually believing them. And that children playing a Wild West game do not actually believe themselves to be Indians and cowboys fighting in a real war, but simply imagine that. They never stop believing to be children living at home with mum and dad, but – as long as the game goes on – they imagine themselves to be Indians and cowboys instead.

---

3   Derek Matravers (2010) has questioned that imagination plays the central role in our engagement with fiction that most authors take it to play. He argues that readers/film viewers do not *need* to – nor typically *do* – imagine the contents of the fictions they engage with. According to Matravers readers/film viewers do just 'understand' (or 'engage with') such contents; and this is something they do both with fictions and with non-fictions. In fact, I wonder whether what Matravers calls 'understanding' or 'engagement' is not, in the end, a basic form of imagining. Matravers does not clearly spell out what the critical difference between *understanding* and *imagining* is supposed to be. And my impression is that it is not really a substantial difference. If ask you to understand a proposition p, and then I ask you to imagine that p, am I asking you to do two essentially different things? Arguably not. Whilst granting that a proper refutation of Matravers' view would require more extensive discussion, here I will simply note that this view is not mainstream. And I will assume the otherwise widely accepted view according to which our engagement with fiction is, indeed, a paradigmatic example of imagination's exercise.

Appeals to the imagination are not limited to playful cases like the ones just seen. Imagination is often appealed to also to explain 'more serious' phenomena, such as our capacity to create and understand thought experiments, to form counterfactual thoughts about what might have happened, to hypothesise about what might happen in the future.

So for example we say that we imagine the existence of Twin Earth – a planet where the liquid that people drink and call 'water' is not H_2O; that we imagine how our life would have been if we had met a different partner; that we imagine getting a new job and moving to a different country. We sometimes also say that we imagine 'putting ourselves in someone else's shoes', to indicate that we see the world from the perspective of someone else.

I take all these to be rather uncontroversial examples of imagination's exercise. Less uncontroversial and less obvious is the question of what are the essential features by virtue of which they classify as such; and, notably, by virtue of which they differ from cases that we explain in terms of belief.

2. *Same contents, regarded in the same way*

One thing we can notice immediately is that in none of the previous examples the crucial differences between imagination and belief seem to concern their contents.

Take the daydream case. My imagining and my belief here have two different contents – I imagine THAT I AM A DUCHESS, while I believe THAT I AM AN ACADEMIC PHILOSOPHER; but this is *not* what makes the critical difference between them. It is not the case that being a Duchess is a kind of thing that can only be imagined, while being an academic philosopher is a kind of thing that can only be believed. I can imagine that I am an academic philosopher, as well as believing it; and I can do both things at the same time. I do this now: I imagine that I am an academic philosopher who is writing her book with pen and ink. Part of the content of this imagining – the bit THAT I AM AN ACADEMIC PHILOSOPHER WHO IS WRITING – is also something that I believe.

This is possible insofar as imagination and belief's contents are isomorphic: they are both propositional contents, and the same propositions that can be believed can also, in principle, be imagined.[4]

---

4   The reverse might not always be true; maybe I can imagine, but not believe, that I do not exist, or that $5 + 7$ does not equal 12. But these are quite exceptional cases; and anyway they do not undermine the claim that in most cases imaginings and beliefs cannot be distinguished just on the basis of their contents.

Belief and imagination do not only have the same kind of contents; they also seem to 'look' at their contents in rather similar ways. They are both cognitive attitudes, which 'regard' their contents *as true,* differently from conative attitudes – such as desires or intentions – which regard their contents as *to-be-made-true,* or from aversive attitudes – such as (some) negative emotions – which regard their contents as *to-be-prevented-from-becoming-true.*[5] Whether we believe or imagine something, we represent it as *being the case*; we represent the world in a certain way – e.g., as a world where (it is true that) I am an academic philosopher working on her book, or as a world where (it is true that) I am the Duchess of Sussex on the day of her wedding. This seems to be what Hume was hinting at in the passage quoted above, observing that "imagination can feign a train of events *with all the appearance of reality,* ascribe to them a particular time and place, conceive them as existent".

What precisely does such 'conceiving-as-existent' – or, as contemporary philosophers more often say, 'regarding-as-true' – characteristic of both belief and imagination amount to?

I take it to involve at least two aspects. First, a *phenomenal* aspect: there is something that it is like to regard *p* as true (which is, arguably, what makes us intuitively grasp the similarity in this respect between beliefs and imaginings, as opposed to desires and intentions). Second, a *cognitive* aspect: insofar as a proposition is regarded as true, it is available to play some specific roles in our cognitive economy – and notably in our theoretical reasoning – in ways that I am going to clarify.

Let's then say something more on these two aspects of regarding-as-true, and see how imagination and belief are alike in both of them.[6] I will

---

The view that imaginings and beliefs do not (intrinsically) differ at the level of the content – but are rather distinguished by their functional roles – is accepted by most cognitive accounts of imagination in the contemporary debate (see e.g. Nichols and Stich 2000, Currie and Ravenscroft 2002, Schroeder and Matheson 2006, Weinberg and Meskin 2006, Doggett and Egan 2007, Van Leeuwen 2013, Liao and Doggett 2014, Kind 2016 – and indeed many others). Two interesting exceptions to this widespread consensus are Leslie (1987, 1994, 2002) and Langland-Hassan (2012), which however I will not discuss here.

5   I take this taxonomy and terminology from Velleman and Shah (2005); see also Velleman (2000) and Van Leeuwen (2009) for analogous distinctions/terminologies. A distinction similar to (if not fully coincident with) the distinction I am drawing here between cognitive and conative attitudes has been captured by some philosophers in terms of different *directions of fit* – mind-to-world vs. world-to-mind (see Anscombe 1957, Searle 1983, Humberstone 1992).

6   Here it is worth noticing that my characterization of regarding-as-true is (partially) different from others that has been suggested. The notion of regarding-as-true is

discuss the phenomenal aspects in §§ 3 and 4; § 5 will be devoted to the cognitive aspect.

3. *Regarding-as-true: phenomenal aspect (I)*

A first, phenomenal, aspect of regarding-as-true can be characterized in terms of a disposition to undergo certain kinds of conscious experiences in response to the relevant proposition which is regarded as true. Notably, a disposition to feel emotions that would be appropriate if the proposition in question were true (e.g. grief in the case of propositions describing a loss, fear in the case propositions describing a danger, joy in the case of propositions describing positive things, and so on).

Imagination and belief are widely recognized to be alike in this respect. Imagining that my next bouldering competition will be terribly tough, can produce unpleasant feelings very similar to those generated by believing that it will be terribly tough. Imagining that Harry Potter eventually manages to save his friend Ginny can make me sigh of relief as I would if I believed a young life to be saved. Apparently, the same proposition can elicit similar – if not identical – emotional responses whether it is believed or imagined.

This is something we are all familiar with. It is also attested in a number of psychological studies, showing, among other things, that that the same physiological arousal underlies our emotional responses to beliefs and to

---

often associated to that of *acceptance*, which in turn has been characterized in somewhat different ways by different philosophers (see e.g. Stalnaker 1984, Cohen 1989, Bratman 1992, Velleman 2000). Velleman himself, to whom much of my views here are inspired, uses 'regarding a proposition as true' and 'accepting a proposition' interchangeably, analysing them in terms of a disposition to act in ways that would promote the satisfaction of one's desires if the proposition in question were true: "Regarding a proposition as true – or, to introduce a term, accepting a proposition (…) involves a disposition to behave as would be desirable if the proposition *were* true, by doing things that would promote the satisfaction of one's desires in that case. We can thus interpret the locution 'regarding as...' to mean 'representing in a way that disposes one to behave as *would be desirable if...*' – or just '...as if...' for short." (Velleman 2000: 250, 255). I agree that regarding-as-true disposes us to act in the ways Velleman describes: this is indeed what I am going to argue in the next chapters. But here I won't commit myself with the view that such behavioural dispositions are *constitutive* of regarding-as-true in the way Velleman suggests. At least for present purposes, I take the phenomenal and cognitive dispositions that I will describe to be sufficient for regarding a proposition as true.

imaginings.[7] And the assumption of a close similarity – if not identity – between such responses informs common experimental practices. Psychologists in their trials do often rely on (acknowledgedly) fictional scenarios in order to elicit emotions that subjects would be expected to have if they believed such scenarios to really obtain (see Izard 1991; Harris 2000: Chapter 4).

Importantly, imaginings and beliefs are not alike just in that they can elicit emotional responses, but also in that they can justify, or rationalize, them. Such responses will be more or less appropriate depending on how well they can be understood in the light of what the subject believes/ imagines. So, for example, fear can be quite an appropriate response to my belief that there is a psychopath killer at large, but not to the belief that today is a sunny day. It can also be appropriate to my imagining – in watching *Psycho* – that Norman Bates is approaching Marion's shower; but it does not seem appropriate to my imagining that Winnie the Pooh happily flies in a balloon.

Note that here I have been oversimplifying things a bit. I have been ignoring some complexities concerning, respectively, the status of our affective responses to imaginings, and the role that other mental states – notably other conative states – play in generating such responses. In §§ 3.1 and 3.2 I shall address these complexities.

3.1. *Real emotions or quasi-emotions?*

I said that fear can be an appropriate emotional response to my imaginative engagement with *Psycho*'s shower scene. But it is a controversial question whether I can literally *fear* for Marion as I fear for the intended victims of a killer I believe to be around.

---

7   Lang (1984) and Vrana and Lang (1990), for example found the same reactions in terms of heart-rate, skin-conductance and startle responses. For a review and discussion of various classic studies on emotional reactions to imagined scenarios, see Harris (2000): Chapter 4. Damasio (1994) provides compelling evidence of how imaginative engagement with hypothetical scenarios/courses of action can produce emotional responses which match very closely those that would be produced by actual engagement with such scenarios/actions. Damasio also stresses the great adaptive value of our emotional sensitivity to imaginary stimuli (for further philosophical discussion of Damasio's findings, see Gendler and Kovakovich 2006; Currie and Ravenscroft 2002: Chapter 9). Matheson and Schroeder (2006) discuss some evidence of the fact that emotional responses to acknowledgedly fictional stimuli and emotional responses to acknowledgedly *non*-fictional stimuli have the same or very similar neural correlates.

According to some authors, the answer to this question is no, because genuine emotions require beliefs in the existence of their objects. So, as I do not believe, but merely imagine, that Marion exists, I cannot really fear for her: what I experience, though phenomenologically (and physiologically) alike to fear, is a different kind of state – call it 'quasi-fear', in Kendall Walton's famous terminology (Walton 1978 and 1990: Part II; for a more recent defence of this 'quasi-emotions view', see Friend 2003).

Other authors reject the idea that genuine emotions require beliefs in the existence of their objects. As Richard Moran (1994) pointed out, emotions are a broad and heterogeneous category. Some emotions might not require any belief at all: think of disgust at the perception of something rotten, surprise for something unexpected, or the discomfort most of us feel in witnessing surgery, though not believing that the patient is suffering. Other emotions – such as remorse, regret, or nostalgia – seem to involve beliefs about things that might have existed/happened but ultimately didn't, or about things that existed in the past but do not exist anymore. Given the breadth of states that we are happy to count as genuinely emotional, Moran argues, it is unclear why affective responses to imaginings should be denied that status (Moran 1994: 76-79; for other more recent defences of this sort of 'genuine fictional emotions view' see Currie and Ravenscroft 2002; Gendler and Kovakovich 2006).

Perhaps the disagreement here is less radical than it may prima facie seem to be. After all, most parties in the debate agree that beliefs and imaginings can produce the same sort of *phenomenological and physiological responses*. We have seen that this is indeed something that also advocates of quasi-emotions concede (see in particular Walton 1978: 6; Friend 2006: 35). And of course, on the other hand, advocates of genuine emotions must concede that such phenomenological and physiological responses are functionally distinct at least in this respect: they are generated by different (i.e. believed vs. imagined) stimuli. As I see it, the critical question here is then the question whether this is *the only difference* between such responses: i.e. the question whether what we have are phenomenological and physiological responses which *only* differ in that some of them are generated by beliefs while others are generated by imaginings.

If this is indeed the only difference, then we could arguably conclude that beliefs and imaginings have the same emotional effects, after all. The reason why advocates of quasi-emotions reject this conclusion is that in their view the difference between the two classes of emotional responses here in question has not to do just with their (imagined vs. believed) inputs, but has also to do with their action outputs. When I 'fear' for Marion I do not call the police as I would do (plausibly) if I feared for a real intended victim. As Walton puts it: "Fear is motivating in distinctive ways. (...) It puts pressure on one's behaviour (even if one resists). To deny this would be radically to reconceive the notion of fear. Fear emasculated by subtracting its distinctive motivational force is not fear at all" (Walton 1990: 201-202).

But is it actually true that emotional responses to beliefs systematically differ from emotional responses to imaginings in motivational force? I do not think so. Arguably, the distress that I feel when I *imagine* that my next bouldering competition will be tough can motivate me to undertake intensive training precisely as it would do the distress caused by the *belief* that the next competition will be tough.[8] Admittedly, though, a proper defence of this claim is not straightforward, and requires a more careful investigation of the relations between belief, imagination, and action. Indeed, here it should be noted that what motivates us to act, strictly speaking, are not just (nor indeed directly) our emotions; but are rather the patterns of cognitive and conative attitudes in the context of which our emotions arise.

Distress at the idea of a tough competition would not in itself motivate me to undertake intensive training, *unless I also desired to do well in the competition.* If I desired to forget about bouldering and turn to more relaxing activities, my distress might motivate the decision to give up any intensive training and to begin a yoga course, instead. And my desire to do

---

8   Here one could also observe that the *Psycho* example I considered before does not really show the difference between 'fictional' and 'genuine' emotions that it is supposed to show, either. Indeed, what I imagine in watching *Psycho* might not (and indeed, ought not to) be that there is a killer in action *right now*, approaching his victim in the shower. Perhaps what I imagine is rather that a real killer did such things in the past, and the film *reports* them (or something like this). If this is the case, then the fact that I do not call the police does not in itself reveal a difference between the motivating force of emotions elicited by imagination and the motivating force of emotions elicited by belief: arguably, I would not call the police even if I *believed* that I am watching a documentary film reporting a frightening crime that really happened in the past (for considerations along these lines, see Matravers 1997). Now, I grant to Walton and friends that it is not hard to find better examples of cases where imagining and believing *the very same thing* produce the very same emotion (or emotion-like) experience, yet lead to different action outputs (e.g.: now I hear a footfall in the basement, I *imagine* that there is burglar there, and I feel scared; but this may not motivate me to call the police as it would do the scary *belief* that there is a burglar in the basement). However, as I shall argue in Chapter 5, I think that also in cases like this the fact that imaginings and beliefs do not motivate the same actions is not due to their having intrinsically different motivating and emotional powers, but it is rather due to contingent differences in the sets of the other mental states to which the imaginings and beliefs in question belong (on this, see Chapter 5: §2).

well in the competition, in turn, would not be enough to motivate me in any way, unless I could represent ways to fulfil it – e.g. *unless I believed that intensive training increases my chances of success.*

The question of imagination and belief's emotional powers, then, turns out to be strictly related to – and in various ways dependent on – the question of their motivational powers upon action.

This latter question will be the focus of my discussion in Chapters 3, 4, and 5 – where I shall argue that imagination and belief's *motivating* powers are identical. Insofar as my arguments there will be successful, they will support a similar conclusion with respect to imagination and belief's *emotional* powers.[9] For the moment, I shall leave the question about emotional powers open. And I shall go on briefly discussing another related question, which has just emerged, concerning the relationships between belief, imagination and *desire*.

3.2. *Real desires or 'make-desires'?*

As my action of training for the competition depends on my desire to do well in it, so does my feeling of distress. Indeed, when I said that such a feeling can be explained by the *belief* that the competition will be terribly tough, I told just part of the story. Such a belief disposes me to feel distressed only in conjunction with a desire to do well in the competition, or with some other desire of that sort. If I did not care about doing well in the competition, the belief that the competition will be terribly tough might not distress me at all.[10]

Something similar will be true for the distress generated by my *imagining* a tough competition: whether it is believed or imagined, the scenario of a tough competition seems to be distress-generating only insofar as I desire to do well in the competition itself (or I desire something else of that sort).

---

9   This is true insofar as the basic difference to which advocates of quasi-emotions appeal is a behavioural difference: if I will show that in fact there isn't any behavioural difference between imagination and belief, this will undermine their argument for the emotional difference. Though admittedly there may be different sorts of arguments to differentiate our affective responses to imagination from our affective responses to belief, which may not be undermined by my arguments.

10   Note that I am not arguing that all emotions depend on beliefs and desires. I am just suggesting that, when emotions depend on beliefs, they typically depend on desires as well. In the next section I will discuss a kind of emotional response to belief (and to imaginings) that does not seem to depend much on desires: i.e. an emotional experience of *conviction* (see § 4 below).

In the case of imaginings, however, things get more complicated, because it is not always clear what desires could play the relevant explanatory role. The problem is most evident with imaginings concerning fictional entities. My relief when Harry Potter saves Ginny's life seems to be naturally explained by saying that I desire Ginny to be saved. And, indeed, we do commonly give explanations of this sort. But postulating a desire like the one just mentioned raises perplexities somewhat similar to those just discussed in relation to emotions: can I really desire that Ginny is saved, while not believing that she exists?[11]

This looks problematic. And it is not obvious how a real desire about a 'non-existent entity' could be satisfied – as indeed it seems to be – by what I make-believe (or by what the story makes true) about such entity, thereby generating my relief. This is why various authors have argued that it is not by appealing to desires like this that we can explain what goes on here. Currie (2002) and Doggett & Egan (2007) suggested that, in order to account for emotional responses like my relief for Ginny's final rescue, we should recognize the existence of a mental state which is to desire as make-believe is to belief: call it 'make-desire'.[12] On this view what happens is that I make-believe that Ginny is in danger and make-desire that she is saved. Therefore, when eventually I make-believe that she is indeed saved, I have a reaction of relief (whether it is real-relief or quasi-relief).

---

11 The problem here is not so much with having desires involving things that we know to be non-existent. At least some kinds of desires concerning non-existent things are quite common and unproblematic. Take, for example, my desire to have a baby and call him Fred: I do not believe that a baby called Fred exists – what I desire is that such a currently non-existent thing as 'my baby' comes into existence and has the property of being called Fred. But in cases like Harry Potter and Ginny I do not seem to desire that such person as Ginny exists and that she has the property of being in danger and then being saved. Apparently, I simply desire that Ginny – whom I do not believe exists – is saved. This looks more problematic.

12 As I noted above (footnote 2, this chapter), this term is due Currie (1990), who will then shift (in Currie 2002) to talk in terms of 'desire-like imaginings' (see also Currie and Ravenscroft 2002). Doggett and Egan (2007) talk of 'i-desires'. Here I take all these terms to refer to one and the same thing: an imaginative counterpart of real desires (analogous to the imaginative counterpart of real beliefs that I have been discussing). Since I am calling the imaginative counterpart of belief 'make-believe', for uniformity I will use the term 'make-desire' for the imaginative counterpart of desire. Later on, I will sometimes talk in terms of belief-like and desire-like imaginings, adopting the terminology used by the authors I will be discussing.

Many authors are sceptical about the existence of make-desires, though. Nichols (2004), for example, argues that make-desires are unnecessary to explain reactions like my relief for Ginny's rescue, which can been more economically explained by real desires such as the desire that *in Harry Potter's story* Ginny is saved ('more economically' insofar as we do not add a new category to our ontology of the mind).

Sceptics like Nichols suggest that make-desires are also unnecessary to explain other phenomena for which they are postulated by their advocates, and point out a number of problems that emerge when we try to characterize them properly.[13]

Like the debate on real emotions vs. quasi-emotions, the debate on real desires vs. make-desires has been very live in recent years, with a number of different arguments provided from both parties.[14] I will discuss some of such arguments later on (see Chapter 3, §4.4). For the moment, though, without taking a definite side in either of those two debates, I will ignore the complications that they raise, and simply assume the following, on which I take all parties to agree. Belief and imagination are alike in that they both can – generally in conjunction with desires, *or* desire-like states – explain (i.e. cause and rationalize) certain kinds of emotions, *or* emotion-like states. Both believing and imagining that p dispose me to undergo emotional experiences that would be appropriate if p were true, given my p-related desires (roughly, they dispose me to undergo positive reactions in cases where I take the truth of p to fulfil my desires, negative reactions otherwise). Such emotional experiences are a first important aspect of my regarding-as-true that p.

---

13   Other phenomena that make-desires are supposed to explain include our capacity to understand other people's practical reasoning, and – as we shall see in Chapter 3 – pretence behaviours. Further opponents of make-desires who provided extensive arguments against them include Tagliafico (2011) and Kind (2011). See also Kind (2016) for a general overview of the debate.

14   The controversy on real vs. quasi-emotions can be dated back at least to Colin Radford's seminal paper "How can we be moved by the fate of Anna Karenina?" (1975); and was very live in the Eighties and the Nineties. The controversy on real vs. make-desires is more recent. The existence of make-desires was first defended by simulations theorists (such as Gordon 1986, Goldman 1989, Currie 1995, 2002), who took them to be necessary to explain our capacity to predict and explain other people's behaviour. As it has been observed, this controversy marks "one of the most important fault lines" between different theories of imagination: "one of the main parameters on which different accounts of imagination differ" (Nichols 2006: 9; Schellenberg 2013: 500).

4. *Regarding-as-true: phenomenal aspect (II)*

Among all the emotional experiences appropriate to the truth of p that we are disposed to undergo when we regard p as true, there is one that is sometimes described in terms of 'feeling it true' that p (Cohen 1989; see also Ramsey 1926, Schwitzgebel 2002, Bayne and Pachérie 2005). This particular kind of phenomenal disposition deserves special attention in my discussion here, for at least two reasons.

On the one hand, this disposition to feel-it-true plays an especially important role in the phenomenology of regarding-as-true. On the other hand – differently from other phenomenal dispositions such as those discussed so far, which are widely recognized to be associated both with belief and with imagination – the disposition to feel-it-true has often been taken to be an exclusive prerogative of belief, if not even *the* mark of belief, necessary and sufficient to distinguish it from imagination and other mental states.[15] In order to argue that belief and imagination are alike in that they both regard their contents as true, I shall argue that a disposition to feel-its-content-true characterizes also our imaginings.

4.1. *Feeling it true*

To begin, we need to be clear on what such 'feeling that a proposition is true' consists in. Describing it in relation to belief, Jonathan Cohen says:

> Feeling it true that *p* (...) takes different forms. One may feel convinced by the evidence of its being true that *p*, one may feel surprised to learn of an event that is evidence against its being true that *p*, one may feel pleased at its being true that *p*, and so on... (Cohen 1989: 368)

Admittedly, from this description it is not obvious that a disposition to feel it true that p is anything over and above the general disposition to undergo any emotional experiences appropriate to the truth of p (such as, to

---

15 This is for example Cohen (1989)'s view. Other authors who take the disposition to feel-its-content true to be a key feature of belief are Schwitzgebel (2002) and Bayne and Pacherie (2005); see also Ramsey (1926), who talks of a "belief-feeling, or feeling of conviction". Schwitzgebel takes this disposition to feel-true to be one of the most central dispositions belonging to what he calls beliefs' "dispositional stereotypes" (though he grants that it is not strictly speaking sufficient for belief, as indeed in his view no behavioural or phenomenal disposition in itself is: see Schwitzgebel 2002: 252-253).

continue Cohen's list, *disappointment* if p is undesired, *fear* if p describes a danger, *admiration* if p describes something remarkable, and so on...).

However, I think that we can, among all the emotional experiences appropriate to the truth of a given proposition p, identify one which is most peculiarly characterized by the feeling that p is true – one, we could say, which has as formal object the persuasiveness of p:[16] that is what Cohen calls a feeling of *conviction* concerning p. We can also describe it as a feeling of *assent* to an 'internal utterance' of p: something like what one experiences in telling silently to herself "Yes: p!" (see Schwitzgebel 2002: 252).[17] It is this peculiar kind of experience that I will refer to here with the expression 'feeling it true that p'.[18] Of course, there is likely to be a strict relation between such a feeling and all other emotional reactions to p that one might have: plausibly, the more one feels confident that p is true, the more intensely she will respond emotionally to it in a number of different ways. It might even be the case that a minimal degree of feeling-p-true is necessary in order to undergo any other possible emotional experience directed towards p (so that, e.g., I can't really fear the dog snarling at me if I don't feel at all true that a dog is snarling at me[19]). Yet, none of this means that one's feeling true that p can simply be factorized into her other p-related feelings/emotions.

4.2. *Conditions of manifestation: the 'Occurrence Condition'.*

A feeling of confidence/truth like that just described can be observed clearly in some newly acquired beliefs. While waiting for a response about a paper I submitted to a conference, I might wonder whether it has been accepted and hope that it has; but I don't feel assent to the proposition that

---

16   Formal object of an emotion is the evaluative category under which all the particular objects that are appropriate for that emotion fall (see Lyon 1980). So, if the formal object of fear is 'the dangerous', and the formal object of love is 'the appealing', the formal object of conviction/feeling of truth will be something like 'the persuasive'. That is: particular objects are feared insofar as they are experienced as dangerous, they are loved insofar as they are perceived as appealing, and they are felt-true insofar as they are perceived as persuasive.

17   Note that this feeling of conviction that makes me tell silently to myself p, in turn, is likely to dispose me to openly assert it: we are generally disposed to sincerely assert what we feel convinced about (in appropriate circumstances).

18   Here I will use such expressions as 'feeling it true that...', 'feeling of truth about...', 'feeling convinced about...', 'feeling confident that...' interchangeably.

19   This is indeed why I said that feeling it true plays an especially important role in the phenomenology of regarding-as-true.

MY PAPER HAS BEEN ACCEPTED. Then, when eventually, reading an email, I come to believe that it has been accepted, I am likely to think silently to myself: "Yes: it has been accepted!", feeling a kind of internal assent to this.

Of course, I won't actually feel like that for all the time that I hold such belief. When I make holiday plans with my friends at dinner, I don't think about the conference and I don't have any feeling about it. I still believe that my paper has been accepted, but the disposition to 'feel it true' is not expected to be manifest now, unless the relevant proposition comes to my mind (e.g., in case a friend at some point asks me whether I've got any news about the paper I submitted). Indeed, it is important to specify that believing that p disposes me to feel it true that p *on the condition that I pay some attention to p, that p is occurrently present 'before my mind'*. Call this the 'occurrence condition'.

If this occurrence condition is not met, a lack of manifestation of the disposition to feel it true can be 'excused', without thereby compromising the holding of the disposition itself.[20]

Note that this 'occurrence condition' holds also for the manifestation of 'standard' emotions such as those discussed in the previous section: fear, distress, happiness, etc... In relation to such emotions, I only mentioned a 'desire condition' – observing that the belief that the competition will be tough makes me feeling anxious *if I desire to do well in the competition*. But another relevant condition is that the idea of a tough competition is occurrently before my mind: when I am not thinking about it, I might well not feel anxious at all – and this would not mean that I'm not disposed to feel anxious in response to the tough competition idea.[21]

---

20 I am not arguing that the satisfaction of such 'occurrence condition' is in itself *sufficient* to guarantee that the disposition to feel it true is manifested (for, as we shall see, there are also other relevant conditions). Nor am I arguing that the satisfaction of such 'occurrence condition' is *necessary* for the manifestation of that disposition to be possible. (My guess is that it wouldn't be possible to feel it true that p without having p before your mind; but if it were possible, that wouldn't be a problem for my view.) Probably the best way to understand the condition in question is in terms of the 'excusing condition' to which it gives raise if it is not met: *if the 'occurrence condition' is not met, this constitutes an excusing condition for the non-manifestation of the disposition to feel it true.* The same holds for the other conditions that I am going to discuss.

21 Note also that if on the one hand the occurrence condition holds for any kind of emotions, on the other hand the 'desire condition' does not seem to hold for the disposition to feel it true: it seems that if I believe that my paper has been accepted and this proposition is occurrently before my mind, I will feel it true anyway, irrespective of what I desire (see footnote 11 above).

Also the other conditions of manifestation that I am going to discuss in relation to the disposition to feel it true apply to 'standard' emotional dispositions as well. In my view, indeed, the disposition to feel it true is not substantially different from all other emotional dispositions. Most importantly, like all other emotional dispositions, it is associated both with belief and imagination.

Here is where my view differs from most others: while (almost) everyone would agree that both believing and imagining that my paper has been accepted dispose me to experience some pleasant feelings (whether feelings of satisfaction or of 'quasi-satisfaction'), no one I know would agree with me that both believing and imagining that my paper has been accepted dispose me to feel it true that it has been accepted. It is commonly assumed that only believing, but not imagining, that it has been accepted would dispose me to feel that true. Against this common assumption, I shall argue that *imagination disposes us to feel its contents true basically as belief does.*

Note that of course this feeling-true – as any other emotional experience – comes in degrees. But, for the sake of simplicity, I am now going to treat it as an 'all-or-nothing' matter (as I have done with all emotional experiences so far). My point is that belief and imagination do not differ in disposing us to feel their contents true, nor do they differ in the intensity of the feeling-true they dispose us to undergo: it is not the case that believing p disposes us to feel *more* convinced about p than imagining p does. This feeling of truth/conviction and the different degrees in which it comes depend on factors/conditions that are the same for belief and for imagination.

4.3. *Imaginings which feel true...*

The fact that we *can* feel what we imagine to be true is, I take it, a common experience. Consider again a classic case of daydreaming. Maria is falling in love with John, and thinks of him all the time. Now she attends a lecture, but she doesn't follow a word of it. Instead, she fantasizes that John surprises her, calling for her at the University, and taking her out for dinner. Actually, she knows that John is not even in town today, but this doesn't affect her daydream, where she vividly represents him waiting for her at the end of the lecture. She imagines their meeting in great detail – how John is dressed, what he tells her, her first reaction in seeing him, and so on. The more details she adds, the more she gets carried away by the daydream – which *feels so true*. Indeed, it feels so true that she winces with surprize when all her mates in the classroom get up as the lecture is finished, reminding her that nothing of what is going on in her mind *is really true*.

Though some of us may be 'more daydreamers' than others, experiences like the one just described – of becoming absorbed in something you imagine, feeling it more and more true – are not uncommon. Such experiences might be even more common in cases of engagement with fictions and with pretence games. Works of fiction can make us feel that the stories they tell are true; and enjoying them is often also a matter of leaving such feeling to become phenomenologically predominant. Watching *Psycho,* it is hard not to feel the story of Marion, Norman and all the other characters to be true: especially in some engrossing passages we might feel really convinced that it is. While Norman is approaching the shower, don't we typically think silently to ourselves (and sometimes also aloud) such things as: "Oh, he is approaching the shower! Marion doesn't realizes this! Something awful is going to happen!" – feeling internal assent to these propositions? (And, remember, such a 'feeling of internal assent' is precisely what the 'feeling of truth' amounts to.)

This of course does not mean that we don't know, at some level, that such propositions are false – and not even that we temporarily suspend our disbelief in them; but just that, in that very moment, we are so immersed in the story that we feel it true.[22]

Similarly, a child fully immersed in a pretence game may feel it really true that she is a prisoner in her enemy's hands, waiting for her fellows pirates to free her; or that she is a mother, lulling her new-born baby to sleep. And such things as toy swords and dolls help to enhance that feeling. These are all *paradigmatic* cases of imagination's exercise where what is imagined is felt true.

4.4. ... *And imaginings which feel false*

Admittedly, there are also many paradigmatic cases where we imagine something without feeling it to be true; if not even feeling it to be false, made up, *merely* fictional. That is often the case with counterfactual

---

22 And indeed we would react with surprise if, in the thick of it, the video suddenly blacked-out and the lights in the cinema were turned on, reminding us that the story on the screen is not actually true. If this happened, by the way, we would also be annoyed. The capacity fictional works have to (re)create alternative realities, making us feeling them true, is generally something we value and search in them: that is indeed one reason why many of us enjoy highly realistic representational media, such as stereoscopic 3D – which enhance such feelings of truth.

imaginings, such as those we deploy in thought experiments or hypothetical reasoning. While reading "The Meaning of Meaning", trying to assess Putnam's argument for semantic externalism, we do not typically feel it true that there is a planet like Twin Earth – silently thinking to ourselves such things as: "Oh, yes: I have a Doppelgänger who drinks twin-water!". And, actually, also daydreams, fictions and pretence games are not always felt true as in the examples just discussed.

When, cycling in a rainy winter day in Nottingham, I daydream about my summer bike rides in Tuscany, what I imagine might well feel sadly far from truth. When I play with my little nephew his favourite game – 'the underground' (consisting of opening and closing the kitchen's sliding door, simulating the loudspeaker announcements of the stops) – I might well imagine to be in the underground without feeling this true; differently from him, who apparently is completely identified with the stationmaster.

The fact that in many cases we imagine without feeling what we imagine to be true does not itself undermine the claim that imagination *disposes* us to feel-true as belief does. After all, as we have seen, everyone agrees that belief disposes us to feel its contents true even if many – indeed most – of the things that we believe at a given time are *not* things that we actually feel true at that time. We do not feel our non-occurrent beliefs to be true; but in these cases a lack of manifestation of the disposition to feel-true does not undermine the holding of the disposition itself, because the 'occurrence condition' – i.e. the condition that p is occurrently present before our mind – is not met.

The point, however, is that in the cases just considered of imagining p without feeling it true that p the occurrence condition seems to be always met. If what I imagine about cycling in Tuscany, or about being in the underground, doesn't feel true, this is *not* because the relevant propositions – such as I AM CYCLING IN TUSCANY; I AM IN THE UNDERGROUND – aren't occurrently present before my mind. Indeed, according to some, if these propositions weren't occurrently present before my mind, it wouldn't be possible to imagine them at all, for there are no such things as non-occurrent imaginings comparable (somehow) to non-occurrent beliefs (see Currie 1995a: 160-161).

Actually, I don't think this is quite right.[23] But anyway, whether or not imagining something non-occurrently is possible, we can agree that this

---

23   I am with Walton on this. Walton (1990) convincingly argues that we can have non-occurrent imaginings as well as non-occurrent beliefs (Walton 1990: 16-17). Nichols (2004) also argues along these lines, criticizing Currie (1995).

is not what happens in the cases we are considering, which are certainly cases where I occurrently imagine something and yet I do not feel it true – therefore, cases where the lack of manifestation of the disposition to feel-true is not 'excused' by the fact that the occurrence condition is not met. Shall we then conclude that such cases reveal that imagination does not dispose us to feel its contents true as belief does? No. Let's see why not.

4.5. *Conditions of manifestation: the 'Occurrent Meta-Belief Condition'*

Arguably, the reason why my daydream about Tuscany doesn't feel true as Maria's daydream about John, or why my pretence that I'm in the underground doesn't feel true as my nephew's pretence that he is, is that in both cases there is something that prevents me from being fully immersed in what I imagine in the same way in which Maria and my nephew are: something that keeps reminding me that I am, after all, *just* imagining.

Maria, sitting comfortably in the classroom, is not interested in the lecture. Indeed, she's got just one thing in mind: John. This makes it easy for her to pay no attention to what she believes about her actual situation, and to get completely absorbed in her daydream. Something that is much harder for me, when I cycle with the rain pouring in my face, clearly reminding me that I am in England and not in Tuscany.

Similarly, for my nephew – who is mad about trains and, as all children, keen to pretence play – it is quite easy to get absorbed in his game without thinking that it is *just* a game, therefore feeling it true. Again, this is much easier for him than it is for me, as I do not find the game so exciting and I am not really absorbed in it.

The reason why deeper absorption into one's imaginings is associated with a stronger feeling that they are true should be clear: insofar as one is immersed in what is imagined, one assumes a perspective internal to it, focussing all the attention on it, rather than (also) on the fact of being imagining. From this internal perspective, what is imagined *is just true*. If from an external perspective it is *true in the game* (i.e. *fictionally true*) that the kitchen is a coach, from a perspective internal to the game itself it is *simply true* that the kitchen is a coach – and so it is felt. Of course, this is not to say that the imaginer who takes such internal perspective does not believe any more that she is imagining (rather than believing) to be in a coach; she simply does not *occurrently* believe that.

What the previous examples suggest, then, is that imagining that p disposes us to feel it true that p on the condition that we do not occurrently think about the fact that we are *just* imagining p – or, more precisely, that we do not have the occurrent (meta-) belief that we do not really believe that p. Call this the '*occurrent meta-belief condition*'.

What I argue is that the same condition just described holds also in cases where it is a belief that p which disposes us to feel it true that p. If I believe that p and p is occurrently present before my mind, *but* for some reason I also occurrently believe that I do not believe that p (e.g. if for some reason I mistake my belief that p for an imagining that p), then I might well not feel it true that p. And, I take it, this lack of manifestation of the disposition to feel it true would be excused, since the occurrent meta-belief condition is not met.

4.5.1. *Belief and self-knowledge.*

I can concede that cases in which the occurrent meta-belief condition is not satisfied are less frequent with belief than with imaginings. With belief, a non-satisfaction of such condition means that the subject is wrong about what she believes: she actually believes that p, but also believes that she doesn't believe that p. This something that common opinion takes to be very rare, if possible at all: "Of course I know what I believe!", we are generally keen to think, crediting ourselves with a privileged introspective access to our own minds, and to our beliefs in particular.

In fact, the question whether we really have such a privileged introspective access to our own beliefs and deliberations is controversial. Some deny that we do, insisting that we know them by interpreting our behavior in much the same way in which we come to know of other people's beliefs and deliberations (see Carruthers 2010). And anyway, even granting some form of privileged introspective access, this does not mean that mistakes are impossible, or even very rare: privileged is not the same as infallible. Both common experience and empirical research suggest that a number of factors can blur our view of our own mind, and make us believe – maybe just temporarily – that we do not believe something that in fact we do. When this happens, it seems likely that we won't feel what we believe to be true.

Consider for example the following case, from a famous psychological experiment. Subjects were asked to write an essay in defence of a thesis they initially firmly disagreed with. A first group was asked to do that for a paltry sum of money; a second group for a more substantial sum of money. After having written the essay, they were re-asked again for their opinion about the thesis they defended. The result was that subjects in the first group expressed much more agreement with such thesis than they previously did, while subjects in the second group expressed the same disagreement as before. So, subjects in the first group seemed to lose their initial conviction that the thesis was wrong (i.e.: they didn't feel their initial belief to be true anymore); while subjects in the second group remained just as convinced as they previously were (Cohen 1962; see also Linder et al. 1965 for a replication of these results).[24] How can this difference be explained?

The suggestion that subjects in the first group changed their beliefs about the thesis in question, while subjects in the second group didn't, is not really explanatory – it simply shifts the question: why does defending a thesis for an inadequate pay make you changing your mind more than defending it for adequate pay? If what happened is that writing the essay influenced subjects' beliefs by making them realizing previously ignored good reasons in favour of the thesis in question, it would still remain mysterious why receiving a little pay should make them seeing better reasons than receiving a higher pay.

A more plausible and powerful explanation, suggested by Peter Carruthers, is that subjects in the first group didn't change their beliefs, but formed a wrong meta-belief about what they really believed, on the basis of reasoning like this: "Since I spent all that time writing the essay for a small sum of money, and since it was my choice to do so, it must be the case that I thought it worthwhile to defend the position in question. So I must believe it" (Carruthers 2010: 95). While subjects in the second group didn't form any such belief, as they could easily see a reason for what they did: they were well-paid. This would explain the asymmetry in the answers of the two groups when asked again about their position on the thesis defended.

Now, admittedly there might be other explanations here. I am not claiming to have established that Carruthers' explanation is the best possible one (although I think that it is). But little in my argument depends on this. All that matters for my argument is that if Carruthers' suggested explanation is correct, we have a clear case where subjects (those in the first group) believe that p (THIS THESIS IS WRONG), but believe they believe not p (SINCE I WROTE THE ESSAY, I MUST BELIEVE THIS THESIS IS NOT WRONG); and this seems to justify the fact that – at least for the time in which the mistaken meta-belief is occurrently present in their mind – they do not feel it true that p. If you are not persuaded that this was what actually happened to subjects in the experiment, you might probably think of different cases where someone is mistaken about her own beliefs; and even if you had it such mistakes about your own beliefs are psychologically impossible, or almost never happen, what is important for my argument is

---

24 See footnote 17 above on the relation between feeling-true that p and asserting that p.

that you agree with me that in the hypothetical case where such mistakes happened, they would justify a lack of feeling it true that p.

My suggestion so far is then the following: both believing and imagining that p dispose a subject S to feel it true that p *insofar as:*

(i)   S has p occurrently present before her mind *(occurrence condition)*; and

(ii)   S does not have an occurrent belief that she doesn't really believe that p *(occurrent meta-belief condition).*[25]

In cases of belief, condition (ii) is often met, since we generally know what we believe (though mistakes here might be more frequent than we tend to assume). While condition (i) often fails to be met, since – due to the limits of our attention – most of the propositions we believe at a time *t* are not occurrently present in our mind at *t* (and indeed many of them might almost never be occurrently present).

With imagination, the opposite seems to be the case. Condition (i) is often met, at least by the imaginings that we commonly ascribe to each other, which are generally occurrent (even without assuming that imaginings are *by necessity* occurrent). While condition (ii) sometimes is met (when we are immersed in our imaginings), and sometimes is not (in cases where we consciously think of our imaginings as imaginings).

But these differences do *not* indicate that imagining p doesn't dispose us to feel p true as believing p does. Imagining and believing dispose us to feel p true on the same conditions; the differences between them are in the satisfaction of such conditions.[26]

4.6. *Other relevant conditions of manifestation*

Note that (i) and (ii) are not the only relevant conditions of manifestation for the disposition to feel true associated to belief and to imagination. A number of cases where we do not feel what we believe/imagine to be true suggest that there are various other conditions which, if not met, might excuse a lack of manifestation of such disposition.

---

25 For a clarification about how to understand these two conditions, see footnote 20 above.

26 In Chapter 5 I shall argue that the same is true for imagination and belief's dispositional connection to action: imagining and believing dispose us act in the same ways and under the same conditions; the differences between their behavioural manifestations are due to differences in the satisfaction of such conditions. This is a line of argument originally defended by J. David Velleman (Velleman 2000).

Take for example cases where we say things like: "I can't believe that p!". What we mean in such cases is not literally that we cannot (or do not) believe that p, but rather that, though we have come, on the basis of relevant evidence, to believe that p, we still struggle to feel it true that p. So, for example, if I believe with conviction that my paper is going to be rejected, when I am notified that it has been accepted I might come to believe that it has been accepted, but for a while I might still be unable to feel that true: 'it has not sunk in yet'. Believing that p, we can then say, disposes us to feel it true that p insofar as we have enough time to become acquainted with the idea that p is the case. Call this the 'sinking in time condition'. If this condition is not met, we might believe that *p* without feeling p to be true.[27]

Or take another case, widely discussed in the recent philosophical literature: the Grand Canyon Skywalk.[28] People who visit the Skywalk arguably believe it to be safe, but while walking on it they might well struggle to feel it true that it really is. They might keep repeating to themselves that *it is perfectly safe,* without feeling internal assent to this proposition. The lack of feeling of conviction in such a case seems to be due to a conflict between beliefs and perceptions: people believe that the Skywalk is safe, but they see a precipice which they perceive as dangerous, and such perception has a stronger power on their feelings than their belief has. This suggests that believing that p disposes us to feel it true that p insofar as we don't have perceptions which conflict with such belief in the way just seen. Call this the 'no rival perceptions condition'. If this condition is not met, we might believe that p without feeling it true that p.[29]

---

27 Admittedly this is a rough and just approximate formulation of the condition in question (and the same holds for the other condition I'm going to introduce in this section). I am just trying to give an idea of a few further conditions that might be relevant for feeling our beliefs/imaginings to be true.

28 That is a popular attraction in the Grand Canyon: a mile-high glass-bottom walkway extending 70 feet from the Canyon's rim, overlooking the Colorado River, seemingly unsupported. The example has been brought to contemporary philosophers' attention by Tamar Gendler, who introduced it among her paradigmatic examples of *alief*-driven behaviours; though as she notes, 'precipice-cases' like this were discussed by philosophers (e.g. Hume) since early-modern period (see Gendler 2008a: 561-562).

29 Note that cases like this need not be perception-dependent: someone who fears flying might well believe that the aircraft is safe, and repeat this to herself during the flight, without feeling this to be true. Probably in such a case the lack of feeling of truth might be explained by a rival imagining concerning dangers of flying. We might then hypothesize a 'no rival imagining condition' analogous to the 'no rival perception condition' just discussed. This would explain why an actor who believes that he is not Ulysses may not feel this belief true when, while

Both the 'no rival perception condition' and the 'sinking in time condition' seem to hold also in cases of imaginings. Watching a fictional movie where characters walk on the Skywalk glass, I might imagine that they are safe – taking it to be true in the story that they are; yet, seeing them suspended in the void might prevent me to feel fully convinced that they are. When, at the end of Hitchcock's *Stage Fright*, Jonathan Cooper turns out to be the murder, contrary to what we had been led to think up to that point, we might have a moment where we struggle to feel it true that he is the murder, even if we imagine this to be true in the story.[30]

It is worth noticing, again, that in all these examples the relevant feeling of truth/conviction is not really an all-or-nothing matter as I have treated it for the sake of simplicity. It actually comes in degrees. Although I might feel somehow unconvinced that Skywalk is safe, or that my paper has been accepted, this doesn't mean that I don't feel it to be true at all.

But what matters to my point is that these different degrees of conviction do not depend on whether the proposition is believed or imagined; they depend on a number of conditions which are the same for belief and for imagination. Belief and imagination, dispose us to feel their contents true in much the same ways – i.e. on the same conditions – differing only with respect to the satisfaction of such conditions.[31]

4.7. *Summing up*

Where are we? I started from the observation that in paradigmatic cases belief and imagination are alike in that they have the same kind of contents and they both 'regard such contents as true'; and I am trying to spell out what, plainly speaking, such regarding-as-true amounts to. So far, I have considered a first important dimension of it: *a phenomenal dimension*. In §§ 3 and 4 have argued that both belief and imagination regard their contents as true in the sense that they dispose us to undergo certain kinds of conscious experiences in response to such contents: experiences that

---

performing Ulysses' role on the stage, he tells to the Cyclops Polyphemus "I'm not Ulysses".

30   In fact, the question whether it is really true in Hitchcock's story that he is the murder may be controversial (Hitchcock's use of flash-back here makes it hard to settle the issue). Here I am just assuming that some viewers (like me) imagine it to be true in the story that he is the murder, yet (for a while at least) they struggle to feel it true.

31   Here I have discussed just some of the relevant conditions. I take the burden of the proof to find conditions that make a difference between belief and imagination to be on my opponent.

include various kinds of emotions and a peculiar sense of conviction/ feeling of truth. In § 5 I am going to consider another important dimension of regarding-as-true: *a cognitive dimension*.

5. *Regarding-as-true: cognitive aspect*

Regarding a proposition as true does not involve only being disposed to respond emotionally to it in ways that would be appropriate if it were true, but it also involves being disposed to treat it as true in one's reasoning: to ignore, at least temporarily, the possibility that it is false, in order to explore the consequences that would follow from its being true.[32]

This is another respect in which belief and imagination are widely recognized to be alike. If I come to believe that black truffles are cheap, I shall conclude that most people can afford black truffles every day. If I read a fictional story which says that black truffles are cheap, I may well draw the same conclusion: most people can afford black truffles every day. Of course, in this latter case I don't come to *believe* this conclusion as I did in the first case: now I just imagine it to be true in the story.[33] But I draw the same inference in both cases. While I wouldn't draw that inference if I *desired* black truffles to be cheap. That is because in desiring black truffles to be cheap I wouldn't regard it as true that they are. And the conclusion that most people can afford truffles every day only follows if I consider the consequences of it being true that truffles are cheap.[34]

Here it is worth noticing that when, reading the fictional story where truffles are cheap, I conclude that most people can afford them, a tacit premise of my inference is something I *believe* about cheap things – namely, that they are things which most people can afford. Inferences of this kind play a crucial role in our engagement with fictional stories. Authors do not have to (nor indeed reasonably could) tell us *everything*

---

32   This is how Stalnaker characterizes the notion of acceptance: "To accept a proposition is to treat it as a true proposition in one way or another – to ignore, for the moment at least, the possibility that it is false" (Stalnaker 1984: 79).

33   More precisely, I imagine it to be true (true *tout court*) – and I believe it to be true *in the story* (see Currie 1990: Chapter 2).

34   Desires *qua desires* do not function as premises in theoretical reasoning: even though, of course, I can draw consequences from a proposition that I desire, in order to do that I need – if only for a moment – to regard this proposition as true in a way in which only beliefs or imaginings can be regarded. Something like this seems indeed what happens in cases of 'wishful thinking', where a proposition that is desired (for the mere fact of being desired) starts being *regarded as true*.

they want us to imagine; they rely on us using our general knowledge to fill out their stories with relevant information that is not explicit in the text (for discussions about the principles that guide such a 'filling out', see Lewis 1978; Currie 1990: Chapter 2; Walton 1990: Chapter 4).[35]

If Holmes is said to receive a bullet wound in his chest, competent readers will infer that he won't recover in hours or days, importing their beliefs about bullets' effects and human physiology into Holmes' story – more or less in the following way:

P1) Holmes has received a bullet wound in his chest. (Something readers *imagine*)

P2) No one who receives a bullet wound in his chest recovers in hours or days. (Something readers believe, therefore also *imagine*)

∴   Holmes won't recover in hours/days. (Something readers *imagine*)[36]

Inferences like this are possible insofar as belief and imagination have isomorphic contents; and inferential mechanisms process propositions only on the basis of their contents, irrespective of whether they are believed or imagined.

Though this doesn't mean that such mechanisms are completely blind to the belief/imagination distinction: when they work properly, they operate in such a way as to ensure that when the premises of an inference are imagined and not believed, the conclusion of the inference, too, will be an imagining and not a belief – as in the example just seen.[37]

Research in developmental psychology shows that children engaged in pretence make similar inferences from a remarkably young age, importing into their games many things they believe to be true in the real world.[38] If

---

35   As Tamar Gendler notes: "The narrator needs to assume that the listener shares a wide range of back-ground beliefs about the world, and the listener needs to assume that the narrator assumes this, and so on, in a familiar Gricean fashion" (Gendler 2000: 76).

36   See Currie (2002): 206-207.

37   Though note that things can go wrong, and we sometimes end up believing conclusions drawn from imagined premises (for a discussion of cases like this occurring in our engagement with fictions, see Currie and Ichino 2016). Note also that it is not clear that all inferences which have an imagining among their premises *should* end up with an imagined conclusion. If it is true that imaginability entails conceptual possibility, then there would be modal inferences where from imagined premises (I imagine q) we come to believe some conclusions (I believe q to be possible).

38   The classic reference here are Alan Leslie's seminal studies (Leslie 1987, 1994). See also Harris (2000): notably Chapter 2. The literature on these topics is really vast; for some further references see my discussion of pretence in Chapter 3, §4.

(in the game) Sam takes a shot at Rob, they will both spontaneously infer that Rob is now wounded, drawing on their beliefs about the effects of shooting (unless, of course, special assumptions were made in the game, such as the assumption that Rob is invulnerable).

Will they also infer that Rob won't recover in hours or days? Perhaps; but not necessarily. Maybe for the sake of the game it is rather better to 'allow' Rob being back in full form within seconds, ignoring that a consequence of being shot is to be out of action for a long time.

Here it is worth noting that a *decision* of this sort would not be possible if they *believed*, rather than merely imagined, that Sam has been shot. Indeed, when we believe something it does not seem to be up to us to decide what consequences we draw from it. Although factors such as interest and attention do arguably play a role in determining what inferences (among the myriad possible ones) are deployed in different cases, ignoring the *obvious* consequences of something we believe cannot *just* be a matter of conscious deliberation.

An important difference between imagination and belief seems finally to be coming out, then. I will return to this in the next chapter. For the moment, though, I would rather conclude by emphasizing the striking similarity that has emerged so far, which I have described as a cognitive dimension of 'regarding-as-true': both when we imagine and when we believe that p we can – and are somehow disposed to – draw theoretical inferences from p.[39]

The parallel between belief and imagination in this respect seems to be even closer – and, indeed, more uncontroversially recognized – than the parallel in the emotional respect considered above (§ 2). If, as we have seen, some deny that a proposition can have the same emotional effects whether it is believed or imagined, no one really questions that a proposition can make the same contribution to our theoretical reasoning whether it is believed or imagined: no one would argue that inferences drawn from imagined propositions are not real inferences but *quasi*-inferences.

It is sometimes said that imagination 'preserves' (or 'mirror') [40] the inferential role of belief; but this should not – nor, I take it, is meant to – suggest that our inferential mechanisms are primarily suited to process beliefs, while

---

39 The specification 'theoretical' here is necessary because propositions that are not regarded as true – but, for example, as to be made true – play crucial roles in practical reasoning; while only propositions regarded as true enter in theoretical reasoning.

40 See e.g. Currie (2002); Gendler (2003); Currie & Ichino (2013): strictly speaking, both preservation and mirroring are asymmetric processes (imagination preserves/ mirrors something that is originally a feature of belief).

imaginings exploit such mechanisms in a kind of parasitic, subaltern way. Indeed, inferences from imagined premises do not occur just in the context of engagement with fiction and pretence games, but are pervasive in our thinking: they are what make all our counterfactual or hypothetical thinking possible. So, imagination and belief regard their contents as true also in this 'cognitive' sense: we can include both imagined and believed propositions into bits of our theoretical reasoning, drawing inferences from them.

Conclusion

In this Chapter I have introduced the so-called Hume's Problem, which will be a central thread of this book: how does imagination differ from belief? I have sought to explain how the problem arises, considering some striking similarities between imagination and belief that make it hard to set the one apart from the other. I have argued that imaginings and beliefs have the *same sort of contents:* they both have propositional contents. And that they *'regard'* *such contents in the same way:* they both regard such contents as true. Talking in terms of 'regarding-as-true' is, of course, metaphorical. As David Velleman observes, surely this locution shouldn't be understood as positing "an inner eye that squints at propositions or raises its eyebrow at them so as to regard them in different ways" (Velleman 2000: 182). Most of my discussion in this chapter has then been devoted to clarifying this metaphor.

I have suggested that regarding a proposition p as true involves at least two aspects. First, a *phenomenal* aspect: insofar as I regard p as true, I am disposed to undergo emotions that would be appropriate if p were true (emotions which include also a peculiar feeling of conviction about p). Second, a *cognitive* aspect: insofar as I regard p as true, I am disposed to treat p as true in my reasoning, drawing theoretical inferences from it. I take these two aspects to be both necessary and jointly sufficient for regarding a proposition as true. I do also take it that (leaving aside the disposition to feel convinced about p –which is often taken to be an exclusive prerogative of belief) most parties in the debate agree that imagination and belief are alike in the phenomenal and cognitive respects here in question: i.e. most parties in the debate agree that imagination and belief regard their contents as true in at least these two senses.[41]

---

41 While, on the other hand, not everyone agrees that both imagination and belief
      regard their contents as true in the sense of disposing us to *act* as if their contents
      where true, as Velleman (2000) argues. Here I meant to offer a characterization of
      'regarding-as-true' which remains neutral on the controversial question of

But how do imagination and belief differ, then? Why, in spite of the striking similarities just discussed, do we say without hesitation that I believe that I am an academic philosopher, while I just imagine that I am a Duchess?[42] Now that we have clarified how Hume's problem arises, we should find a way to solve it. This will be the business of the next three chapters.

---

imagination's motivating power. Although I agree with Velleman that a disposition to motivate relevant actions is indeed characteristic of states – like beliefs and imaginings – which regard their contents as true, I do not take this to be necessarily part of what regarding-as-true amounts to. Therefore, even if eventually you were not fully persuaded by my arguments for the motivating power of imagination, you could still agree with me that imagination regards its contents as true as belief does.

42   Again, note that the question here is *why,* not *how* we distinguish imagination from belief in that way: it is a question about the *reasons* that *justify/explain* our ascriptions, not about the *mechanisms* that are *causally responsible* for them. And my answer to the 'why' question is neutral with respect to the 'how' question.

3.
IMAGINATION AND BELIEF: WHERE IS THE DIFFERENCE?

We all agree that subjects imagine rather than believing, the relevant contents of the daydreams, fictions, pretences, and thoughts experiments they engage with. So far, however, I have highlighted only the respects in which, in all such cases, imagination and belief are alike. That still leaves us without an answer to Hume's problem: what is that makes the critical difference between them?

In this chapter I shall consider two sorts of differences that might look as good candidates to answer this question. On the one hand, differences in cognitive *inputs* – concerning the ways in which imagination and belief are formed (and maintained). On the other hand, differences in behavioural *outputs* – concerning the ways in which imagination and belief influence our actions. My aim is to show that, in spite of appearances, output differences do not actually hold, and the critical difference between imaginings and beliefs lies at the inputs level.

Though my main argument for this view will come in the next two chapters, here I will bring some initial support in its favour on the basis of the analysis of pretence actions – notably of children's games of pretence. After having clarified what the (supposed) inputs and outputs differences between imagination and belief amount to (§§ 1-2), I will argue that the best possible explanation of pretenders' behaviours requires us to recognize the autonomous motivating power of imagination, thereby challenging the idea that the production of action outputs is an exclusive prerogative of belief (§3).

Along my discussion I shall examine in detail the dynamics of motivation by imagining – considering the role that desires and 'desire-like imaginings' play in it. This will pave the way for next chapters' more general argument in favour of the identity of imagination and belief's motivating powers.

1. *Input differences: sensitivity to evidence*

Let's go back to my daydream that I am the Duchess of Sussex. Why do we say without hesitation that I just *imagine* that I am a Duchess, while I *believe* that I am an academic philosopher? Two orders of considerations seem to be most relevant here – which I will discuss, respectively, in this section (§1) and the next (§2).

A first sort of relevant considerations concern the ways in which my two representations (I AM A DUCHESS; I AM AN ACADEMIC PHILOSOPHER) are formed/maintained, and the normative constraints to which they are subjected.

All the evidence available to me strongly suggests that I am an academic philosopher and not a Duchess; and my representation of myself as an academic philosopher seems to be formed and maintained in response to such evidence. I first formed that representation when I was notified that my application for a philosophy academic position had been successful, and I now maintain it insofar as I have some relevant evidence (e.g. the University keeps paying me), or at least insofar as I don't get relevant counter-evidence. If I received a notice of dismissal from my Head of Department, for example, I would not represent myself as an academic philosopher any more. Or, better: I might continue representing myself as an academic philosopher, but my attitude towards this representation could not be belief anymore. I might imagine that I (still) am an academic philosopher; or wish that I (still) were an academic philosopher. But how could I still *believe* that – after having read and understood notice of dismissal I received? It seems that I simply couldn't: the very belief status of my attitude crucially depends on its being sensitive to the evidence available to me – and that notice is an obvious piece of counter-evidence.

In fact, things here are a bit more complex than that. To say that after having read and understood the University notification I *could not* believe that I am an academic philosopher anymore is not strictly speaking true. What is true is that I could not *just decide* to maintain my belief in the same way in which I can just decide, say, to raise my arm. As Bernard Williams famously observed: "belief cannot be like that; (...) I cannot bring it about, just like that, that I believe something" (Williams 1970: 148).

But while it seems undeniable that I could not *consciously* decide to ignore contrary evidence and keep believing that I am an academic philosopher, it is not hard to think of cases where some evidence insensitive factors *not (fully) consciously recognized as such* cause me to maintain such belief. Think for example of a case where my strong desire to keep my job, and my consequent disappointment at the idea of losing it, lead me to discount – more or less consciously – the evidence provided by the notice I receive. But then, when more compelling evidence becomes available to me – e.g. when I receive a further official notice from the Head of School – I do eventually respond to it, changing my attitude accordingly.[1] In a case like this, my initial resistance to abandon my 'academic philosopher representation' in the face of contrary evidence, *although admittedly far from perfectly rational,* would not in itself compromise the very belief status of my attitude towards that representation. And indeed, looking at the thing retrospectively, I may well feel embarrassed for having *unreasonably* continued to *believe* that I had a position as academic philosopher.

Cases like this, where the formation and maintenance of our beliefs is influenced *also* by motivational (i.e. evidence *in*sensitive) factors like desires or emotions, seem to be quite common. Think for example of what psychologists call 'self-serving beliefs', or of many other familiar instances of wishful thinking.[2] It doesn't sound right to say that any supposed belief that is affected by such motivational factors is, in fact, not a belief at all. What we shall say is rather that, insofar as they are affected by such motivational, evidence insensitive factors, the beliefs in question are somehow epistemically defective: they are, to some extent, *irrational* – as I observed my belief that I am an academic philosopher would be, if I maintained it in spite of the evidence (i.e. the notice of dismissal) I received.

All this suggests that we should distinguish two senses in which the sensitivity to evidence of a representation is relevant for its belief status. The first is a *constitutive* sense: some degree of sensitivity to evidence seems to be a constitutive, necessary feature of belief, so that an attitude

---

1   I might for example ignore it, reading the email very quickly and immediately forgetting it (like in Freudian cases of repression); or I might read it carefully and tell myself that it must be a mistake, that surely the notification doesn't really mean what it seems to mean, hence put it in a corner and, again, forget about it for a while... Till when I receive the new notification.

2   What psychologists call 'self-serving beliefs' are, roughly, beliefs about ourselves which are formed on the basis of a biased consideration of the available evidence, due to a need/desire to enhance self-esteem and preserve a positive self-image (see e.g. Taylor and Brown 1988). So for example it seems that healthy, non-depressed subjects tend to form beliefs of this sort about their own past, concentrating on evidence of good performances, and neglecting evidence of poor ones. I think that in various cases there may be room to question whether so-called 'self-serving beliefs' are actually best described as belief; but at least some instances of them surely are. For a review and discussion of the literature on self-serving bias, see Bortolotti (2010): 143-148.

which doesn't display any degree of such sensitivity cannot thereby count as belief. The claim that after having read and understood the notice of dismissal I *cannot* believe that I am an academic philosopher anymore appeals to this constitutive role of sensitivity to evidence. But it overlooks the important specification that what is constitutively necessary for belief is not *perfect* sensitivity to evidence; it is just *some degree* of it.

The fact that an attitude does not change in response to one relevant piece of evidence does not, in itself, necessarily mean that it is completely insensitive to evidence; so it is not enough to conclude that such attitude is not a belief.

On the other hand, as we have seen, insofar as an attitude classifies as belief, the fact that it does not change in response to one relevant piece of evidence makes it somehow defective. This has to do with the second, *normative* sense in which sensitivity to evidence is relevant to belief.

If perfect sensitivity to evidence is not a constitutive requirement for belief, it seems to be at least a normative one: a normative ideal to which rational beliefs should conform. Ideally, a rational subject ought to form her beliefs just on the basis of an objective assessment of the evidence available to her, not influenced by what she desires, or fears, nor by any other non-evidential factors.

Why ought she to do that? This can be understood in relation to another key norm that governs belief – a 'norm of truth'. When we classify a state as belief, we apply to it a standard of correctness which is satisfied if and only if its propositional content is true. A reason why beliefs ought to be perfectly sensitive to evidence can be seen in the fact that responding to the available evidence is the best way for them to track truth. My attitude towards the representation of myself as an academic philosopher seems to be normatively governed by these sorts of rationality and truth standards: which is why, if I maintain such an attitude in spite of the notification of suspension, I can be criticized in the ways we have seen – I can be criticized for holding an irrational and false *belief*.[3]

My attitude towards the representation of myself as a Duchess is not similarly constrained – either constitutively or normatively – by evidence and truth. That representation is not formed in response to the evidence available to me. It just depends on how I *decide*, for a while, to represent the world, or perhaps simply on what happens to 'come to my mind' at

---

3   To say it, again, with Williams: "Truth and falsehood are dimensions of an assessment of belief as opposed to many other psychological states" (Williams: 1970: 136). I will discuss more in detail these norms and the relation between the constitutive and the normative dimensions of belief's sensitivity to evidence in Chapter 4: §2.3.

a given time. Indeed, I obviously don't take newspapers' articles about the Royal Wedding as a source of evidence about myself; what happens is just that such news somehow prompt me to form a representation – the representation of myself as a Duchess – which I then, more or less deliberately, enjoy entertaining for a while.

And, importantly, there is nothing wrong with that: there is nothing irrational in my *imagining*, for a bit, that I am a Duchess; and the fact that this proposition is false does not put me in a defective epistemic condition.

So this seems to be a first important difference between my two representations, which might explain why one of them is classified as imagining, and the other is classified as belief: my representation of myself as a Duchess is not, nor ought to be, sensitive to real-world evidence as my representation of myself as an academic philosopher is, and ought to be.

1.1. *Inferential integration and holistic coherence*

There are different kinds of evidence to which beliefs can be sensitive. One is perceptual evidence. My belief that I'm sat in front of this computer, for example, is formed in response to my visual perception of the computer, together with my proprioception of myself in front of it – in a rather unreflective process, which doesn't seem to involve any conscious inference (if any inference at all).

My belief that I am an academic philosopher, on the other hand, is the result of a more reflective response to a different kind of evidence, which does not amount to perceptions, but to *reasons:* let's call it 'inferential evidence'. That belief seems to follow as a consequence from various other beliefs I hold – such as the belief that my job application for a philosophy academic position was successful, the belief that if one's job application is successful, then one gets the position for which she applied, etc... These beliefs constitute reasons for me to form and keep the belief that I am an academic philosopher; which in turn constitutes a reason to form other beliefs (e.g. the beliefs that I should pursue academic research, that I should teach the courses I am expected to teach, and so on), as well as a reason to abandon any other belief that is in tension with it (e.g. the belief that I am unemployed).

As it turns out, a direct consequence of belief's sensitivity to inferential evidence is that our beliefs tend to be *integrated into a holistically coherent system.*

This system, of course, includes also perceptual beliefs. Although perceptual beliefs might not be formed on the basis of inferential reasoning, once they are formed they become sensitive to it, being integrated with other pre-existing beliefs. This is how, e.g., the false belief that I might form the first time I look at the Müller-Lyer arrows is revised when I learn that they involve an optical illusion.[4]

And the same is true of beliefs formed in response to other kinds of evidence, like what we can call *testimonial* or *introspective* evidence – intended quite loosely to indicate such stimuli as 'other people's words', or 'the inner perception of one's own feelings'. These sorts of stimuli may – rightly or wrongly, and more or less consciously – be taken as an evidential basis for one's beliefs (as with the belief that my application was successful formed in response to an email from the University Human Resources Office; or the belief that I feel happy for that success, formed by introspecting my own emotions/feelings).

Whether forming beliefs on the basis of testimony (or indeed of introspection) does in itself involve inferential processes of some sorts is a controversial question, which I won't tackle here. But it seems uncontroversial that, once testimonial and introspective beliefs are formed, they become sensitive to inferential reasoning, integrating with the rest of our beliefs (as we have seen with the testimonial belief that my application was successful, which – together with my pre-existing beliefs on the consequences of successful applications – becomes a premise for further inferences about my academic position).

Apparently, then, among the different kinds of evidence to which beliefs can be sensitive, what I have called 'inferential evidence' has an especially important status.[5] It is a kind of evidence to which *all* beliefs, from the moment in which they are formed, become sensitive. While the other sorts of evidence just considered (higher-level testimonial evidence, or lower-level perceptual/introspective evidence) do not play a relevant role in *all* cases.

So, for example, general abstract beliefs (e.g. the belief that $2 + 2 = 4$) may not be sensitive to perceptual evidence; introspective beliefs (and maybe some evaluative beliefs, like moral or aesthetic ones) may not be sensitive to testimonial evidence; but all those beliefs, no matters how they are initially

---

4   While, on the other hand, the lower-level perceptual representation of the two arrows remains the same, due to cognitive encapsulation.

5   I am not claiming to have provided an exhaustive taxonomy of all the possible kinds of evidence to which beliefs can be sensitive (nor indeed a taxonomy that carves the nature of such kinds of evidence at its joints). Another relevant kind of evidence, arguably, comes from *memory*.

formed, will be to some extent sensitive to the inferential evidence constituted by the holistic system of a subject's pre-existing beliefs.

All this, again, should be understood in a *normative* as well as in a *constitutive* sense. Being *fully* inferentially integrated into a holistically coherent system is a norm to which the beliefs of a rational subject should conform; and *some degree* of inferential integration and holistic coherence is a necessary, constitutive condition for a given state to classify as belief.

Local inconsistencies are possible and, indeed, happen rather often.[6] But they put the subject in a defective epistemic condition: a rational subject who recognizes them should feel a pressure to solve them. And, beyond a certain limit, inconsistencies and lack of inferential integration cast serious doubts on the very belief status of the states that are involved. Indeed, one reason why my representation of myself as the Duchess of Sussex does not classify as belief is that it is at odds with many other important beliefs I have (about myself, my life, the UK's Royal family, etc...).

2. *Output differences: dispositions to action*

Another respect in which my representation of myself as the Duchess of Sussex seems to differ from my representation of myself as an academic philosopher has to do with the effects that such two representations have upon my actions.

This morning I did not wear an elegant white dress and looked for my chauffeur in order to be taken to Westminster Abbey. I wore my usual attire and I cycled to University, where I spent all day at my desk, doing such things as writing my book and updating my academic CV – a CV where, of course, I declare to be an academic philosopher working at the University of Milan, not the Duchess of Sussex. My representation of myself as an academic philosopher apparently motivates me to act in certain ways – ways in which my representation of myself as a Duchess does not. This seems to be, *prima facie* at least, a reason why we classify the one as belief and the other as imagining.[7]

6　The extensive psychological literature on human reasoning shows that we are all subject to rather systematic mistakes in deductive as well as probabilistic reasoning, which often lead to the formation of inconsistent beliefs (for an extensive discussion of psychological studies in this area, see Kahneman 2011).

7　Note that when I talk about *motivation* here I refer to the *actual* role that a given cognition has in bringing about action: imaginings in cases of daydream like this do not motivate in the sense that, as it happens, they do not bring about any action.

Here it is worth noting that the belief that I am an academic philosopher will motivate my action to work on my book only in conjunction with other representational states: including other beliefs – e.g. the belief that academic philosophers are expected to write books, and, notably, some relevant desires – e.g. the desire to do what I am expected to do. If I desired to disappoint my employers, instead, or if I believed that academics are not expected to write books, but farming the land, then the belief that I am an academic philosopher would not motivate me to write my book. Nor would it motivate me to write on my CV that I am an academic philosopher, unless I also desired to have a truthful CV. If I desired to fake m CV, I may well write on it that I am a professional dancer.

A good way to describe the motivational power characteristic of belief might then be in terms of a dispositional connection *via desire* to action: believing that p disposes one to act in ways that, if *p* were true, would promote the satisfaction of one's desires (see Stalnaker 1984: 82; Velleman 2000: 255; Van Leeuwen 2009: 219). Indeed, if it is true that I am an academic philosopher, writing my book will (help to) satisfy my desire to do what my employer expects me to do. And writing on my CV that I am an academic philosopher will (help to) satisfy my desire to have a truthful CV.[8]

Importantly, belief's dispositions to action may fail to be manifested even in the presence of the relevant desires. So, for example, I might well believe that I am an academic philosopher who is expected to write books, and desire to do what I am expected to do, yet fail to perform the action of writing my book because my computer is broken and I spend the entire day trying to repair it.

In a case like this, the lack of manifestation of the disposition to act upon my belief might be excused by the physical impediment to perform the relevant actions, and it wouldn't indicate that I am not disposed to perform such actions.[9] But the holding of such disposition, even though not manifested, seems to be necessary to ascribe to me the belief that I

But – as I shall argue in Chapter 5 – that does not mean that imaginings lack *motivating force* – i.e. that they do not dispose to act in the relevant ways. In §3.1 below I shall better clarify what precisely the motivation here in question amount to, introducing the so-called Humean Theory of Motivation.

8   This latter action, by the way, is of a kind that plays a key role in our practices of belief ascription: indeed, as I noted in Chapter 2 (§4), we tend to credit people with a reliable knowledge of their own beliefs (and inner lives more in general), therefore we take sincere assertions as a reliable guide to people's beliefs.

9   There is a large (arguably, indefinitely large) number of 'excusing conditions' of this sort, which may justify lacks of belief's behavioural manifestations. I will discuss this point at length in Chapter 5.

am an academic philosopher. If I never even thought to work on a book, I never said that I am an academic philosopher, nor I wrote it into my CV, this would probably mean that I am not disposed to perform such actions; hence, that I do not believe that I am an academic philosopher, after all.

This, we have seen, may indeed be a reason why my representation of myself as a Duchess does not qualify as belief: this representation does not motivate any action, hence the natural thing to say seems to be that it does not *dispose* me to act in the relevant ways (the natural thing to say, I shall argue, is wrong; but for the moment let's grant its *prima facie* plausibility).[10]

2.1. *Some doubts about output differences*

So, in a paradigmatic case of daydreaming like the one I have been discussing, my imaginings seem to differ from my beliefs in two notable respects. On one hand, they seem to differ with respect to their cognitive inputs (and the normative constraints which govern them): my imaginings are not (nor ought to be) formed and maintained in response to real-world evidence as my beliefs are (and ought to be). On the other hand, they seem to differ with respect to their behavioural outputs: my imaginings do not motivate me to act as my beliefs (jointly with my desires) do.

Similar considerations on inputs and outputs might be taken to explain also other paradigmatic cases where the belief/imagination distinction looks straightforward.

Readers' imaginings of Harry Potter's story, for example, are obviously unresponsive to real-world evidence (they are indeed formed in response to the fiction) and disconnected from action. Readers typically enjoy the story for the sake of fun and recreation: their engagement with it is not contingent on their taking it to be true (and there is nothing irrational with that: that's precisely what competent fiction's readers should do). Nor does readers' engagement with the story motivate them to act upon it: they do not take precautions against Lord Vordemort's evil curses, or ever consider applying for a job at Hogwarts School of Witchcraft and Wizardry. And, of course, they would not sincerely assent to most of the propositions that are part of the story. If invited to speak truthfully, they would not say that somewhere in the UK, near to a black forest, there is a famous school of witchcraft and wizardry.

---

10 Indeed, in Chapter 5 I shall argue that this is just a case where the relevant disposition fails to *manifest* itself.

And so it goes with the more 'serious' instances of imagination's exercise introduced above – such as thoughts experiments and other forms of counterfactual thinking.

The view that imaginings and beliefs critically differ both with respect to the ways in which they are formed and with respect to their behavioural outputs is almost universally accepted. So much that Shaun Nichols (2006) describes these two differences between imaginings and beliefs as one of the "central *facts* about the propositional imagination that have shaped almost all theorizing in the recent literature" (Nichols 2006: 6).[11]

This almost universal agreement notwithstanding, however, I wish to distance myself from the view in question.

As I already hinted, I think that motivational differences between imagination and belief, far from being 'a fact', are actually merely apparent. Even if in the paradigmatic cases just considered imaginings do not motivate any action, there are many other cases where they do motivate, suggesting that imagination has the same motivating *power* as belief, though this power is not always exerted. But remember that it is not always exerted in cases of belief, either – since belief's connection to action outputs is a dispositional one. I characterized it as a disposition to act in ways that would promote the satisfaction of our desires if what we believe is true, noting that in many cases such disposition holds without being actually manifested. Imagination – I shall argue – disposes us to act in the same ways.

Some initial evidence and intuitive plausibility for my view comes from the consideration of another paradigmatic case of imagination's exercise I introduced in Chapter 2: the case of pretence.

---

11   Introducing a collection of key contributions to the ongoing debate on propositional imagination, Nichols (2006) observes: "Most people working in this area agree on several substantive claims about the nature of imagination. (...) Imaginational representations are distinguished from belief representations by their *functional roles*. (...) Further, the central facts reviewed in Section 3 provide us with some of the critical functional differences between believing and imaging. *The inputs to the imagination are at the whim of the intention, but this is not the case for belief, and the imagination and belief make different contributions to action tendencies. These are major differences in the causal roles of imaginational representations and belief representations...*" (Nichols 2006: 8-9). For more recent endorsements of this 'Standard View of Imagination' (as I shall call it in Chapter 5), see e.g. Sinhababu (2012, 2016); Schellenberg (2013), Liao and Doggett (2014). Basically, as I shall say, I know just one author who does not conform to this view: J. David Velleman (2000).

3. Pretence

Children playing the Wild West game seem to act upon their imaginings: cowboys twirl round their jests, Indians throw their darts, they chase each other... That's indeed what the game crucially consists in. So, one may argue, the fact that children imagine, rather than believe, that they are cowboys/ Indians, cannot be explained by the fact that their representations of themselves as cowboys/Indians do not motivate them to act in the relevant ways. It can only be explained by the fact that such representations are formed as a result of what children decide to enact in their games, rather than in response to real-world evidence (and there is nothing irrational in that).

If this is right, then, the case of pretence may be taken to support my view that considerations about behavioural outputs are not sufficient to distinguish imagination from belief, while only considerations about epistemic inputs are sufficient.

We should be careful in drawing such a conclusion, though. One thing is to say that a child imagines, rather than believes, that he is a cowboy. Quite another thing is to say that this very imagining is what motivates him to act in cowboy-like ways. While the former thing is rather uncontroversial, the latter is not: many deny it, arguing that the only mental states that can motivate action are beliefs in conjunction with desires. In §§ 3.1 and 3.2 I will critically discuss these arguments and explain why I take them to be, ultimately, unconvincing.[12]

3.1. The 'Humean theory of motivation'

The idea that the only mental states with motivational power upon action are beliefs and desires is at the basis of a very influential view of psychological motivation, known as 'Humean theory of motivation' (see Davidson 1963; Smith 1987, 1994).

This view looks very plausible, prima facie, at least if we start from the assumption that actions are by definition *intentional* doings. Indeed, it seems that, insofar as an action is something that an agent does intentionally, it must involve some *desire* of the agent towards an intended end; and this desire, in turn, will only motivate the relevant doing if such doing is seen as a way to fulfil the desire – which is why a *belief* seems to be

---

12 In what follows I will focus mostly on children's pretence. However, I take what I am going to say to hold more in general, also for adult's pretence (more precisely, for *many paradigmatic instances* of it).

also necessary.[13] Therefore, on this view, any action A must be motivated – i.e. caused and rationalized – by a desire-belief pair: more precisely, by a desire to ϕ and a belief that ϕ can be obtained by performing the action A.

So, for example, if my cycling to the swimming pool is an action, rather than something that merely happens to me (like an autonomic behaviour), this is because it is motivated by a desire-belief pair of the kind just seen: e.g. by my desire to swim and my belief that if I cycle to the swimming pool, then I can swim.

The specification that such a *motivation* amounts both to a *cause* and a *reason* for my action is important. This is a point famously defended by Donald Davidson (1963). My desire to swim, together with my belief that I can swim if I cycle to the pool, certainly constitutes a *reason* for that action – call it reason R. But I might well have also a number of other reasons S, T, W... to act in that way: I might well have a number of other belief-desire pairs that would rationalize my action – e.g. the desire to try my new bike and the belief that I can try my new bike by cycling to the swimming pool. Yet, on this occasion *the* actual reason for my action is R, and nothing else: I cycle to the pool *because* I want to swim, and not because I want to try my new bike (nor for any other reason either). The only way to account for this – Davidson suggests – is to recognize that R is not just a reason, but it is also what actually causes my action. *Motivating reasons* are not just reasons that justify actions; they are also causal factors that produce them.

It is also worth noticing that on this view not all beliefs have a *direct* motivational power upon action. Strictly speaking, only beliefs of the form "ϕ can be obtained by performing action A" can – in conjunction with the relevant desires (desires *to* ϕ) – motivate actions. This however doesn't mean that we should revise the *general* claim that beliefs dispose us to act in ways that would promote the satisfaction of our desires if the believed

---

13   Belief-desire pairs like this are what Davidson calls "primary reasons" of an action (Davidson 1963: 686). It is controversial whether such primary reasons are enough to motivate actions, or whether it is also necessary to form, on the basis of such primary reasons, an *intention* to act. In contrast with Elizabeth Anscombe (1957), Davidson argues for a reduction of intentions to primary reasons: on this view, acting with intention is just acting on the basis of a belief-desire pair; there isn't any distinctive state of intending over and above beliefs and desires (later on, Davidson will change his mind; see Davidson 1980, Essay 5). It is worth noticing that also the definition of *action* is controversial: some authors question the idea that actions are necessarily intentional (see e.g. Romdenh-Romluc 2013). However, here I sidestep this debate. What I am interested in is the 'Humean' claim that only belief-desire pairs can motivate intentional doings; and I call all intentional doings 'actions'.

contents were true, claiming instead that only beliefs of that particular form dispose us to act in such ways. Indeed, as we have seen, a crucial feature of beliefs is their holistic (coherent) inferential integration. Our beliefs about how to satisfy our desires (i.e. beliefs of the form "φ can be obtained by performing action A") will be connected with – and, in many cases, derived from – the other beliefs we have about the real world (notably, beliefs about the nature of φ, about the effects of action A, about ourselves and our own capacities, and other similar matters). All these other beliefs can then be taken to play a role, more or less direct, in disposing us to act in particular ways – since they are (or at least are available to be) taken into account into our practical reasoning.

Take the case where I desire to eat some pie, I walk to the kitchen, take a piece of pie, and put it in my mouth. Presumably, what happens in this case is that *my desire to eat pie* makes occurrently present before my mind some beliefs relevant to the satisfaction of that desire, e.g. the belief that there is some pie left over from yesterday, the belief that the pie is in the kitchen, the belief that if something is in the kitchen I can get it by walking to the kitchen, and so on. From these beliefs, I come to form the further belief that *I can eat some pie by going to the kitchen, taking a piece of pie and putting it in my mouth.* This latter belief is surely the one that makes maximally close contact with my action; but all the other beliefs from which it is derived are also responsible for my action (in a *causal* as well as in a *rational* sense). All these beliefs are part of a system which, as a whole, is dispositionally connected to action.

So, far from contradicting the view that dispositional connection via desire to action is a necessary feature of beliefs, the Humean theory of motivation pushes that view even further, suggesting that dispositional connection via desire to action is also sufficient to set belief apart from the other cognitive attitudes, since that disposition to action is an exclusive prerogative of belief. Anything that counts as an action is motivated by a belief-desire pair of the kind just seen.

3.2. *A Humean account of pretence?*

If anything that counts as an action is motivated by a suitable belief-desire pair, this must be the case also with pretence actions. This doesn't commit Humean theorists to denying that imagination plays any role in explaining pretence. But it does commit them to denying that imagination plays a straightforwardly *motivational* role.

An influential account of this Humean kind has been defended by Nichols and Stich (2000) (henceforth, "N&S"). While granting that a child who chases his friend, shooting (toy) arrows at him and shouting: "Give yourself up!" imagines – and does not believe – that he is an Indian fighting with a cowboy, N&S argue that it cannot be that imagining *by itself* which motivates him to act in such a way.

Indeed – they notice – there may be plenty of cases where the child has precisely that same imagining without acting it out at all. If in this particular case he does perform the relevant actions, that must be due to the fact that now he *desires* to act in accordance with what he imagines, and *believes* that he can do that by chasing his friend, shooting toy arrows at him, and shouting at him "Give yourself up!". More precisely, what happens according to N&S is that when the child imagines that he is an Indian fighting with cowboys, he comes to form various beliefs about how he would behave if he really were an Indian fighting with cowboys; and, desiring to behave in a way similar to the way in which he would behave if he really were an Indian fighting with cowboys, he ends up performing the relevant pretence actions.

On this view, then, imagination drives pretence actions just indirectly – *via* beliefs and desires: what directly motivates pretence actions are beliefs and desires about what is imagined and pretended.

3.2.1. *Some problems for the Humean view*

Such a Humean picture of pretence faces various objections. A common objection is that it credits pretenders with very implausible – if not even impossible – beliefs and desires. Some authors have pointed out that crediting children with desires and beliefs about pretence is highly implausible, because children start engaging in pretence games at a remarkably young age (normally at about fifteen-months-old), when they still haven't mastered the concept of pretence.[14] As Currie and Ravenscroft observe: "if young children lack the concept of pretence, they can hardly be credited with the desire to pretend" (Currie and Ravenscroft 2002: 127).[15]

---

14   There is evidence that children by the age of fifteen month are able to engage in primitive games of pretence (cf. Friedman and Leslie 2007; for a great overview of the research on children and pretence, cf. Lillard 2002).
15   In a similar vein, Velleman (2000) argues that a Humean explanation like the one here at stake "is wrong developmentally, in that it credits the child with a precocious mastery of the distinction between fact and fiction" (Velleman 2000: 257).

Admittedly, to this N&S can reply that crediting children with a desire to pretend does not necessarily mean requiring them to possess the concept of pretence.

To understand this point we should distinguish between two different senses in which "pretence" is used within this debate: (1) a *behavioural sense* – for which 'pretence' is used to refer to the action of pretending, and (2) a *mentalistic sense* – for which 'pretence' is used to indicate the mental states that underlie pretence actions ('pretence' in this mentalistic sense is generally used as a synonym of 'imagination'). Arguably, these two senses of pretence are strictly related at the conceptual level: a proper conceptual understanding of pretence actions seems to require an understanding of the mental states that underlie them (i.e. it seems to require understanding them as actions performed with an intention to pretend, or anyway as involving a pretence/imaginative representation in the agent's mind). But it is not obvious that performing pretence actions (and recognizing them when performed by others) requires the possession of the concept of pretence. N&S endorse a 'behavioural account of pretence' – which is opposed to 'mentalistic accounts' precisely in that it maintains that engaging with pretence doesn't require to recognize it as driven by mental states of a certain kind, or by intentions to pretend, but only requires an ability to *behave as if* the pretended contents were true (and recognizing pretence actions when performed by others only requires an ability to recognize them as actions that would be appropriate if the pretended content were true).[16]

On this view, the desires and beliefs about pretence that we should ascribe to pretenders are nothing but desires *to behave as if something were the case* and beliefs about *how to behave in that way*. A child who pretends that P will do that simply insofar as:

(i)   (having imagined that P) she forms a conditional belief with a content of the form: *If it really were the case that P, then it would be the case that Q, R, S... And I would behave in ways v, w, z*;

(ii)   she has a desire *to behave in ways* similar to *v, w, z*;

---

16   The question of what mental capacities underlie children's (and adult's) pretence is a rather controversial one, which has been extensively discussed in the recent psychological and philosophical literature. Here I am particularly interested in the following aspect of that general question: does a good account – whatever it is – of the mental capacities underlying pretence require us to recognize the autonomous motivating power of imagination?

(iii)   she has a belief like: *I can behave in ways similar to v, w, z...* by
        performing actions v1, w1, z1...[17]

Desires and beliefs like these are 'about pretence' *de re* – they concern
something that, as a matter of fact, counts as pretence; but not *de dicto*
– they do not require children to have the concept of pretence explicitly
deployed in their mind.[18] So they do not involve any sophisticated
mentalistic concept. They simply involve the concept of *behaving as if,*
which even young children do plausibly possess.[19]

However, even if desires and beliefs like (i), (ii) and (iii) are not
developmentally implausible, there are other reasons why they do not seem
to be good candidates to explain what motivates children's (or also adults')
pretence. Such desires and beliefs do not seem to be neither necessary nor
sufficient to motivate pretence.

As various authors have observed, we can – and often do – pretend that
P without having the relevant conditional beliefs about how we would
behave if P were actually the case; or maybe having beliefs about how we
would behave if P were the case, but not desiring to act in ways similar
to such ways, and indeed acting in very different ways. So, for example,
it seems that I can pretend to be a dinosaur even if I don't have any
specific belief about how dinosaurs behave. Or, having just a few boring
beliefs about possible dinosaurs' behaviours (e.g. just the belief that
dinosaurs are very heavy and static creatures), I might not want to base
my pretence upon them, and pretend to behave in ways dissimilar from
those in which I believe dinosaurs would do. The view that pretending
that P is motivated by desires to act *similarly* to how one would act if P
were true (and beliefs about how to do that) cannot explain all the kind
of creative, bizarre behaviours that pretenders engage in, which can be

---

17   See Nichols and Stich (2000): 128. Note that N&S only indicate (i) and (ii).
     However, strictly speaking a belief-desire pair like (i) and (ii) is not of the right
     'Humean' form to motivate action. In order to work, N&S's account also needs
     (iii).
18   See Nichols and Stich (2000): 129, footnote 8. For similar behavioural accounts,
     see also Perner (1991) and Harris (2000).
19   Schellenberg (2013) has a different strategy to reply the 'developmental' objection
     just discussed, based on the idea that there can be 'non-conceptual states with
     conceptual content': i.e. states that have a conceptual content but are such that a
     subject can be in those states also without having the conceptual tools necessary
     to articulate that content (Schellenberg 2013: 516-517). This sounds interesting.
     However, from Schellenberg's brief discussion of this point I can't clearly
     understand how mental states of this sort are possible.

very different from (and even incompatible with) what they believe to be true in the real world.[20]

Moreover, even if beliefs and desires like (i), (ii) and (iii) above do not require the child to conceptualize what she is doing as pretence, they still require her to have occurrently present in her mind the idea that what she is doing is not an authentic and effective action, but is just *similar* to what could be an authentic and effective one. This makes it hard to see how pretenders can become fully immersed in their pretences: i.e. how children can 'lose themselves in their games' as they typically do. It seems that a child who acts on the belief that what he is doing is similar to what he would do if he were an Indian cannot be fully immersed into the Wild West fictional world, since within that world he is not just *similar* to an Indian and doesn't just perform actions *similar* to those that would be appropriate if he were an Indian. Within the game he rather *is* an Indian and performs authentic Indian actions. This is why Velleman argues that Humean accounts (like the one we are discussing) give a picture of pretence which is 'depressingly unchildlike':

> As I see it, the desire-belief explanation of pretending makes the child out to be depressingly unchildlike. According to this explanation, the child keeps a firm grip on reality while mounting an appearance conceived as such. He puts on an act conceived by him as a means of impersonating something that he is not. (...) I call this explanation depressing because it denies that the child ever enters into the fiction of being something other than it is.
>
> A child who was motivated by such a desire would remain securely outside the fiction, thinking about it as such. (Velleman 2000: 257)[21]

---

20 For criticisms along these lines, see Velleman (2000); Doggett & Egan (2007); Van Leeuwen (2011). Van Leeuwen gives a nice example of pretending to do things that we don't believe to be similar to anything that we would ever do: "A student who gets a bad grade on her test may, in private, pretend she is shooting the professor with a gun: 'Bang, take that!'. What would her conditional belief be? Presumably: *if I had a gun, I would shoot my professor.* But surely it is not a requirement that she believe this in order to engage in such pretending. In fact, it is perfectly common for people to pretend to do things that they do *not* believe they would do under any circumstances. Sometimes, that is the point." (Van Leeuwen 2011: 59).

21 To this, Currie & Ravenscroft reply that children do not necessarily have to consciously and reflectively attend the beliefs and desires (of kind i-iii above) that drive their pretence actions (Currie and Ravenscroft 2002: 124). However, I think that if such beliefs and desires play the relevant motivational role, causing and rationalizing the pretence actions here in question, they must have an impact on the ways in which children see those actions, hence on the experience they have in performing them.

Finally, then, beliefs and desires like those that N&S ascribe to pretenders are not only unnecessary and insufficient to motivate pretence; they even seem to make it hard to understand some important characteristics of pretence – such as the creativity of pretenders and the possibility for pretenders to become fully immersed into their games.

Now, admittedly all these criticisms only show that the beliefs and desires that N&S attribute to pretenders are implausible; they do not establish that pretenders are not motivated by beliefs and desires. However, it's not easy to see what other beliefs and desires we could postulate to explain pretenders' behaviours, if we exclude – as I am assuming everyone would – that pretenders literally believe the contents of their pretences and have genuine desires about them (e.g. that children really believe they are Indians and cowboys, and desire to kill each other, etc.).

All the attempts to provide Humean explanations of pretence that I am aware of end up ascribing to pretenders beliefs and desires with implausibly complicated and conceptually sophisticated contents.[22] This makes it tempting to conclude that a better explanation of pretence is rather in terms of what pretenders imagine – with no mediation of beliefs and desires. It is this view which I explore in the remainder of this chapter, as a first step on the way to my final conclusion, in subsequent chapters, that belief and imagination are not distinguished at the level of outputs.

3.3. *The* Imagination-as-Motivation *view of pretence*

On this view, the child who chases his friend, shooting toy arrows at him is not motivated by beliefs and desires, but by imaginings. What happens is simply that he imagines that he is an Indian, and he *acts this imagining out.*

---

22   Funkhouser and Spaulding (2009), for example, suggest that: "the children's pretense is often accounted for by a desire to pretend (e.g. for its own sake, as a way to socialize with others, etc.), the imagination that guides it, and a belief that following the imagination is a good means of achieving the end specified as the content of the desire" (Funkhouser and Spaulding 2009: 309-310). This seems to require pretenders to possess (at least) the concepts of pretence and imagination – and to have such concepts deployed in the contents of their beliefs and desires when they pretend. Schellenberg (2013) argues that pretenders are typically motivated by "desires to make fictional" and beliefs about how to satisfy them (Schelleneberg 2013: 515). It is not hard to see how (at least some of) the problems I have raised in relation to N&S's account can affect also these other Humean accounts. Though admittedly a fair assessment of such accounts would require a more extensive discussion.

Following Currie and Ravenscroft (2002), let's call this "the imagination-as-motivation view" of pretence.

I think that some version of this view is likely to provide the best possible explanation for many central cases of pretence. Here I shall present and defend the version of this view proposed by Currie and Ravenscroft (2002; henceforth, "C&R"); though what I am going to say draws also on discussions from Velleman (2000) and Egan and Doggett (2007).[23]

What exactly does "acting out of imagination" mean? Advocates of the imagination-as-motivation view must clarify that, explaining how imaginings can motivate us to act in consequent ways.

As we have seen, beliefs do not motivate alone, but only in conjunction with relevant desires. My belief that I can kill you by hitting you with this paperweight does not motivate me to hit you with this paperweight. Fortunately, it would motivate me to do that only if I wanted to kill you. It is my *wanting* that outcome, in a sense, which constitutes the real *motor* of motivation. If there are cases where imagination motivates, then, we should expect a similar motor to be at work there, too.

Take again the child's imagining that he can kill his 'cowboy enemy' by shooting arrows at him. If it is this imagining that motivates his pretence action of shooting arrows, then we should expect it to do that in conjunction with some relevant desire – a desire which the content of such an imagining somehow indicates how to satisfy (in the same way in which the content of the belief that *I can kill you by hitting you with this paperweight* indicates a way to satisfy a desire *to kill you*). But what plays the relevant desire role in this case?

---

23   In fact, note that Currie and Ravenscroft (2002) do not claim to have conclusive arguments for this imagination-as-motivation view. They provide various reasons to endorse it, but they eventually leave the question open: "Further arguments might decide the matter, but for now making a choice seems more a rhetorical move than a rationally dictated one. Nor we do have to make a choice. (...) We can base our claims on a disjunction: either imagination motivates pretence, or the beliefs and desires that motivate pretence are guided by imaginings" (Currie and Ravenscroft 2002: 130-131). For the sake of simplicity, here I shall treat Currie and Ravenscroft as fully committed with the first disjunct (this is indeed how they are generally treated by their opponents: in the debate on pretence, they are always considered as convinced advocated of the imagination-as-motivation view). Note that also my final position on these matters will remain to some extents open. As I shall say, I don't take my arguments in favour of the imagination-as-motivation view of pretence to be conclusive. Nor I need them to be conclusive, since my main argument in favour of the motivating power of imagination is based on the consideration of a different sort of actions, which I will introduce in Chapter 4.

According to C&R, it is not a real desire to kill his 'cowboy enemy'. Indeed, it seems perfectly possible (indeed plausible) that the child performs that action without having any real desire to kill: you don't need to be an aspirant killer in order to engage in a pretence of killing. Most importantly, C&R notice, a *real* desire to kill "would *not* normally explain an action of *pretending* [to kill]"; it would rather explain an action of *really* trying to kill. Therefore, the motivating force of the child's imagining must depend on something other than a real desire – which is why C&R appeal to an imaginative counterpart of desire: a kind of 'make-desire' like those I introduced in Chapter 2 (which they now call "desire-like imagining"):[24]

> A motivating reason to pretend to Ψ might be that the agent has the desire-like imagining to φ and the belief-like imagining that he can φ by Ψ-ing. (Currie and Ravenscroft 2002: 116)[25]

So on this view the child who makes-believe (i.e., in the new terminology, has a belief-like imagining) that he is an Indian armed with arrows to kill his cowboy enemy does also make-desire (i.e. have a desire-like imagining) to kill his cowboy enemy; and this imaginary belief/desire pair motivates his action of pretending to shoot arrows.[26]

Here it is important to notice that actually C&R do not seem to exclude categorically that a real desire might play the relevant role in explaining pretence actions. Indeed, what they say is that "a real desire [to φ] would not *normally* explain pretending to [to φ]" (C&R 2002: 116, my emphasis); thereby suggesting – I take it – that a real desire *could* in principle, jointly

---

24 Remember that in Chapter 2 the introduction of make-desires was suggested to explain how imagination disposes us to react emotionally in various ways.

25 Note that in C&R's text this sentence appears as a question: "We can ask whether a motivating reason to pretend to Ψ might be that...". C&R do then defend a positive answer to this question, even if in a cautious and admittedly tentative way (as I noted before, in footnote 23). More convinced advocates of the imagination-as-motivation view of pretence are Doggett & Egan (2007) and, even more, Velleman (2000).

26 From now on I will use the terms "belief-like imagining" and "desire-like imagining" to indicate the imaginative counterparts of belief and desires. I will keep using the terms "make-believe" and "make-desire" (introduced in Chapter 2) to indicate the corresponding verbs. So, just to be clear: a subject who makes-believe that p and makes-desire that q has a belief-like imagining that p and a desire-like imagining that q. I will sometimes talk also of "imaginary beliefs" and "imaginary desires", as N&S do.

with a belief-like imagining, motivate pretence, though this is not what happens most of the time, in normal cases.[27]

This sounds very right to me. If Sam is annoyed with Tom, his real desire to hurt Tom might well explain his pretence action to shoot a (toy) arrow at him: that is, it seems plausible that Sam's desire to hurt Tom, together with his (belief-like) imagining that he can do that by shooting a (toy) arrow at him, is what actually motivates his pretence (while, presumably he doesn't try to *really* hurt Tom with a *real* arrow because he has higher-order desires to control himself, to obey the social rules he has been taught, to avoid being punished... And perhaps partly also because a real arrow is not so readily available to him!). Indeed, as children's genuine desires obviously play an important role in determining what games they engage with, it would be surprising if such desires did not – at least sometimes – also played a role in determining their actions within the games.

Pushing this line of thinking, Velleman (2000) has suggested that some species of real desires – what he calls 'wishes' – are always what plays the relevant motivating role in pretence. Still, I agree with C&R that real desires are not likely to be what *normally* motivates pretenders' actions. Indeed, the conative states that typically motivate pretence seem to differ from real desires in two important respects – which have emerged in the discussion so far.

First, pretenders' 'desires' and real desires seem to differ in the ways in which they are formed and controlled. Pretenders seem to have a deliberate control upon the 'desires' that they endorse in their games, which they do not typically have upon their real desires. It seems at least possible for a child engaged in a pretence fight to bring about (more or less consciously and deliberately) a 'desire' to kill that is at odds with her own inclinations and natural feelings towards her friend; while a *real* desire to kill cannot be elicited in this way.

Moreover, pretenders' 'desires' and real desires seem to differ with respect to their satisfaction conditions (see Currie 2010). In most cases, the 'desires' that motivate pretence seem to be fully satisfied by what turns out to be fictionally true *within* the pretence itself. Again, this wouldn't be possible if they were real desires. A 'desire' to kill a cowboy, which motivates the pretence of shooting a toy arrow at him, will generally be totally satisfied by

---

27   C&R make this point using the example of a pretence to eat a (mud) pie: "There may be no real desire for the belief-like imagining to combine with so as to motivate: the child who pretends to eat may not really want to eat anything. Anyway, wanting to eat would not normally explain *pretending* to eat." (C&R 2002: 116). I will come back to the mud-pie example shortly, in §3.4.

the cowboy's *pretence* of falling down dead, which makes it true in the game the he has died. A real desire to kill a cowboy would not be satisfied by it merely being true in the game that the cowboy has died.

These differences with respect to formation and satisfaction conditions suggest that, if we want to argue that children's pretence actions are motivated by their (belief-like) imaginings, we must appeal to desire-like imaginings as well.[28]

I will have more to say on the relation between desire-like imaginings and real desires shortly (§3.4). For the moment, let's conclude the presentation of the imagination-as-motivation view of pretence by emphasizing once again that such pairs of belief-like and desire-like imaginings constitute proper *motivations* – i.e. both causes and reasons – for actions, as we have seen that genuine belief-desire pairs do.

This suggestion, by the way, does not seem to involve any particularly new or implausible revisions of our concept of imagination. After all, as C&R observe, it is already widely accepted that imaginings can *cause* various sorts of behaviours. This is how, for example, the so-called phenomenon of 'motor mimicry' is explained: the fact that we tend to conform our facial expressions and postures to those of people around us is typically explained (roughly) by saying that we imagine ourselves to be in other peoples' situation, and this move us to behave accordingly (think e.g. of when we move so as to defend our own body at the sight of a blow aimed at another; see Goldman 2006: Chapter 11). Moreover – as we have seen in Chapter 2 – it is also widely accepted that imaginings can *rationalize* emotional responses (as with *Psycho* shower scene rationalizing a fearful response, rather than an envious one). But then, if we are ready to credit imaginings with such *causal and rational* powers, why deny that they can exert the two powers together in motivating proper actions?

---

28   Here I must notice that the origin of *real* desires is a difficult and much debated question (notably for what concerns intrinsic, non-instrumental desires; see Schroeder 2015 for an introduction to this topic). My suggestion that pretenders' desires differ from real desires with respect to the ways in which they are formed, then, is not based on a clear positive view about how real desires are formed. It is based on the more modest consideration that, however they are formed, real desires are not (straightforwardly) sensitive to our will and conscious deliberations in the ways in which pretenders' desires seem to be. However, I see that more work would be needed to properly support this claim: both the extents to which pretenders' desires are, and the extents to which real desires are not, subject to the will, would require further discussion.

Cowering from a blow aimed at another suggests that imaginings have the capacity to generate behaviour, if not to rationalize it, and the emotions case suggests that imagination has the capacity to rationalize if not to generate behaviour. Put the two together, and you have imagination as motivation. (Currie and Ravenscroft 2002: 130)

3.4. *Problems (and solutions) for the* Imagination-as-Motivation *view*

Criticisms of the imagination-as-motivation account of pretence have focused mostly on the notion of desire-like imaginings – which we have already seen to be a rather controversial one (see above Chapter 2, §3.2). Here I will discuss some problems raised by Nichols and Stich (2000) (as before, 'N&S' for short), which will allow me to clarify some important points on the nature of desire-like imaginings and, more generally, on how imagination motivates.

3.4.1. *Desires and desire-like imaginings: same motivating powers?*

The first objection raised by N&S is that if desire-like imaginings and real desires with the same contents have the same motivating powers, then we should expect them to produce the same behaviours, and this would obviously be a wrong prediction. Considering the case of a child who pretends that a gob of mud is a pie, N&S note:

An (imaginary) desire to eat some pie, along with an (imaginary) belief that the gob of mud is a pie would presumably lead the pretender to actually eat the mud pies. But pretense behaviour of this sort is rarely seen in children and almost never seen in adults. (Nichols and Stich 2000: 134)

So, N&S conclude, the imagination-as-motivation account of pretence makes the wrong predictions about the behaviour of pretenders.

C&R have a reply to this. They concede to N&S that *if* desire-like imaginings and real desires with the same contents had the same motivating powers, then we should expect them to produce the same behaviours *and this would be a wrong prediction about pretenders' behaviours.* But they reject the antecedent of the conditional, arguing that we need not assume that desire-like imaginings and real desires have the same motivating powers:

Why should we assume that the motivating powers of desire-like imaginings and of desires with the same contents are the same? (...) Imaginings might be type-individuated partly by their *distinctive* motivating powers. In particular, where the desire to P is apt to motivate one to ϕ, the imaginary desire to P may motivate one to pretend to ϕ. (Currie and Ravenscroft 2002: 116)

I find this reply unconvincing. But a better one is available to C&R. In my view, C&R should reject N&S's conditional altogether: for it is not true that if we assume that real desires and desire-like imaginings have the same powers, we make the wrong predictions about pretenders' behaviours. What is wrong, rather, is the story N&S's tell us about the 'mud-pie pretence game'.

N&S say that if the motivating power of real desires and desire-like imaginings is the same, then a child who makes-believe that the gob is a pie and makes-desire to eat a pie would actually eat the mud. But this doesn't sound right. A child who makes-desire to eat a pie and makes-believe that the gob is a pie, will presumably also make-believe that she can eat that 'pie' by putting it close to her cheek and saying "yum-yum" (or something like that). Strictly speaking, it is this belief-like imagining that, together with the desire-like imagining to eat the pie, motivates her pretence action. And if we assume that this belief-like/desire-like imagining pair has the same motivating power of a belief/desire pair with the same contents, we make precisely the right prediction about the child's behaviour.

If the child desired to eat that pie and believed that she can eat it by putting it close to her cheek and saying "yum-yum", she would behave precisely in that way: she would put the mud-pie close to her cheek and say "yum-yum".

Of course, in this latter case the child would not be pretending to eat a pie; she would rather be trying (unsuccessfully) to eat one. These seem indeed to be two rather different actions (though based on the same observable behaviour). But the difference between them does not depend on the fact that one is motivated by a real desire and the other by a desire-like imagining; it seems rather to depend on the fact that in one case the child believes (falsely) that the action she performs will allow her to eat, while in the other case she just makes-believe that it will.[29] The pretence status of her action depends on how the child 'sees' the action itself, not on the imaginative nature of the desire that such action is supposed to satisfy.

And indeed, as I have argued in §4.3, it seems that also real desires can motivate pretence actions, if they operate in conjunction with belief-like imaginings. Remember the example of Sam who is (really) annoyed with

---

29   Note that I am not suggesting that the fact that she make-believes that is *sufficient* to make her action a pretence; I am suggesting that it is necessary.

Tom and pretends to shoot a toy arrow at him. Or – to take a case which parallels the mud-pie pretence – think of a situation where, waiting for pizza at the restaurant and being very hungry, I grab the (empty) plate in front of me and pretend to bite it, saying "Mmm, this pizza is good!". What makes this a pretence action, rather than a genuine unsuccessful attempt to eat, is clearly the fact that I don't believe, but just make-believe that I can eat the 'pizza-plate' – even if my desire to eat is a real one.

How can we tell that my desire here is a real one, while children's 'desires' to eat (mud) pies are imaginary? As I suggested before, one clear criterion here has to do with their different satisfaction conditions. My desire to eat at the restaurant is *not* satisfied by the fact that in my mini-pretence it becomes true that I have had a bite of pizza. While (in many cases) children pretending to eat mud-pies can thereby satisfy their 'desires' for pies. Moreover, such 'desires' for pies seem sensitive to children's will and control in a way in which my desire for pizza isn't. Children engaged in a mud-pie pretence seem able to bring about 'desires' for pies irrespectively of whether they feel hungry, and even of whether they actually like pies; something that arguably I couldn't do with my real desire for pizza.[30]

All this might suggest that desire-like imaginings are always easily and straightforwardly satisfied: you never have to wait for a pretend-pizza; all you need to do is to pretend to eat it. But things are obviously not that simple. At least in the context of pretence games, desire-like imaginings are satisfied by what is fictionally true in those games, and what is fictionally true in a game does not always depend on what a pretender spontaneously makes-believe to be true. Generally, it also depends on what other players make-believe, as well as on a number of somewhat 'objective' rules: such as rules on which children agreed, more or less explicitly, in advance – e.g. "Sam *is* the chef, Jules *is* the diner" – or more conventional rules typically holding for given kinds of games – like the rule I have been assuming to hold in my examples, according to which putting something close to your mouth and saying "yum-yum" *is* eating.

---

30 In relation to this, note that while my pretence of eating at the restaurant is likely to start precisely because no pizza is available to me, children might very well play mud-pie games also in cases in which real pies would be easily accessible to them. Indeed, children who are fussy eaters and never finish their meals may well engage in cooking/eating pretences. Of course, one might argue that such pretences reveal a suppressed real desire to eat; but this doesn't look plausible to me as a standard explanation. All that said, though, here note again the doubts and complexities that I pointed out before concerning the differences between real-desires and pretence-desires' formation (see footnote 28 above).

So, if Sam is slow in preparing pizza, Jules's will have to wait in order to satisfy her imaginative desire for pizza, as I have to wait to satisfy my real desire at the restaurant. And note also that if Jules didn't realize that the game she is playing is one where people are used to eat from their feet, her pretence to put food close to her mouth wouldn't make it fictionally true that she is eating: in the game, she would be unsuccessfully try to eat. As Currie (2004) notices, like 'competent believers' are those whose beliefs correspond to what is true in the real world, 'competent pretenders' are those whose make-beliefs corresponds to what is true in the game they are playing (Currie 2004: 205).

Now we are also in the position to better understand the intuitive plausibility of N&S's objection. Their example of the mud-pie pretence is plausibly referred to cognitively normal children, who are competent believers (in particular, who correctly believe that to eat you should put food *into* your mouth), and competent pretenders (in particular, who correctly make-believe that to eat you should put food *close* to your mouth). For such competent children (and, note, here I am not questioning that even very young children are normally that competent), a desire to eat a pie and a belief that something is a pie will indeed motivate an action of putting that thing into their mouth, while a desire-like imagining to eat a pie and a belief-like imagining that something is a pie will motivate an action of putting that thing close to their mouth. So, N&S are right that desire/belief pairs and imaginary desire/belief pairs will normally motivate different actions.

But now we can appreciate that these differences are not due to the intrinsically different motivating powers of those two pairs, but rather to contingent differences in the sets of representational states to which those two pairs normally belong. (Incidentally, note that paying attention to the whole set of mental states in the context of which imaginary belief/desires pairs motivate is crucial for dealing with another important question that advocates of the imagination-as-motivation view must be able to answer: namely, the question of *why* imagination motivates actions in cases of pretence, but not in many other cases. I will come back to this important point in Chapter 5: §3).

3.4.2. *Dead cats (and some tentative conclusions)*

A second problem that N&S raise for the imagination-as-motivation view is that there are cases of pretence for which an appeal to desire-like imaginings is utterly implausible – such as the case of someone pretending to be a dead cat. Even if we grant that a child pretending to be an Indian who shoots arrows at his cowboy enemy is motivated by Indian-like imaginary desires and beliefs, a similar explanation is not available for a child pretending to be a dead cat. Dead cats have no desires – nor, of course, beliefs about how to satisfy them; so whatever the child does in such a case (presumably something like lying on the floor, muttering "I am dead") cannot be explained by his taking on, *in imagination*, the desires and beliefs of a dead cat and acting out of them. It should instead be explained – according to N&S – in terms of a real desire to behave as you would if you were a dead cat, and real beliefs about how to do that.

C&R have a reply also to this objection. And, this time, it's a persuasive one. They grant that cases like the dead cat pretence are not plausibly explained in terms of motivating imaginings and seem to require belief-desire explanations. But this, they argue, is not in itself a problem for the imagination-as-motivation view, since this view was explicitly offered to explain one particular kind of pretence: namely, pretence that involves role taking – pretence that involves acting out the part of an intentional agent. This, C&R suggest, is a sufficiently distinctive kind of pretence for it plausibly be thought of as having a distinctive kind of explanation" (Currie and Ravenscroft 2002: 117).

Indeed, it is not obvious that all cases of pretence must have the same kind of mental causes. And surely defending the imagination-as-motivation view does not amount to deny that there are cases of pretence motivated by beliefs and desires.

Nor, importantly, does it amount to denying that beliefs and desires can influence pretence in a number of ways. As Humeans can allow that imaginings play a role – even an important one – in explaining pretence, advocates of the imagination-as-motivation view can allow the same for beliefs and desires.

We can probably all agree that beliefs about Indians and cowboys' behaviours are likely to influence what children imagine when they pretend to be Indians and cowboys. And we may also agree that such imaginings do – at least sometimes – bring about further beliefs like those postulated by N&S (*If I were a cowboy, I would behave like that...*). All these beliefs and imaginings will play a role in explaining children pretence. The point is to understand which, among these representational states, make maximally close contact with behaviour. And what I have argued so far suggests that imaginings are more likely to be the ones.

Have I *established* that pretence is, in some cases at least, motivated by pretenders' imaginings? Admittedly not. The debate on the cognitive motivation underlying pretence is very extensive and live, and my defence of the imagination-as-motivation view hasn't dealt with all the objections that have been raised against it, nor with all the available alternative views which have been proposed.[31]

However, I have provided good reasons to think that an explanation of pretence in terms of what pretenders imagine can avoid some serious problems that affect most Humean explanations in terms of belief-desire pairs, without involving theoretically expensive moves (i.e. without requiring any dramatic change in our view of imagination's powers), since both the causal and the rationalizing powers of imagination are already widely accepted. For the moment, I would be happy to have persuaded you of this, and I won't go further into the debate on pretence. As I said, indeed, I take the case of pretence actions to provide some initial evidence and intuitive plausibility for my view that imagination and belief do not critically differ in action outputs; but my main argument for such view is not based primarily on pretence. Vice versa, insofar as I will be able to persuade you, on a somewhat independent basis, that imagination has the same motivating powers of belief, this will provide further reasons to accept that such powers are exerted also in cases of pretence.

Conclusion

In this Chapter I have started addressing the 'Hume's Problem' of how to distinguish imagination from belief. I have discussed two orders of considerations that look relevant to solve this problem: (i) considerations concerning the cognitive inputs that are responsible for imagination and belief's formation; and (ii) considerations concerning imagination and belief's behavioural outputs. I have first clarified what reasons we might have to think that in paradigmatic cases of daydream, engagement with fictions, and counterfactual/modal reasoning imaginings differ from beliefs in both these respects. Then I have focussed on cases of pretence, asking whether they challenge the idea that imaginings and beliefs can be distinguished on the basis of behavioural outputs, and whether they

---

31   Another interesting account of pretence is the account defended by Van Leeuwen (2011), according to which imaginings do influence pretence behaviour without the mediation of beliefs, but the imaginings that do that are sensory/perceptual imaginings, rather than propositional imaginings. Van Leeuwen also raises various criticisms against the notion of desires-like imaginings, arguing that they cannot explain the two phenomena that he calls "semi-pretence" and "pretence-layering" (Van Leeuwen 2011: 55-56).

might be taken to support my view that imaginings and beliefs differ just with respects to cognitive inputs. I have argued that such cases do indeed provide some *initial* evidence (and some intuitive plausibility) in favour of my view, because the best available explanation of pretence requires us to recognize that imagination is not motivationally inert, but can cause and rationalize actions in ways very similar to the ways in which belief does – thereby revealing that the differences between imagination and belief with respect to action outputs are much smaller than they might prima facie seem (and have traditionally been taken) to be.

This initial evidence is not conclusive, though: it does not prove that imagination and belief are totally alike with respect to action outputs. According to the version of the imagination-as-motivation view of pretence that I defended, when imaginings (belief-like ones) motivate pretence they generally do so in conjunction with desire-like imaginings; while beliefs – we have seen – typically motivate in conjunction with real desires. So, cases of pretence do not reveal that imagination and belief motivate action *in the same ways*. Actually, I did also argue that imagination *can* sometimes motivate pretence in conjunction with real desires (and I mentioned reasons why, according to some, this is what happens all the time). But this still does not prove that there are no motivational differences between imagination and belief.

Indeed, beliefs' dispositional connection (via desire) to action holds across contexts: as various authors pointed out, "beliefs can enter into action choice in any sort of context whatsoever" (Van Leeuwen 2009: 224; see also Bratman 1992). If imagination motivated actions only in cases of pretence, its motivating power would be much more limited than that of belief. In order to show that imagination's motivating power is really the same as belief's, then, I need to consider whether and how imagination's power is exerted across different contexts also outside the domain of pretence – as belief's power is. This is what I am going to do in the next chapter.

4.

WISE PENS, EVIL CARDIGANS, THOUGHTFUL DOORS, AND OTHER STRANGE THINGS

So far, I have defended a view according to which imagination and belief are alike in important respects. They have the same kinds of contents: i.e. propositions.[1] And they both 'regard such contents as true' – in the phenomenological as well as in the cognitive sense I specified: both imagining that p and believing that p dispose us to undergo emotional experiences that would be appropriate if p were true, and they both dispose us to 'treat p as true' in our reasoning, drawing theoretical inferences from it. I have also argued that imaginings and beliefs have similar motivating powers: cases of pretence reveal that imaginings can motivate us to act in ways very similar to the ways in which beliefs, jointly with desires, do (even though I granted that in pretence cases imaginings are more likely to motivate in conjunction with desire-like imaginings, rather than with real desires). Thus, on this view imagination and belief turn out to have very similar emotional and behavioural outputs. The most critical difference between them has to do with the cognitive inputs in response to which they are formed and the related normative constraints that govern them: imaginings are not (nor ought to be) formed and maintained in response to real-world evidence as beliefs are (and ought to be).

In fact, as I anticipated already, I think that output similarities between imagination and belief can be pushed even farther. They can be pushed so far that, rather than talking in term of 'similarities', it may become more appropriate to talk in terms of 'sameness': imagination and belief have basically the same behavioural/emotional outputs and can only be

---

1   Here remember that with 'imagination' without further qualifications I refer to propositional imagination which is belief-like. As I said in Chapter 1, I do also recognize forms of propositional imaginings that are desire-like (as well as forms of non-propositional imaginings). But when I want to talk about these latter forms of imaginings I shall always make this explicit.

distinguished with respect to cognitive inputs (and related normative constraints).

In this chapter I will introduce my main argument for this view, based on the consideration of a number of cases different from the paradigmatic ones on which I have been focussing in the last two chapters. As I have it, the same imaginative state that we invoke to explain cases of daydreams, engagement with fictions, pretence and modal reasoning, plays the relevant explanatory role also in a number of other cases (/activities/experiences) that are not at all marginal in our lives. The analysis of such cases reveals something important about the nature and powers of imagination.

Here is the plan. In § 1 I will introduce the relevant cases and overview a number of possible explanations for them. In §§ 2 and 3 I will focus on explanations in terms of belief, arguing that they don't work. In § 4 I will argue for my own explanation in terms of imaginings, and raise some general questions about the motivating force of imagination as compared to that of belief, which I will then answer in the next chapter. Before moving on to this, though, in § 5, I will address a radical challenge to my view, which is raised by Tamar Gendler's arguments for the existence of *aliefs*.

1. *Superstition and magic*

When I was in High School, I used the same pen for written tests as I took notes with in my classes, since 'it already knew the right answers'. During my BA at university, I used to wear the same red T-shirt on the days of exams. I also have a T-shirt (a different one, of course) that I use when I go on difficult climbing expeditions in the mountains. At the supermarket, I always take the second item in the row on a shelf. And I read Rob Brezsny's horoscope on *International* every Thursday.

I feel slightly ashamed in reporting these small rituals and superstitious actions that punctuate my everyday life; but, at least, I know that I am in good company. Barack Obama is famous for his ritual of playing basketball on the morning of every important vote; David Beckham for wearing a brand new football outfit at each match.[2] And apparently Beckham's fans

---

2   Along with students, politicians, athletes, musicians, financial investors, and fishermen are all categories of people well-known for the propitiatory rites and lucky charms they perform before and during their performances (see Vyse 2014: Chapter 2). A nice, detailed discussion of athletes' superstitions is provided by the anthropologist and former baseball player George Gmelch in his popular essay "Baseball Magic": "As I listened to my professor describe the magical rituals of

are ready to pay significant amounts of money to possess his 'old' outfits – as indeed people are ready to do for such things as Princess Diana's wedding dress or John Lennon's hand-written lyrics.

As these particular objects seem to mean a lot to us, by the way, so we tend to charge with special meanings some particular events in the lives of their owners: think of the many conspiracy theories circulating about Princess Diana's car crash (which, obviously, 'couldn't be *just* an accident').[3] We are also all familiar with a number of traditional superstitious actions, like touching wood, crossing your fingers, throwing a coin into a fountain before leaving a nice place you visited, avoiding travel on Friday the 13th, and so on.

Psychological research over the last decades has provided more systematic evidence of how widespread among educated Western adults is the tendency to behave in superstitious ways more or less similar to those just described. In a series of seminal experiments Paul Rozin and colleagues found most subjects to be reluctant to throw darts at the photograph of a loved one (although explicitly recognizing that action to be harmless); unwilling to drink from a bottle labelled 'Poison' (although knowing that it actually contains just sugared water); or unwilling to wear an acknowledgedly fully sterilized sweater that they were told previously belonged to Adolf Hitler (see Rozin, Millman, and Nemeroff 1986, Nemeroff and Rozin 2002).[4]

Superstitious behaviours have also been pointed out to be characteristic of some forms of obsessive-compulsive disorder (a pathological condition which affects about 2% of European and U.S. populations), involving such rituals as turning the light on and off a certain number of times before exiting a room 'to prevent something bad from happening', or compulsive

---

the Trobriand Islanders it occurred to me that what these so-called primitives people did wasn't all that different from what my teammates and I did for luck and confidence at the ballpark..." (Gmelch 1978: 33).

3   This, by the way, is something we do with our own lives as well: like when we say that such things as running into a long-lost friend in a *so unlikely* place, or *miraculously* escaping an accident, 'can't be sheer coincidences'.

4   Similar findings are informally replicated by the psychologist Bruce Hood during his talks, which he uses to open by offering his audience to wear, for a substantial reward, a cardigan that has belonged to the serial killer Fred West, unvaryingly obtaining a vast majority of refusals (See Hood 2012: Chapter 2). See also Haidt (2012) for other evidence of this sort. For further extensive evidence about the pervasiveness of superstitions in cognitively normal population, see Risen (2016).

hand-washing 'to kill all bacteria that assault your skin every time you touch something'.[5]

What all these otherwise disparate actions, which I have gathered under the broad label of *superstitious actions,* have in common, is the peculiar kind of 'magical' thinking that they all seem to presuppose.[6] A kind of thinking, that is, which departs in various ways from the natural view of the world supported by contemporary science, ascribing supernatural properties to things and agents: taking, for instance, action at distance to be possible, or treating inanimate things as sentient objects and brute physical processes as teleological ones; most generally, seeing meaning, reasons and intentionality where in fact there seem to be none, and more of them where there seem to be less.

1.1. *Other 'magical' actions*

At least some aspects of the kind of thinking just described seem to be very pervasive in our cognitive life, underlying also many actions and behaviours that would not typically classify – if not very loosely – as *superstitious.*

Consider for instance all those cases where we happen to talk to (or talk about) inanimate things as if they had a mind and could understand us – like when we insult the printer for 'not understanding that we want

---

5   I will say more on the relation between superstition and obsessive-compulsive
      disorders in §3.2. below.
6   Here the question arises whether all these cases are properly characterized as
      actions. Aren't at least some of them better described as unintentional *reactions* –
      i.e. sorts of instinctual reflexes? This might be true in a few of my cases. Take for
      instance the Rozin' experiment where subjects were hesitant to eat faeces-shaped
      fudges. Some of these subjects might have just displayed a quick-and-dirty
      disgusted reaction – a reaction upon which they then did not end up acting (e.g.:
      they might have just turned their nose up at a faeces-shaped fudge, hesitated a bit,
      but then ended up eating it). These cases of course wouldn't count as actions. But
      most participants in the experiment definitely refused to eat the faeces-shaped
      fudge, and ate instead the other one. What I am concerned with here are the
      behaviours of those subjects, which I think would count as actions on any account
      of this notion. If you don't think that *refusing* is an action, you should nonetheless
      agree that *choosing the other one* is. More generally, I think there is little doubt
      that most of the superstitious/magical behaviours I described do count as
      intentional actions: in most cases we can identify a deliberate doing on the part of
      the subject – something for which, indeed, she can be taken to be *responsible* for.

an A6 format', or ask the door to 'please remain shut'.[7] Or consider other similar cases that Velleman calls "expressive behaviours" – i.e. behaviours expressive of an emotion – like: tearing up your boyfriend's letter when you are angry with him, yelling at the driver in another car who obviously can't hear you, or loudly encouraging the players of your favourite team while watching a match in TV.[8]

Admittedly, describing all these cases as manifestations of magical thinking might sound a bit odd: where is the magic in the screams of an enthusiastic sport fan? But the apparent oddity eases off if we take, as I shall do here, the term "magical" as a sort of term of art: a term indicating something that might involve typical magical constructs/properties – such as ghosts, spirits, supernatural gifts of second sight – but might also just amount to exaggerating the degree to which some properties that are not themselves magical – such as consciousness, understanding, rationality – are manifested in the world around us, whether it is a door or the image of a soccer player on a TV screen.

1.2. *Magical thinking: general principles and particular contents*

Lots of interesting work has been devoted to spelling out what precisely this sort of 'magical thinking' amounts to – i.e. which categories and principles underlie it. Anthropologists from Levi-Strauss have emphasized its fundamentally *anthropomorphic* nature (see e.g. Guthrie 1993). Currie and Jureidini (2004) introduced the category of *over-coherence* to describe its characteristic tendency to overestimate the world's coherent design and rationality. Lindeman and Aarnio (2007) identified its most distinctive feature as a systematic tendency to *category mistakes* where the core attributes of mental and physical a processes are conflated. Rozin and Nemeroff famously argued that much of this thinking conforms to what they call "laws of sympathetic magic": notably, a "law of contagion" – according to which things that *once* have been in contact may influence each other permanently through transfer of non-physical essences to each other (as with the cardigan permeated by Hitler's wicked essence); and a "law of similarity" – according to which objects that are superficially similar in some respect do also share a deeper essence, so that the action taken on one

---

7   As we ascribe consciousness and mindedness to inanimate things, we also exaggerate the degrees to which such properties are possessed by sentient beings, at various levels.

8   Some of the examples here are due to Rosalind Hursthouse (1991), who calls these "arational actions".

can affect the other (as with a photograph sharing the essence of the person it portrays; or with a name sharing the essence of its referent[9]). Various authors have recently suggested more detailed articulations of these two laws into a number of more specific principles.[10]

Which, if any, of these principles and categories are better suited to describe the logic and contents of our magical thinking, is a fascinating question; but not one that I am going to discuss any further here.[11] Arguably, to say that our thinking in this domain presupposes some or some other principles/categories does not necessarily mean that such principles/categories are internally represented by us in the abstract form we have just seen – let alone that abstract representations of such principles/categories are what directly motivates our 'superstitious actions'.

On the contrary, as Currie and Jureidini have persuasively argued, our magical, over-coherent thoughts typically take the form of unsystematic little narratives concerning the interactions between particular individuals/objects/events (generally represented as intentional agents – or, at least as goal-directed entities), whose behaviours are coherently and somehow teleologically related to one another.

And indeed, whatever our views of the general underlying principles are, I think we can all agree in ascribing to the agents in the cases I described particular magical thoughts more or less like these:

---

9   Following Piaget, Nemeroff and Rozin describe this as a case of 'nominal realism' (Nemeroff and Rozin 2000: 6).

10   Such as Huston (2012)'s seven principles of magical thinking: objects carry essences; symbols have powers; actions have distant consequences; the mind knows no bounds; the soul lives on; the world is alive; everything happens for a reason. See also Rozin and Nemeroff's re-elaboration of their original theory (Nemeroff and Rozin 2002).

11   Here note that such principles/categories are not necessarily alternative to each other. Moreover, it is worth noticing that, beyond the disagreements, there are also some important points on which most parties in the debate seem to agree: (1) the superstitious/magical thoughts here in question are extremely pervasive in our thinking; (2) in spite of their falsity and irrationality, holding such thoughts and acting upon them can yield a number of pragmatic benefits. Such benefits include psychological benefits (e.g. it has been argued that personal superstitious rituals may generate a sense of control which has positive effects: wearing his 'lucky new outfit' may make David Beckham actually feel better and play better in the match); social benefits (when the rituals are collective, they can constitute a "useful glue that binds us together as a society" Hood 2012). I will say something more on the benefits of superstitious thinking at the end of Section 2.

– *This pen* – who *attended all the lessons* – *will help me to write down the correct answers* (my thought when I take that particular pen out of my writing case for the exam);
– *Throwing this coin here will make sure that I return to Rome* (the tourist's thought when she throws one euro into the Trevi Fountain);
– *This door can understand what I say: if I talk to her gently I might persuade her* (my thought when, trying to close the door for the third time, I ask her to 'please remain shut eventually').

1.3. *The explanatory options*

The plausibility of the thought-ascriptions just suggested, of course, depends on the fact that it seems to be in the light of thoughts like these that subjects' actions make sense.

No doubt, there might be a number of different explanations for such actions, some of which might have nothing whatsoever to do with those thoughts. One might have never heard about the legend that throwing coins into the Trevi Fountain is a way to make sure that one returns to Rome, and might well throw a coin there *just* because she sees all the other tourists doing that; or perhaps in order to test whether coins can float into water. But this is not what happens most of the time.

Typically, people are aware of the fountain legend, and the reason why they throw their coins there has something to do with that very legend. Similarly, the reason why people avoid travelling on Friday the 13th has typically something to do with the idea that it is a day of bad luck; the reason why people touch wood has typically something to do with the idea that this brings good luck; and so on and so forth.[12] After all, we call all these actions 'superstitious' precisely insofar as they involve such sorts of superstitious thoughts. And something similar holds also for the

---

12   Here note that subjects themselves do sometimes appeal to such ideas in explaining their actions (as I've done in telling you that I insisted in using that particular pen in my exams *because* it was the same who had previously heard the lessons'). And even if – as we shall see – subjects may be reluctant to avow such ideas explicitly, other people do appeal to such ideas in order to make sense of what subjects do: I take it that most of us would agree that the thought that *the pullover has been touched by Hitler and is somehow contaminated* does typically play some role in determining people's refusal to wear it, whether they explicitly recognize this or not. After all, the same people would probably accept to keep in their hands books describing Hitler's atrocities in detail, and featuring pictures of him. Their problem with the pullover seem to be related to the idea that it has been touched, hence *contaminated*, by such an evil person as Hitler.

other actions I mentioned, which do not straightforwardly classify as 'superstitious'. When I ask the door to please remain shut, I obviously somehow think of it as *able to understand me:* this thought clearly has some role in explaining my action of talking 'to her'.

What role precisely? Well, this is much less obvious. While it seems clear that thoughts like those just seen do generally play *some* relevant role in explaining the actions we are considering, spelling out precisely what that role amounts to is much trickier. So far, I have been referring to them in the generic terms of 'thoughts' or 'ideas'. But what kinds of mental states such thoughts and ideas exactly are? And, whatever they are, how do they interact with the subjects' other mental states in order to motivate action?

In my view, the thoughts in question are *imaginings*, which motivate action directly in conjunction with subjects' desires. When I ask the door to remain shut, I (really) want it to remain shut, and – though I obviously don't believe that it can understand me, I *imagine* that it can: this is what motivates my verbal action. Similarly, I *imagine* that my pen will suggest me the right answers in the exam, and this – together with the desire to give the right answers – is what motivates me to use it.

An explanation along these lines is available for all the cases here in question; and, I shall argue, is generally the best available one. But I am aware that, for some cases at least, this is controversial: especially for cases of superstitions, which are normally explained in terms of belief. I wouldn't be surprized if you agreed that I don't really believe that the door can understand me, but you took the pen case to be different. In the pen case, many would say that I simply used to have a superstitious *belief*, as students typically have when it comes to exams.

Alternatively, some may grant that I merely imagined that the pen would have helped me, yet still deny that this imagining played the direct motivating role I suggest: perhaps what happened is simply that I realized that using such a pen made me feel less anxious (since the mere fact of imagining that it would have helped me in the exam had a relaxing effect), so I just used it to relieve my exam-related anxiety.

Or else, some may think that neither imagination nor belief are the relevant categories here: I obviously didn't believe that my pen would have helped me, but I did not *just* imagine that, either; my attitude towards that proposition should be described in rather different terms. But then, in what terms?

As it turns out, contrary to what happened with the paradigmatic cases considered in the previous chapters, which we straightforwardly explain in terms either of imaginings or of beliefs, our intuitions concerning the cases introduced in this chapter are not always so clear, and might vary from subject to subject. From what I have just said, the following explanatory options have emerged.

i)   *Standard Humean explanation.* The 'magical' thoughts in question are beliefs, which motivate the relevant actions in conjunction with subjects' desires.
(In a Humean fashion: I believe that using that 'wise pen' will help me to do better in the exam, I desire to do better, I use that pen).

ii) *Sophisticated Humean explanation.* The thoughts in question are imaginings, but they motivate the relevant actions just indirectly, via belief-desire pairs.
(Again, in a Humean fashion: I imagine that using that pen will help me to do better in the exam. This imagining – which typically becomes occurrent when I use that pen – elicits a positive emotion, reducing my exam-related anxiety. I then come to believe that using that pen makes me feel better. This belief, together with the desire to feel better, is what motivates me).

iii) *Explanation in terms of imaginings.* The thoughts in question are imaginings, which motivate action directly, in conjunction with subjects' desires, with no mediation of belief.
(I imagine that my pen will suggest me the right answers in the exam, and this – together with the desire to give the right answers – is what motivates me to use it).

iv) *Radically new explanation.* Neither belief nor imagination can play the relevant explanatory role here – neither of these categories can capture the hybrid status of subjects' attitudes towards the thoughts in question; we need a new cognitive category. What category, then? Tamar Gendler has suggested one: *alief.*
(So: I *alieve* that the pen will help me to do better in the exam; and this *alief* alone drives my behaviour – in the ways that Gendler describes).

In what follows I shall discuss these four different explanatory options (i)-(iv). My aim is to defend (iii), showing that superstitious actions are explained at best in terms of (directly motivating) imaginings. In order to do that, I shall first discuss and reject the two Humean explanations, (i) and (ii). Then, after having laid out and defended my view (iii), I will also criticize (iv).

Since the most controversial part of my claim concerns superstitions, I will initially focus on them. Once argued that they are *not beliefs*, I will defend a unified account in terms of imaginings for all the sorts of 'magical actions' that I have described.

'Unified', note, does not purport to mean 'universal'. The claim that these actions and behaviours are imagination-driven is in important respects an empirical claim that – as such – goes subject to exceptions. But while not denying that we ever hold (and are motivated by) genuine superstitious/ magical *beliefs*, I shall argue that in most cases our superstitious/magical thoughts are better understood as (directly motivating) imaginings.

2. The standard Humean explanation[13]

As I have noted, the thoughts here in question are often called 'beliefs'. We commonly ascribe to each other superstitious *beliefs*. For example, we say that people *believe* that Friday the 13th is a day of bad luck, or that it is a popular *belief* that throwing a coin into the Trevi Fountain is a way to ensure a return to Rome.

This talking in terms of belief is quite standard also among psychologists and anthropologists working in this area. Stuart Vyse's seminal book on the psychology of superstition is indeed called '*Believing* in magic'. Paul Rozin talks interchangeably of 'sympathetic magical thinking' and '*belief* in the laws of sympathetic magic'. Bruce Hood talks of "supernatural *beliefs* operat[ing] in everyday reasoning, no matter how rational and reasoned you think you are" (Hood 2012: 10).

Philosophers, too, (though with some notable exceptions I shall discuss) when discussing superstitions do generally treat them as beliefs. Lisa Bortolotti, for instance, includes superstitions among the uncontroversial instances of ordinary beliefs that she uses as benchmark to assess the doxastic status of delusions (Bortolotti 2010: 85).[14] The list of examples could continue, but I don't think I need many more than these to persuade

---

13   Some of the ideas presented in this section are also discussed in Ichino (2018).
14   To be fair, what Bortolotti claims is that superstitions are uncontroversially *ascribed* as beliefs. At the beginning of her book, she makes clear that she is interested in our practices of belief ascription, and she is open to the possibility that what we commonly call belief is better described in a different way (Bortolotti 2010: 2). I take her point to be a conditional one: *if* you are happy to call all these things 'beliefs', then you should do the same with delusions. I argue that the antecedent of this conditional, in many of the cases she considers, is false. My worry concerning Bortolotti (2010)'s discussion is precisely this: that many things which (apparently) we are happy to call 'beliefs' in fact are better described in other terms.

you that talking of superstitious, magic, or supernatural *beliefs* is very common, and indeed quite natural.

Arguably, the reason why it is so common and natural to describe superstitious thoughts as beliefs is that they seem to motivate actions in conjunction with subjects' desires, as beliefs typically do. The superstitious thought that throwing a coin into the fountain will ensure a return to Rome seems indeed to be what – jointly with a desire to return to Rome – is most directly responsible for my action of throwing the coin. The thought that Hitler's pullover is contaminated, together with a desire to avoid contamination, seems to be what motivates people's refusal to wear it. And so it goes, plausibly, for the other superstitious thoughts (together with the relevant desires) in the other cases I introduced.

Among these cases, remember, there are also instances of *verbal* actions – which (as we have seen in Chapter 3) play a key role in our practices of belief ascription (see above, Chapter 3: §2). Even though, as psychologists have long recognized, people may be reluctant to explicitly avow their superstitions (for fear of ridicule and of negative social evaluation – cf. Vyse 2014: 14-19), at least some kinds of more 'fashionable' and socially accepted superstitious thoughts (e.g. those on horoscopes, or on hidden conspiracies) do often find more or less explicit verbal expression. And when they do, they are generally taken as evidence to credit people with the corresponding beliefs. Why, indeed, would someone ask you what your astrological sign is – and comment on it: "Aha, Sagittarius! So you must be introverted and creative…" – if she didn't *believe* that horoscopes can tell something relevant on people's personality?

However, if on the one hand superstitious thoughts like those just considered seem to play the paradigmatic motivational role of beliefs, on the other hand, they seem to lack another crucial feature of paradigmatic beliefs – actually two strictly related features: what I have called 'sensitivity to evidence' and 'inferential integration' (or 'holistic coherence'). Differently from paradigmatic beliefs, superstitious thoughts do not seem to be formed and maintained in response to the evidence available to us. Most notably, they seem to be unresponsive to that kind of inferential evidence which makes our beliefs integrated with each other into a (more or less) holistically coherent system. The lack of such epistemic features casts serious doubts on the doxastic status of superstitious thoughts – as I am about to show.

2.1. *Doubts on the doxastic status of superstitions: inferential evidence and holistic (in)coherence*

The fact that superstitious thoughts do not cohere with the contemporary scientific view of the world is fairly obvious and, in a sense, given by definition: as we have seen in § 1, it is also and importantly because they clash with such a view that they classify as 'superstitious' (or 'magical', 'supernatural', etc.).[15]

Ideas about the influences of horoscopes and lucky charms, the contagious powers of invisible essences, the bad luck attached to a particular date in the calendar, and other such things, are clearly at odds with basic physical laws (e.g. laws of causation, space-time homogeneity, etc.), as well as with basic methodological principles of scientific inquiry (which require systematic observation and reproducibility of results as a basis to accept hypotheses).

Of course, the obvious fact that superstitious and scientific propositions are inconsistent does not *in itself* imply that superstitious people hold inconsistent thoughts. After all, we can imagine someone whose thinking is consistently non-scientific, holding a fully coherent system of superstitious/ magical thoughts. This is precisely how James Frazer famously depicted people of what he calls 'primitive' cultures: characterized, in his view, by the endorsement of a globally consistent (as well as globally mistaken) magical view of the world, which has then evolved over time into a more rational naturalistic view.

This picture of the 'primitive mind', however, is highly controversial: few contemporary anthropologists would still endorse it.[16] And anyway, whether or not it has any plausibility for some individuals belonging to the 'primitive' cultures that Frazer was concerned with, surely it doesn't for the

---

15 So for example Vyse adopts the following definition (coming from the *Encyclopaedia Britannica*) of superstitions as "beliefs or practices groundless in themselves and inconsistent with the degree of enlightenment reached by the community to which one belongs" (Vyse 2014: 19). And one of the two major components of Nemeroff and Rozin's working definition of 'magic' is the idea that 'magic does not make sense in terms of contemporary understanding of science' (Nemeroff and Rozin 2002: 5).

16 In fact, there is even room to argue that a 'primitive creature' like that depicted by Frazer is highly evolutionarily implausible. And indeed, while acknowledging the importance of Frazer's huge work, contemporary anthropologists and psychologists have criticized it in many ways: few would now endorse Frazer's views (on this, see e.g. Nemeroff and Rozin 2002, or Vyse 2014. For the most famous philosophical criticism of Frazer's conceptual framework, see Wittgenstein 1967).

superstitious people I am considering here: people living nowadays in our Western society, otherwise committed to a scientific, natural view of the world. As we have seen, this category of 'superstitious people' is likely to include most of us; interestingly, there is not even consistent evidence of an inverse correlation between superstitious thinking and levels of scientific education.[17] For people like us, superstitious thoughts will then surely conflict with many other beliefs (not only, note, beliefs that are strictly speaking scientific, but also various ordinary beliefs which follow more or less directly from them[18]).

The inferential isolation of superstitious thoughts with respect to the whole system of our beliefs is also evident to the extent that we typically fail to draw the consequences that would follow from such thoughts – even very obvious consequences. Those who move their bed in order not to sleep with their feet towards the door, *thinking that this would lead to death in seven days*, do not consistently worry about other people (including loved ones!) who happen to sleep in that position, apparently failing to appreciate that the same tragic consequences might follow for everyone. Similarly, those who avoid travelling on Friday the 13th *thinking of it as a day of bad luck* do not seem to conclude that other people travelling on that day are foolhardy, nor that flying companies are blameworthy for lowering the tickets' prices on such day, even though they surely believe that travelling in well-known dangerous conditions is foolhardy and that encouraging someone to do something dangerous is blameworthy.

From all these examples, the lack of consistent integration between superstitious thoughts and ordinary natural beliefs seems hardly deniable; and it seems indeed to be something of which superstitious people are generally aware. Their reluctance to publicly avow (and, in some cases,

---

17   Indeed, the vast majority of published studies on superstitious thinking are conducted on college students. And actually, some forms of superstitious thinking are even more common within subjects with higher level of intelligence, education and socio-economic status (on this, see Vyse 2014: 67; see also Huston 2013: Introduction).

18   Think for example of common folk-psychological beliefs on the relation between our mind and other minds, or between our mind and the physical world, in relation to such ideas as: *crossing your fingers can influence someone else's decision,* or *speaking ill of a person can make it happen.* Moreover, there is a growing body of empirical data concerning our intuitions about the future, free-will and determinism (see in particular research by Shaun Nichols and Joshua Knobe). Apparently our intuitions are not fully clear. But it seems that at least for such things as our own actions we are not determinist. If this is true, this would conflict with many superstitions – which seem to presuppose some form of determinism.

tendency to explicitly disavow) their superstitions, which we noted before, is likely to be due precisely to that awareness: to their realizing that such thoughts are in obvious contrast with many other (more sensible?) ones which they themselves would not seriously put into question.

2.1.1. *Coherent superstitions?*

Admittedly, some of the thoughts that I included in my category of 'superstitions' may look different in this respect. Take for example thoughts concerning horoscopes, or conspiracy theories (like those circulating on Princess Diana's death, or on 9/11). As we have seen, these are thoughts that many subjects are not reluctant, but actually quite willing, to express publicly – even 'very publicly', as on magazines and social networks. This willingness is likely to be due also to the fact that such thoughts do not look so obviously inconsistent with their other beliefs. On the contrary, they seem to make coherent sense of at least some such beliefs. Ideas on the influences of stars upon human life and character, for example, can well make sense of subjects' beliefs about other people's behaviours; ideas about hidden conspiracies behind an event like someone's death can well make sense of one's other beliefs concerning the complex circumstances of that event. If so, thoughts concerning astrology and conspiracy theories might turn out not to be so inferentially isolated, after all. And indeed we call them 'theories' – a term indicating systems of propositions which are somehow logically related to one another. At least in this respect, they differ from traditional superstitions like those concerning Friday the 13th, which typically involve isolated propositions that do not constitute premises for further reasoning.[19]

Without denying this difference (nor indeed many others that I recognize into my heterogeneous category of 'superstitious thoughts'), however, I'm still convinced that superstitious ideas like those on horoscopes or conspiracy theories cannot be taken to be sensitive to inferential evidence and integrated into a holistically coherent system as beliefs typically are.[20] Ideas on horoscopes are as inconsistent with

---

19   In all the respects just mentioned these more structured and 'theory-like' superstitious ideas on astrology or hidden conspiracies are somewhat similar to systems of religious beliefs. I'll return to this in Chapter 6.

20   In relation to this, it is interesting to note that that apparently this sort of 'theory-like superstitions', like those on horoscopes or other New Age ideas are particularly popular among people with higher levels of education (Vyse 2014: 47).

basic scientific propositions as the other traditional superstitious ideas I considered are;[21] and apparently they are even more likely than traditional superstitions to be endorsed by subjects with higher levels of education – hence presumably higher levels of scientific beliefs. Moreover, also the image of astrology as an internally consistent theory is in fact bogus; hence, the body of astrological views endorsed by a single subject is likely to be a bundle of contradictory claims, too.[22]

And something similar seems to hold for 'superstitious conspiracist thoughts'. The work by Karen Douglas and her colleagues at Kent show that the ideas endorsed by conspiracy theorists are typically characterized by dramatic internal inconsistencies. Subjects who distrust the 'official stories' of Princess Diana's or Bin Laden's death, for example, tend to *simultaneously* endorse contradictory accounts of such events (e.g. in a study, those who thought that Diana faked her own death in order to retreat into isolation with Dodi turned out to be *also* significantly more likely to agree that Diana was killed by business enemies of the Fayeds *and* marginally more likely to agree that she was killed by British intelligence).[23] And these subjects do not seem much concerned with supporting their conspiracist views with positive reasons, either: they simply tend to *state* such views in the form of slogans – slogans which then, not surprisingly, they are not really open to abandon or revise in the light of contrary reasons.[24]

Overall, then, while acknowledging relevant differences between the various superstitious thoughts I have been considering, I think we can conclude that none of them is really sensitive to reasons and inferential evidence as paradigmatic beliefs, instead, are.

---

21 McGrew and McFall (1990) provide many compelling examples of the incompatibility of astrology and science.

22 There is little doubt that self-proclaimed astrologists contradict each other all the time. And their own theories do often include contradictory claims, as you can easily appreciate by reading 'zodiac profiles' that ascribe to one and the same sign incompatible properties. Note that these contradictions are generally openly recognized.

23 See Wood, Douglas and Sutton (2012). Similarly, subjects who thought that Bin Laden was already dead at the time of the American raid were more likely to agree he is still alive now.

24 Wood and Douglass (2013). In relation to this, see also Haidt (2012); although Haidt does not focus on conspiracy theories, but discusses ideologies (political and religious) more in general.

2.2. *Further doubts: other sources of evidence and the origin of superstitions*

My discussion so far about superstitious thoughts' insensitivity to inferential evidence has been referring to the way in which they are *maintained:* I have argued that we *keep* such thoughts without revising/ abandoning them in the face of contrary reasons as instead we typically do with beliefs. I haven't said anything about how they are initially *formed,* though. How do superstitious thoughts enter our mind in the first place? If they are not maintained in response to inferential evidence, are they at least initially formed in response to it, or in response to any of the other kinds of evidence to which beliefs are sensitive?[25]

These are widely debated questions in psychology and cognitive anthropology. Without taking a definite position in this debate, I shall briefly consider some influential hypotheses that have been advanced concerning the origin of superstitious thinking, and discuss their implications for the non-doxastic view I am defending.

2.2.1. *A natural mind design*

When considering the origins of superstitious thoughts at a quite general level, various authors – including for example Guthrie (1993), Vyse (2014), Hood (2012), Risen (2016) – have suggested that they come about as products of our 'natural mind design': i.e. of the ways in which our minds naturally respond to external and internal stimuli, forming representations at various levels.

At the heart of these suggestions is a widely accepted view of human cognition, according to which the mind is not a blank slate which passively receives amorphous information from the real world, but is a rather active machine which constantly tries to make sense of such information, filling its gaps in coherent ways and detecting in it meaningful patterns – the most meaningful ones for us generally being patterns having to do with human agency and intentionality.

This can be observed from the lowest levels of our cognition, with, for example, our visual system automatically responding to anything that is even remotely face-like (whether it is a cloud, a tree trunk, some lines and spots on a piece of paper...) making us *seeing a face in it*; or – at an even lower level – our mirror neurons being activated by agent-like movements

---

25   I discussed these different sorts of evidence in Chapter 3, §1.

such as reaching and grasping. It is not difficult to see how superstitious thoughts fit within this general framework: their characteristic tendency to posit meaning, reasons and intentionality behind 'brute' facts/events can be seen as a sort of higher-level manifestation of the natural interpretive strategy I just described in relation to the perceptual/sensory level. As we tend to *literally* see faces and human-like features in the objects around us, we also tend to *cognitively* 'see' hidden meanings, reasons and human intentions into a variety of facts/events in our lives – whether they concern someone's death, the stars' position at the time of our birth, or even just such mundane things as spilling some salt on the table.

This is why, when we come to know that Princess Diana died in a car crash, we are naturally keen to think that someone orchestrated this; and so we are naturally keen to think that 'apparently irrelevant' facts such as salt spilling may mean something important for our lives. No doubt, in cases like this latter one our superstitious ideas are also in important respects the product of cultural transmission: traditional superstitions are typically acquired from what we are told by other people. But – many authors argue – the reason why their cultural transmission is so successful is that they are precisely the sort of ideas which we are naturally keen to form ourselves. As Hood puts it:

> [Superstitious] beliefs are not simply transmitted by what other people tell us to think. Rather, I would argue that our brains have a mind design that leads us naturally to infer structures and patterns in the world and to make sense of it by generating intuitive theories. (...) Yes, we can believe what others tell us, but we tend to believe what we think could be true in the first place. (Hood 2012: 236)[26]

Now, what I have just said may be taken to indicate that superstitious thoughts are actually *initially* formed in response to inferential evidence and reasoning (though obviously flawed ones); and, in the case of traditional superstitions, also in response to some sort of testimonial evidence. But I do not think this would be quite right – and actually I do not even think that this is what Hood is suggesting in the passage just quoted.

The fact that we are naturally keen to form some thoughts does not in itself mean that such thoughts are inferred from beliefs to which we are

---

26 Note that actually the expression Hood uses is 'supernatural' beliefs; but his category of supernatural basically coincides with my category of superstition. This basic suggestion about the 'epidemiology of cultural transmission' is originally put forward by Sperber (1996). See also Boyer (2001).

seriously committed; they may simply be *triggered* by such beliefs and/ or by other bits of our cognition like emotions and desires, as imaginings often are (so, for example, a belief about Diana's tragic death together with a pervasive feeling of distrust towards authority and medias may well prompt us to imagine an alternative story...).[27]

Nor, on the other hand, everything that other people say and do reveal the serious commitment on their part which seems to be required for *testimonial* transmission (even broadly conceived).[28] If I form the idea that there was a child called 'Little Red Riding Hood' in response to your telling me a story about her, we wouldn't typically say that I formed such an idea in response to testimonial evidence. We would rather say that your reading the story prompted me to imagine that. Similarly, the naturalness with which superstitious thoughts are formed in response to such stimuli as other people's sayings/doings does not really prove them to be evidence-sensitive as beliefs are (and ought to be). I'd rather suggest, again, that these thoughts are naturally *prompted* by such stimuli in a way more similar to that in which imaginings typically are. After all, there are also many things that we are naturally prone to imagine.

2.2.2. *Supersense*

What I have just argued is in line with the psychological accounts defended by the authors I am discussing, who – although not talking in terms of *imaginative* prompting – emphasize the role of evidence-insensitive factors such as emotions, desires, or 'need for control' in the formation of superstitions (see Vyse 2014; Hood 2012; Huston 2012). Admittedly, as we have seen in Chapter 3, all these factors can play *some* role in the formation of genuine beliefs; but not the *systematic,* central role that they are suggested to play in the case of superstitious thinking.

Take again Hood's account of the origin of superstitions.[29] Far from suggesting superstitious thoughts to be rational responses to inferential

---

27 Admittedly, Hood uses the term 'inference'; but his use of this term is quite sloppy.
28 Here by the way remember that traditional superstitions, which are the ones supposedly sensitive to testimonial evidence – are also those that people are more reluctant to explicitly avow, or even tend to explicitly disavow and dismiss as 'mere rituals' or 'bits of fun'– something that makes the idea of testimonial transmission even less plausible (on this, see Hood 2012: 20).
29 The reason why I focus on Hood (2012)'s account is that, as I said, it constitutes one of the most recent and extensive discussions of these issues, drawing on a

or testimonial evidence, Hood's basic suggestion (which gives the title to his book) is that they are formed through the operations of what he calls our "supersense": a sort of faculty that doesn't coincide neither with our five senses nor with our rational thinking, but has rather to do with the affective and low-level associative dimensions of our mental lives. Indeed, Hood variously characterizes it in such terms as: "a gut feeling operating beneath the veneer of rationality", an "emotional urge that runs counter to reason", "a physical feeling of knowing" or even in terms of "wishful thinking", insisting on its intrinsic spontaneity and creativity. And his repeated appeals to psychological constructs such as Damasio's *somatic marker* or the so-called 'system 1' leave little doubt that this supersense has more to do with emotions and low-level automatic associations than with any reliably evidence-reflective mechanism.[30]

Here one might point out that also genuine beliefs can be the product of low-level perceptual responses that are impervious to rational reflection. Can't the inputs from our supersense be taken as sorts of low-level responses to real-world evidence, similar (though not identical) to perceptual responses? I don't think so, since, as I said, what Hood calls 'supersense' seems to be a *projective*, rather than a *receptive* mechanism. However, I won't insist on this any further. Even granting that some superstitious thoughts may be formed in response to low-level reality-reflecting stimuli as perceptual beliefs are, a fundamental difference between such thoughts and beliefs would remain in that perceptual beliefs (as all other beliefs) as soon as they are formed become sensitive to inferential evidence and

---

large range of up-to-date empirical findings from developmental and social psychology, cognitive anthropology, and neurosciences.

30   Here is are a few passages from Hood's discussion which can give an idea of the sort of mechanisms he appeals to: "Psychologists have come to the conclusion that there are at least *two different systems* operating when it comes to thinking and reasoning. *One system is believed to be evolutionarily more ancient in terms of human development; it has been called intuitive, natural, automatic, heuristic and implicit.* It's the system that we think is operating in young children before they reach the school age. The supersense we experience as adults is *the remnant of the child's intuitive reasoning system* that incorrectly comes up with explanations that do not fit rational models of the world. (...) Mood is an important factor in triggering supernatural beliefs in those who score more highly on measures of intuition. (...) The supersense lingers in the back of our minds influencing our behaviours and thoughts, and our mood may play a triggering role. This explains why perfectly rational, highly educated individuals can still hold supernatural beliefs. (...) The neuroscientists Antonio Damasio calls this the *somatic marker*: it indicates the way emotions affect reasoning in a rapid and often unconscious way." (Hood 2012: 259-260; 40-41).

coherence constraints. Remember what we do for example with perceptual illusions, rapidly correcting for first appearances which do not cohere with our pre-existing beliefs.[31] Superstitious thoughts, we have seen, are not so sensitive to coherence constraints. The maximum of coherent integration they reach is a temporary and local integration with a few of our beliefs – as indeed typically happens with imaginings.

Even granting (which I don't) that superstitious thoughts were initially formed in response to real-world evidence, then, we should recognize that they stop being so sensitive fairly soon.

2.3. *Belief: epistemic and pragmatic dimensions*

The claim that superstitious thoughts are not sensitive to evidence nor coherently integrated in the system of subjects' beliefs is not terribly controversial. As I have shown, it is supported by the available empirical data. And most of the authors of the studies I considered explicitly agree with that. Hood describes such thoughts as "stubbornly resisting" contrary reasons and critical thinking (Hood 2012: 10). Nemeroff and Rozin observe that they coexist with naturalistic thoughts without influencing them, nor being influenced by them (Nemeroff and Rozin: 2). Huston (2012) does also insist on people's awareness of such inconsistencies.[32] Yet, these authors do not hesitate to call such thoughts "beliefs".

In so doing, they seem to assume – if only implicitly – that the epistemic dimension of belief is not, after all, *constitutive* of it. Indeed, if one recognizes that superstitious thoughts are not sensitive to inferential evidence and holistically coherent, and yet wants to classify them as 'beliefs', then one seems to be committed to the view that these epistemic features are not necessary features of belief, after all. On this view, presumably, *all* that is necessary for belief would be its practical dimension – having to do with motivational connection to action (and emotion).

---

31   See above Chapter 3: § 1.1.
32   "Research shows little correlation between people's levels of rationality or intelligence and their susceptibility to magical thinking. I 'know' knocking on wood has no mystical power. But my instincts tell me to do it anyway, just in case, and I do. A possibly apocryphal tale has the legendary physicist Niels Bohr responding to a friend's enquiry about the horseshoe he'd hung above his door: 'Oh, I don't believe in it. But I'm told it works even if you don't!'..." (Huston 2012: 6). Hutson's discussion is full of anecdotes like this. Even if it weren't true that superstitious thoughts are acknowledgedly incoherent with subject's beliefs, surely Hutson thinks that they are.

But this, I argue, would be an undesirable conclusion: such a 'purely motivational view' of belief misses out something important about its nature. The sorts of cognitive inputs in response to which beliefs are formed and the sort of relations that they have with each other are as important for a proper characterization of beliefs' functional profile as their behavioural (and emotional) outputs are. So, both the practical dimension – having to do with motivating power – *and the epistemic dimension – having to do with sensitivity to evidence* – seem to be necessary to define belief: I don't see why we should privilege one dimension over the other.

Now, admittedly, one may agree that a proper characterization of belief must say something on the inputs responsible for belief formation, but object to the idea that such inputs must *necessarily* be 'evidential' inputs.[33] Bayne and Pacherie (2005), for example, argued that though paradigmatic instances of belief are formed in response to evidential inputs, there can also be beliefs formed in different ways:

> Beliefs are *typically* formed in response to perceptual information or by inference from other beliefs, but we see no reason to think that these are the only routes to belief. (...) We deny that there is a constitutive connection between belief and evidence. As we pointed out earlier, folk-psychology – and indeed, scientific psychology – has little trouble with the thought that beliefs can be innate, and can be formed by motivation mechanisms. (...) Why such states shouldn't be called beliefs is unclear to us – after all, they could guide theoretical and practical reasoning in much the way that standard beliefs do. (Bayne and Pacherie 2005: 169)

In a sense, the dispute here may be taken to be more terminological than substantial: it depends on how fine-grained we want our mental categories to be. Bayne and Pacherie seem willing to adopt a rather broad characterization of belief, which respects (some) common uses of this category. They say:

---

33   There are at least two possible forms of 'purely motivational accounts' of belief (as I intend it here). One is a *dispositional account,* according to which believing that p is *nothing more than* being disposed to act (and react) in certain ways. An account like this completely ignores the inputs dimension (see Schwitzgebel 2000, 2002, 2009, 2013). Another sort of 'purely motivational account' may be a functional account according to which beliefs can be formed in response to a variety of different inputs, and what distinguishes them from other cognitive states are their action (and emotional) outputs (this is the sort of account that I take Bayne and Pacherie 2005 to defend).

> The category of 'belief' is far from homogeneous. As with many terms of folk-psychology (desire, emotion, intention) the states that we are prepared to accept as beliefs differ in various ways. Unfortunately, dominant models of belief obscure the multi-dimensional nature of belief. (Bayne and Pacherie 2005: 179)

But what Bayne and Pacherie consider 'unfortunate', is something that I see as a desideratum for a good account of belief (and of mental states more in general), instead. In my view, the fact that we are ready to call 'belief' a number of states with different features just means that our common linguistic uses are approximate. What a good scientific theory should do is precisely to distinguish the different sorts of states that our common speech tends to conflate. This, at least, is the sort of account of folk-psychological states which I am looking for (as I indicated in Chapter 1).

The idea that belief's inputs must be evidential inputs, by the way, is not really a strict requirement: as we have seen in Chapter 3, there are different kinds of evidence to which beliefs can be sensitive – which correspond to different kinds of beliefs (perceptual beliefs, testimonial beliefs, introspective beliefs, etc.). I think that, insofar as we are aware of these differences, gathering these kinds of beliefs under a unique 'belief' label does make sense; but surely we shouldn't broaden our category of belief even further, including in it even states that are not formed in response to any kind of evidence whatsoever. Hence, we should say that displaying at least some degree of sensitivity to evidence is necessary for a state to count as belief. Recognizing this, arguably, is important also to account for belief's *normative* dimension – as I am going to show.

2.3.1. *What grounds for epistemic rationality norms?*

Authors like Hood, Rozin and the others whose views I discussed in this chapter recognize that superstitious thoughts are typically produced by evidence-insensitive mechanisms. However, they insist in qualifying such thoughts as *irrational,* thereby implying that even if such thoughts are not, *as a matter of fact,* sensitive to evidence, they *ought to* be so sensitive.

This sounds problematic to me. If it is true that superstitious thoughts are not constitutively regulated by evidence-sensitive mechanisms, then normatively evaluating them on the basis of how well they respond to evidence does not seem appropriate. It would be a bit like going to a piano concert and criticizing the pianist for not having served us a good dinner. As a criticism like this would be inappropriate – since the pianist isn't supposed to serve us any dinner, so it seems inappropriate to criticize superstitious thoughts for not responding adequately to evidence – since they are not formed through the operations of a mechanism which is supposed to respond in such ways.

The question here at stake, put in more general terms, is that of what justifies us in applying to a given cognitive state a normative constraint of epistemic rationality according to which it *ought* to be sensitive to evidence. The (admittedly tentative) answer which I suggested with my analogy of the piano concert is that we are justified in applying epistemic norms only insofar as the state to which we apply them is as a matter of fact regulated by mechanisms that are designed to track real-world evidence: only in such a case it makes sense to ask whether the mechanisms in question respond to evidence accurately or not; and, consequently, to criticize them to the extent that they don't.[34]

This seems indeed to be the reason why we do not criticize imaginings for being unresponsive to evidence and for misrepresenting reality in the ways in which we criticize beliefs for that: because responding to evidence and representing reality accurately is not what imaginings are supposed to do. Beliefs can *fail* to track evidence and *mis*represent reality because tracking evidence and reality is (one of) their proper functions. This suggestion is based on the view defended by Velleman (2000), who argued that:

> Belief aims at the truth in a normative sense only because it aims at the truth descriptively, in the sense that it is constitutively regulated by mechanisms designed to ensure that it is true. (Velleman 2000: 17)

Although here I prefer to avoid Velleman's talking in terms of belief's 'aiming at truth', I endorse his basic point according to which the epistemic norms of rationality/truth which apply to belief crucially depend on a descriptive fact concerning (the function of) the mechanisms that regulate its formation and maintenance – i.e. *a descriptive fact concerning beliefs' cognitive inputs*.[35]

---

34   As Velleman says: "A phantasy [i.e. an imagining] and a biased belief are alike in that they fail to track the truth; but the phantasy has no tendency to track the truth at all, whereas a biased belief is diverted from the truth; and something can be diverted from the truth only against the background of a tendency to track it" (Velleman 2000: 254-255). A *type-token distinction* may be helpful to better explain my point here: what I mean is that it is only because a state [*type*] is as a matter of fact the product of a mechanism that has evidence tracking as its proper function that it [a *token* of that type] can fail to track it, and be criticized thereof.

35   The question of what it means precisely to say that beliefs 'aim at truth' is highly controversial, and I won't address it here (see e.g. Owens 2003, Nishi and

In contrast with this, authors like Hood, Vyse, Rozin and the others seem to assume that the epistemic norms of rationality/truth which apply to belief depend on *a descriptive fact concerning belief' behavioural outputs*. The fact that superstitious thoughts motivate action seems indeed to be enough for these authors to say that such thoughts ought to be sensitive to evidence, and to criticize them as irrational insofar as they are not.[36]

However, it is not really clear how a fact about action guidance may be sufficient to ground norms of *epistemic* rationality. Consider the following explanation (the only one I can think of): a cognitive state that guides action in conjunction with our desires has the best chances to do that successfully if it represents reality accurately, and the best way for it to represent reality accurately is to respond to the available evidence; therefore cognitive states that guide action, in order to do that successfully, ought to be sensitive to evidence. Although prima facie plausible, this explanation is actually unconvincing.

For one thing, it is not obvious that responding to evidence and representing reality accurately is *always* the best way for a cognitive state to guide successful actions. On the contrary, we can easily to think of cases where acting on the basis of cognitive states that are unresponsive to evidence and factually inaccurate may be good in various ways.

Velleman 2005, Steglich–Petersen 2006). What matters to my point is Velleman's idea that beliefs are the product of a mechanism *designed* to track-truth in some way. I am aware that this suggestion makes appeal to the functional role of belief intended somewhat differently from how I have intended it so far. While so far I have understood belief's function in terms of its *causal role*, here I am referring to belief's *teleological* function. I think that these two approaches to belief's functional role are not incompatible, though more work would be needed to spell out more clearly the relation between them (for a discussion of hybrid functional accounts of mental states which appeal both to causal and teleological functions, see Polger 2004: Chapter 3). It is also worth noting that I am not suggesting that belief's proper function is *just* to represent reality accurately; arguably, another key function of belief is to guide behaviour.

36   An explicit statement of this sort of view can be found in Bayne and Hattiangadi (2013), who say that: "it is partly because beliefs play the causal role that they do in the production of action that we want them to be evidence sensitive. And it is partly because beliefs' are evidence-sensitive that they are the ideal candidates for playing the causal role that they do." And more generally: "insofar as [given mental states] give rise to behaviour typically associated with belief we *should* care whether they are sensitive to evidence" (Bayne and Attianghadi 2013: 130). However, note that strictly speaking here Bayne and Hattinghadi do not argue that the fact that a given mental state guides action is *sufficient* to apply to it epistemic norms. They argue the fact that beliefs guide action is *part* of the reason why we want them to be evidence sensitive. As I shall say, this is something on which I agree.

Superstitious thoughts themselves seem indeed to provide an example of this sort. Authors like Rozin, Hood, Huston and many others insist that even if such thoughts are utterly false and insensitive to evidence, entertaining them and acting upon them may bring significant benefits – psychological, social and possibly of other kinds as well.[37]

And anyway, even if it happened to be true in this world that being sensitive to evidence and reality is always the best way for a given cognitive state to guide successful action, the following modal argument suggests that that this could not be what *grounds* the relevant norms of epistemic rationality which apply to that state.

> Now consider a subject for whom God is ensuring that actions based on a false belief are nevertheless successful in so far as their unsuccessful consequences are controlled for. So let us say that Katie has the belief that π to three decimal places is 3.147. God makes it the case that any actions Katie engages in as a result of holding this belief (and given certain appropriate desires), will have the same effects as the true belief that π to three decimal places is 3.142. So when Katie claims in a room full of π experts that π to three decimal places is 3.147, or when she writes in her maths exam that π to three decimal places is 3.147, God makes it the case that those maths experts also have a false belief on the matter, or fall asleep, or go temporarily deaf (and the same for Katie's maths teacher), so that in terms of the success of Katie's actions, it is as if she had stated that π to three decimal places is 3.142. Now let us ask whether Katie's belief in this case incorrect. It is, but this time we cannot ground this incorrectness on how the belief fares in guiding Katie's actions, because it fares perfectly well. (...) So if Katie's belief is incorrect in this case, the motivational account cannot explain this. (Sullivan-Bissett 2014: 33)

As this thought experiment makes clear, what justifies us to apply epistemic norms of rationality/truth to belief cannot be *just* a fact concerning belief's behavioural outputs. Hence my alternative suggestion: what justifies us in applying such norms is instead a fact concerning the cognitive inputs responsible for belief formation: the fact of being constitutively formed via the operations of a mechanism that is disposed to track changes in real-world evidence.

This of course does not amount to denying that in many cases it is actually desirable to act upon cognitive states that track evidence and

---

37   Indeed, all these authors argue that not only we cannot, but we ought not want to, get rid of our (supposedly) irrational superstitious thinking (see above, footnote 11). By the way, note that another case where acting upon evidence insensitive representations may be pragmatically beneficial is *pretence* (insofar as the imagination-as-motivation view of pretence that I defended is correct).

reality accurately: arguably, we would be very poor survivors if we didn't do that. My point is not that there can't be anything wrong with the fact that a state which is not regulated by evidence-sensitive mechanisms guides action. My point is just that there can't be anything *epistemically* wrong with that, since epistemic norms only apply to states that as a matter of fact are regulated by mechanisms whose proper function is track evidence and reality: i.e. mechanisms that have an epistemic function.

If this is right, then the constitutive and the normative dimensions of belief's sensitivity to evidence cannot be separated so easily, since the second is somehow grounded in the first. Hence, if one recognizes – as Hood, Vyse and Rozin and many others do – that superstitious thoughts are not constitutively sensitive to evidence and reasons, then one should not criticize them as *epistemically* irrational, either (although of course one may criticize them in other ways). And the lack of these key epistemic features *both at the constitutive and at the normative level* is sufficient for me to conclude that superstitious thoughts are not, in fact, beliefs.[38]

2.4. *Where are we?*

In this section I have discussed the 'standard Humean view' according to which superstitious thoughts are *beliefs* that motivate the relevant actions in conjunction with subjects' desires. On such a view, a superstitious action like my action of using a particular pen for written exams would be motivated by the superstitious belief that *using that particular 'wise pen' will help me to do better in the exam,* together with the desire *to do better in the exam* – in a standard Humean way. I have argued that an account like this has undesirable consequences, forcing us to 'renounce' the epistemic dimension of belief, and that if we want to preserve that dimension, we should recognize that superstitious thoughts are, in fact, *not* beliefs.

At this point, my suggestion that superstitious thoughts are imaginings starts getting some more plausibility. The picture of such thoughts that has emerged from my discussion so far is that of cognitive states which are similar to beliefs in important respects, but differ from them with respect to sensitivity to evidence and holistic coherence – a picture that matches the picture of paradigmatic instances of imaginings emerged in the previous

---

38 Here note that even if you are not persuaded by my argument that the epistemic norms which apply to belief depend on its being *as a matter of fact* produced by evidence-sensitive mechanisms, still the fact remains that superstitious thoughts are as a matter of fact insensitive to evidence. As have it, even only this would be sufficient to deny their doxastic status.

chapters. And, indeed, I guess that the same people who think that I didn't really *believe* that my wise pen could help me in the exam, would say that I did, instead, just *imagine* that.

If this is right, can we then conclude that imaginings, and not beliefs, play the relevant motivating role in the case of superstitious actions?

Not yet. Acknowledging that superstitious thoughts are imaginings and not beliefs is *not* tantamount to acknowledging that superstitious actions are motivated by imaginings and not by beliefs. While it seems clear that superstitious thoughts play *some* role in the explanation of superstitious actions, we cannot take it for granted that they play the most direct motivating role. One may well agree that superstitious thoughts are imaginings and not beliefs, but argue that they motivate superstitious actions just indirectly, via beliefs and desires.[39] In the next section I shall discuss this possible explanation.

3. *A more sophisticated Humean story*

3.1. *Emotion-driven beliefs and desires*

Take again the wise pen case. The fact – if it is a fact – that my action is not motivated by superstitious beliefs and desires does not mean that *no* belief-

---

39   The parallel with children pretending to be cowboys and Indians may help to clarify this point. While it is uncontroversial that the imagining that they are Indians and cowboys plays a crucial role in children' pretence game, what precisely this role amounts to is questionable: is it a direct motivating role (as, e.g., Currie and Ravenscroft argue), or does this imagining motivate only indirectly, via beliefs and desires (as, e.g., Nichols and Stich argue)? One difference between cases of superstitious actions and cases of pretence, though, is that in cases of pretence everyone seems to agree that the relevant thoughts are imaginings, so the debate is just on whether these imaginings motivate directly or indirectly. While in the case of superstitious actions even the very nature of superstitious thoughts is controversial. So with superstitious actions we have more options on the table: (i) superstitious thoughts are beliefs, which motivate action directly, in conjunction with the relevant desires; (ii) superstitious thoughts are imaginings, which motivate action indirectly via beliefs and desires; (iii) superstitious thoughts are imaginings, which motivate action directly, in conjunction with the relevant desires. Having criticized (i) – i.e. the standard Humean explanation of superstitious actions, in the next section I will turn to (ii) – i.e. a more sophisticated Humean explanation – which I will also criticize. Finally, I shall argue in favour of (iii) – i.e. my own explanation of superstitious actions in terms of imaginings.

desire explanation is available for it. Perhaps what happens is this. I imagine and do not believe that using that pen will help me to write down the right answers in the exam. This imagining – which typically becomes occurrent when I use that pen – prompts in me a positive emotional response (as we have seen imaginings can do), reducing my exam-related anxiety. Noticing this, I come to believe that using that pen makes me feel better. This belief, together with a reasonable desire to feel better, is what motivates me to use the pen.

This is a Humean account of my action – I called it 'the sophisticate Humean account' – which differs from the standard, naïve one discussed in § 2 in that here the relevant belief and desire, rather than concerning the superstitious content itself, concern my emotional responses to such content.[40] In a sense, as Currie and Jureidini observed, what an account like this does is not so much to explain superstitious actions, as to *explain them away*, construing them as the result of a rational affect-management strategy, rather than the result of irrational superstitious thinking. On this account, indeed, superstitious thoughts themselves do not play any *direct* role in bringing about my action. They just bring about an emotion; and then what motivates me to act is the belief that such emotion may be supported by performing the action in question – that is, a belief of the form: *by performing action A, I will experience the emotion E* (or a belief of some logically equivalent form) in conjunction with a desire *to experience the emotion E*.

3.1.1. *How plausible is this 'sophisticated Humean account' of my action?*

There is little doubt that a belief like the one just seen (in conjunction with the relevant desire) would rationalize my action: if, when I was at

---

40 An account along these lines is discussed by Currie and Jureidini (2004), who present it as a suggestion originally put forward in informal discussion by Paul Noordhof. For another brief discussion of this account, see also Currie and Ichino (2012), on which I will come back in shortly (see §5 below). Note that several versions of this account can be construed, appealing to different variants of sophisticated beliefs and desires. So for example Hood (2012) discusses a sophisticated Humean explanation of superstitious actions in terms of beliefs and desires concerning the *social* (rather than emotional) benefits of performing such actions. On that view, subjects would refuse to wear the serial-killer's cardigan because they believe that wearing it would be socially blamed and desire to avoid social blame. Here I will focus on a version of the sophisticate Humean account that appeals to beliefs and desires concerning superstitious actions' emotional effects. But I think that what I am going to say applies equally well also to various other versions of that account.

high school, I really believed that using that pen would have made me feel better (and I desired to feel better), of course it would have been rational for me to use that pen. [41] But the relevant question here is: did I actually hold such a belief – and was it what actually drove my action?

Let's put it in more general terms. There is little doubt that a belief like: *By performing action A, I will experience the emotion E* would constitute a reason for an agent (who desires to experience E) to perform action A. However, as we have seen, not all reasons are *motivating* reasons. If the sophisticate-Humean theorist wants to argue that beliefs like this are indeed the agents' motivating reasons in the cases of superstitious actions that we are considering, she must also show that in such cases:

(i)   the agents *actually hold* such beliefs; and
(ii)   such beliefs are, among all the agents' beliefs, the ones that *actually cause* their superstitious actions. [42]

In fact, I have doubts on both (i) and (ii). I shall argue that in at least some cases of superstitious actions (i) is implausible: the agents do not plausibly believe their superstitious actions to produce positive emotional experiences. And, most importantly, even when (i) is plausibly true, (ii) is not: even when it seems plausible that the agents believe that their superstitious actions will produce positive emotions, it seems unlikely that it is this sorts of beliefs that directly drive their actions. Let's consider these two claims in turn.

3.2. *Unpleasant superstitions*

So, my first point is that there are a number of cases where it is not really plausible to say – as the sophisticate Humean account does – that superstitious agents believe that their actions will bring about positive emotions. My argument for this is based on the consideration that there are a number of cases where it seems to be *obviously false* that superstitious actions will bring about positive emotions. Assuming a principle of charity in belief ascriptions, I see no reasons to think that subjects in such cases hold obviously false beliefs. [43]

---

41   Henceforth I will focus on the relevant belief, omitting the specification that it motivates in conjunction with an appropriate desire. But I do of course assume that this is the case.

42   Obviously, (ii) entails (i). But I will consider (and criticize) them separately anyway: even if you are not persuaded by my criticisms towards one of them, you may be persuaded by my criticisms towards the other.

43   With 'principle of charity' here I refer, roughly, to a principle according to which the beliefs that we ascribe to each other should be, *until proof to the contrary,*

Examples of superstitious actions that do not produce relevant positive experiences (and generally produce overall negative ones) can be found both within what I called 'traditional' and 'idiosyncratic' superstitions.

As to traditional superstitions, in § 2 I have noted that they are often associated to some embarrassment and worries about negative social evaluation. These worries, as we have seen, are sometimes so strong that they prevent people from publicly performing the relevant superstitious actions – as with people reluctant to verbally express their superstitions for fear of ridicule.[44] Of course, those negative feelings are not always so strong (otherwise we would hardly ever see anyone avoiding ladders or throwing salt over her shoulders!). But anyway, stronger or weaker that they may be, in many cases they do not seem to be compensated by other sorts of emotional benefits deriving from performing the actions in question. Indeed, differently from some personal superstitious actions which may be invested with important emotional values, traditional superstitions nowadays are often treated as little more than ritual routines, which are, overall, 'emotionally neutral'.[45]

---

rational and true (an alternative way to put it is that they should in line with the evidence available to the subject to which we ascribe them).

44   This is indeed how Vyse explains people's reluctance to answer questionnaires about their superstitions: "Undoubtedly, many believers are reluctant to confess their superstitions for fear of ridicule. (…) Even when they reply anonymously, as in the case of Gallup Polls, survey respondents may imagine that the interviewers are forming judgements about them. This fear makes some people reluctant to reveal their true feelings on questions revealing unconventional beliefs or behaviour. (…) In conventional use, the word *superstition* has a distinctly negative flavour, and superstitious people are often thought to be primitive and ignorant. Unlike belief in the paranormal, belief in superstition is thoroughly unfashionable. (…) Reports of traditional superstitions are thus particularly vulnerable to bias caused by apprehension about being evaluated. Psychologists have long recognized that research participants are sometimes motivated by a fear of negative evaluation" (Vyse 2014: 16-18).

45   With "emotionally neutral" I mean that performing such actions does not, in itself, make a great difference to our pre-existing emotional state. One here may argue that any intentional action will be accompanied by some conscious, phenomenal experience – which must have some emotional value. This may be true, but anyway I think we all agree that there are some actions that make little or no difference to the value of our conscious experience at a given time. Here is an example: now I exit the room and I close the door a little. This is something I do intentionally, but arguably it does little or no difference to my emotional state. Closing the door a little doesn't make me feel either better or worse than I would feel if I left it entirely open. Or at least – which is what matters more to me here – *I don't believe* that it makes me feel either better or worse.

This becomes quite evident in situations where, for whatever reasons, we find ourselves unable to perform them. Though we may be keen to touch wood after having made an optimistic prediction, or to cross fingers when we wish something to happen, an impossibility to perform such actions (due for example to the simultaneous engagement in another activity) is not, for most of us, really distressing. If I can touch wood, well; if I'm driving my car and I can't do that... Well, it's just the same![46] At least in cases like these, traditional superstitious actions do not seem to yield significant emotional benefits; and I do not see reasons to think that superstitious agents mistakenly believe that they do.

Note that this is not the same as to say that superstitious agents in these cases have the definite belief that their actions have negative (or even just neutral) emotional effects – let alone that they do *occurrently* believe so at the time where they act. Indeed, belief has the property to be *negation incomplete:* from the fact one *does not believe A*, we cannot infer that she *does believe not-A* (see Currie 1990: 174). One may simply don't know whether A or not-A. So superstitious agents may, in some cases, simply lack a definite view on the emotional effects of their actions. All what I am arguing is that I don't see why, in cases where *as a matter of fact* superstitious actions seem to have neutral or even negative emotional effects, we should ascribe to the agents the definite and occurrent belief that such effects are good – as the sophisticated Humean account would require.

Cases where the emotional costs of superstitious actions are even more evident and, arguably, disproportionately higher than their possible benefits, can be observed in obsessive-compulsive disorders (OCD).[47]

---

46 Another similar example here is the superstitious action of drawing a cross on pizza's dough before leaving it raising: we do not feel really distressed if we can't perform it. Contrast this with a case where you're unable to perform a personal superstitious action: think of a case where you realize that you've lost your lucky object just before an important performance. It seems that in this latter case you would feel much more distressed. The different emotional investment that we put into traditional vs. personal superstitious actions is pointed out by various psychologists (see e.g. Hood 2012: 31).

47 While the precise relation between OCD and superstitious thinking is debated, many authors agree that some sort of superstitious thinking is a fundamental feature of OCD and that some typical obsessive-compulsive actions – such as turning the light on and off a certain number of times before exiting a room, or washing-hand obsessive rites – classify as superstitious. (see e.g. Einstein and Menzies 2004; Brugger and Viaud-Delmon 2010). Anyway, even if obsessive-compulsive actions did not count as superstitious, these would still remain intentional actions that call for an explanation; and in my view no plausible Humean explanation is available for them.

Psychologists largely agree that compulsive stereotyped actions involving e.g. hand-washing, skin-picking, doors/lights-checking, do not really make the agents feel better, but on the contrary tend to make them feel worse, fostering their doubts and obsessions. The more one repeats those sorts of actions, the more she will feel anxious and in need to repeat them again, without really getting any benefit from that – let alone *emotional* benefits. It is indeed also because of the distress they produce that these actions classify as symptoms of a pathological condition.[48] One of the objectives of the so-called "Exposure and Response Prevention treatment" (EX/RP) – one of the most used and effective treatments for OCD to date – is precisely to make patients fully aware of this, showing them that refraining from performing the relevant actions will reduce their anxiety and make them feel overall much better (see Huppert & Roth 2003).

Admittedly, here we need to distinguish between 'feeling overall much better' and 'getting an immediate relief from anxiety'. Or, in other words, between longer-term, all-things-considered emotional benefits and immediate, though short-lived and shallow, emotional benefits. Moreover, of course, we should also distinguish between the *actual* emotional effects of compulsive superstitious actions (as they may be '*objectively*' assessed by psychologists) and the emotional effects that obsessive-compulsive subjects may *believe* such actions to have. Even if a compulsive action like turning the light on and off five times won't *actually* make one feel '*all thing considered* better' in the long term, one may *(rightly or wrongly) believe* that this action will give her at least an immediate relief from her anxiety.[49] And in order for a sophisticate Humean account of this action to be plausible, it is enough that the agent

---

48   According to the DSM V, in order for the obsessions or compulsions to classify as symptoms of OCD it must be the case that: "they are time-consuming (e.g., take more than 1 hour per day) *or cause clinically significant distress* or impairment in social, occupational, or other important areas of functioning". It is also worth noticing that obsessive-compulsive actions are, in various cases, physically painful: as with compulsive skin-picking producing extensive excoriations, or compulsive hand-washing (with very hot water and aggressive soaps) provoking serious dermatitis.

49   And indeed, one may ask: doesn't the fact that the therapy aims to make the patients aware of the negative effects of their actions suggest that they typically have some belief to the contrary – i.e. that they typically believe that their actions make them feeling *at least in some respects* better? In fact, I do not think this necessarily the case. As belief is *negation incomplete,* the fact that one does not believe that her action is emotionally bad does not imply that she believes that it is emotionally good. Obsessive-compulsive agents may simply lack a definite belief about the emotional effects of their actions.

holds a belief like that (in conjunction with a desire to get an immediate relief from their anxiety).

I don't want to deny that subjects suffering from OCD do ever hold beliefs like that; I grant that in various cases they may do. What I argue, though, is that there are *also* cases in which they don't: cases where they perform their compulsive actions without actually believing that they will get *any* emotional benefits from them (even not shallow, temporary benefits).

Take for example subjects who have 'a good insight into their OCD condition'[50] and are actively trying to get over it – as are indeed many patients willingly engaging in the EX/RP cognitive-behavioural therapy I mentioned. Typically, as a (fairly successful) therapy progresses, such patients become convinced that performing their compulsive rituals won't make them feel better, and vice versa refraining from doing that will. Having got direct experience of this in the first sessions, they are often strongly motivated to achieve the full 'ritual prevention' that the therapy envisages, and think that missing this achievement and repeating their compulsive rituals will make them feeling (immediately!) very bad. Yet, they often slip back into repeating such rituals – and this may happen many times during the recovery process (after which, by the way, relapses can still happen).[51]

One here may want to insist that, insofar as they do that, they must believe that their actions have *some sort* of emotional benefits. But I don't really see on what grounds we could insist on that: in cases like these, I simply don't see any reasons to ascribe to the agents the belief that their actions will have *any sort of emotional benefits whatsoever*. On the contrary, we should recognize that they perform those actions *in spite of* their belief that this will make them feel worse.[52] So here again, as in the

---

50   The DSM V distinguishes three sorts of cases. Patients with: (1) "good or fair insight" into their OCD condition, (2) "poor insight" into their OCD condition, (3) "absent insight/delusional belief" about their OCD condition. Notice that subjects can have a good insight into their condition (realizing that their compulsions make them feel bad) and yet not being actively trying to get over it (e.g. not undertaking a EX/RP therapy), for a number of reasons.

51   Recovery is unfortunately a slow, and not-linear, process. And relapses are not uncommon (see Huppert and Roth 2003: 69-70 – on which my description here is based).

52   Here, again, note that – because of belief's property of *negation incompleteness* which I noted above –the claim that agents *do not believe* that their actions will have any emotional benefits does not straightforwardly imply the claim that they *do* have a definite belief to the contrary – i.e. that they *do* definitely *believe* that

cases of traditional superstitions discussed above, the sophisticate Humean account does not seem to work.[53]

My perplexities on the sophisticated Humean account, however, are not limited to such cases. In fact, I think that this account fails to explain *most* cases of superstitious actions, including also cases where admittedly superstitious agents do believe that their actions will bring about some positive emotions. Indeed, as I shall argue, even when it is plausible to ascribe to superstitious agents the belief that their superstitious actions will be emotionally beneficial, it still doesn't seem plausible to say that *it is because of such belief* that they perform those actions. This was indeed the second doubt I raised above in relation to sophisticated Humean accounts. My argument for this will lead me to introduce, finally, my own explanation of superstitious actions in terms of directly motivating imaginings.

4. *Superstitious imaginings*

While so far I focussed on cases where this seems unlikely, I grant that there are *also* cases where it is vice versa quite plausible that superstitious agents believe their actions to be emotionally beneficial. After all, superstitious actions are *intentional* actions; and generally speaking it may be reasonable to assume that (until proof to the contrary) the actions we perform intentionally are actions that we deem apt to bring about some emotional benefits.[54] So I shall grant that, as when I perform such actions as sitting here writing my book, or answering a phone call, I do plausibly believe that they can produce some positive emotions, similarly when I

---

their actions will *not* have any emotional benefits. But I think that in the case we are considering (i.e. the case of OCD patients engaged in a *successful* therapy) it is plausible to ascribe to the agents such a definite belief.

53   Now, one may raise a fundamental doubt on my argument here, suggesting that it is part of the functional role of desire that satisfying it will produce positive emotions. However: (i) this suggestion is not *obviously* true; (ii) note that I am not talking about desires themselves, but about *our beliefs* concerning desires; and anyway (iii) my argument does not crucially depend on this – as we shall see in the next section.

54   My point in §3.2 was just that in cases of weary traditional superstitious actions and of self-damaging compulsive superstitious rituals we *do* have proof the contrary. In fact, I should say that what seems to me most reasonable to grant is that generally when we do something intentionally we do not (occurrently) believe it to be emotionally harmful. But here for the sake of the argument I concede that we may also have the positive belief that it is emotionally beneficial.

perform superstitious actions like using a lucky pen for exams, wearing a lucky shirt, or reading my horoscope, I do plausibly believe that they can somehow make me feel good.

What I shall not grant, on the other hand, is the idea that such sort of beliefs concerning the emotional benefits of my actions are the cognitive states that (most directly) motivate me to act.

To better understand this point it is worth remembering that belief's connection to action is a dispositional connection mediated by desire (see above, Chapter 3: §2). This means that while an agent A will have, at any time T, a large number of beliefs all of which have some motivating *potential*, which ones among such beliefs end up *actually* motivating her actions crucially depends on what are her strongest, occurrent desires at T. Hence, the reason why I don't think that beliefs concerning the emotional benefits of our actions (i.e. beliefs of the form: *by performing action A, I will experience emotion E)* are, in most cases, the cognitive states that directly motivate us, is simply that I don't think that in most cases our strongest occurrent desires are generic desires concerning the positive emotions which our actions may bring about. Our strongest occurrent desires are more often 'goal-specific desires' – i.e. desires concerning 'external' outcomes related to the particular activities we are engaged in – which do then motivate us in conjunction with cognitive states that represent how to achieve such specific outcomes.

In cases of ordinary non-superstitious actions, we can probably all agree on this. So for instance I think we can all agree that, if now I am sitting here writing, this is likely to be because my current strongest desire is to put down this paragraph; and if I stop a moment to answer my phone, this is plausibly because, as the phone rings, the desire to know who is calling me becomes temporarily predominant. Indeed, I guess that if you had to explain why I act in these ways you would mention these or other similar desires, rather than a generic desire to feel good as the one invoked by the sophisticate Humean theorist. You would not typically say that I answer my phone *because I desire to feel good* and believe that answering the phone will make me feel good.

Of course, you may well think, in line with psychological hedonists, that specific desires like my desire to finish the book, or to know who is calling me, are just instrumental to the satisfaction of an ultimate desire for good feelings/pleasure/happiness. But to say that such a basic desire for positive emotions is my *ultimate* motive does not amount to denying that what most directly motivates me when I write/answer a call are such goal-specific desires as the desire to write this paragraph, or to know who is calling –

which seem indeed the ones that make maximally close contact with the actions of writing/answering.

Why then deny that analogous goal-specific desires play the relevant motivating role also in the case of superstitious actions? I don't see any reasons to deny that. Arguably, my strongest occurrent desire when I sit in the exam-room waiting for the exam to start and I and take my lucky pen out of the pen case is the desire to do well in the exam. David Beckham's strongest desire when he wears his brand-new outfits before a match is to play at his best and win the match. The tourist's strongest desire when she throws a coin into the Trevi Fountain before leaving Rome is to return there soon. And so on and so forth.[55]

There is little doubt that the agents in these cases have goal-specific desires of these sorts – which indeed are manifested also in other of their non-superstitious actions/reactions;[56] and that, in the moment when they act, these desires are stronger than the desire to experience/reinforce a positive emotion.

If my strongest desire at the exam time were to feel better, I could just take a heavy tranquillizer to reduce my anxiety. But I don't do that, because this would hinder my performance in the exam and, after all, it seems that what I currently desire most strongly is to have a good performance.

The fact that I do have such a goal-specific desire, by the way, is not denied even by the sophisticated Humean theorist, but on the contrary is presupposed by her own account: it is precisely because I desire to do well in the exam that the mere fact of imagining that my lucky/wise pen will help me in the exam makes me feel better. Still, the point of the sophisticate Humean theorist is that such a desire cannot be the one that motivates my superstitious action of using the lucky/wise pen, because I do not believe, but just imagine that using that pen is a way to do well in the exam – and, on a Humean perspective, desires can manifest their motivating power only in conjunction with beliefs about how to satisfy them.

But this is a perspective I have already rejected. In Chapter 3 I have argued that there are, plausibly, cases where our actions are motivated by genuine desires in conjunction with belief-like imaginings. And I think that

---

55   And the strongest desire of an obsessive-compulsive subject who repeatedly washes her hands will be, typically, the desire to get rid of germs: this is indeed what her obsession is all about.

56   For example, my desire to do well in the exam is also manifested in my anxious last-minute revision of the exam material. As I will notice, cases like this, where the very same desire motivates almost at the same time in conjunction with some belief and with some imagining, are very common.

this is precisely what happens in most cases of superstitious actions we are considering. Remember Chapter 3's example of my pretence action of biting the empty plate in front of me when I hungrily wait for pizza at the restaurant – an action which seems explained at best as motivated by a desire to eat together with the imagining that I can eat a bite of my 'pizza-plate'.

Similarly, now I suggest that the superstitious action of using my lucky pen in the exam is explained at best as motivated by my desire to do well in the exam *together with my imagining that the lucky pen can help me to do well*; that the tourist's action of throwing a coin into the Trevi fountain is explained at best as motivated by her desire to return to Rome *together with her imagining that throwing the coin will propitiate her return*; that David Beckham's wearing a brand-new outfit before each match is best explained by the desire to play at his best *together with the imagining that the brand-new outfit will make him play better*; and so on.

With this, note, I don't want to deny that superstitious actions are *ever* motivated by desires for positive emotions in conjunction with beliefs like those postulated by the sophisticate Humean account. Admittedly, in circumstances that are heavily 'emotionally charged', our strongest occurrent desires may be desires about (how to enhance/dampen) our own emotions; and we may then be moved to act by beliefs about how to satisfy such desires. So for example in some of Rozin and colleagues' experiments, which were expressly built in order to elicit strong emotional responses of disgust or distress, such disgusted/distressed responses may well have been the objects of participants' strongest desires. A participant in the Poisoned-water experiment may well have had as her strongest desire that of reducing the unsettling feeling provoked by the idea of drinking poison, and her refusal to drink it may have been motivated by the belief that to avoid any contact with it could help to reduce her unsettlement.[57]

But if a sophisticate Humean explanation of this sort may be plausible in particular cases like this, where the agents' only purposeful activity consists in participating into the experiment, I do not think it is plausible in the majority of cases of superstitious actions, which are performed in circumstances where the agents are pursuing specific external goals (such

---

57   See above, §1; I will discuss this 'Poisoned-water' experiment more in detail in the next section: §5.2. Note that also ordinary, non-superstitious actions are sometimes primarily motivated by desires and beliefs concerning our own emotions. For example, roller coaster's goers may typically be motivated by the desire to feel excited together with the belief that roller coasters' runs will make them feel excited.

as taking an exam, playing a match…), and their strongest desires do typically concern such specific goals. Since – this is a point of agreement between me and the sophisticate Humean theorist – the agents in all these cases do not believe, but just imagine, that the actions they perform are ways to satisfy such goal-specific desires, I think we should conclude that the cognitive state which plays the relevant causal role in conjunction with their desires is imagination and not belief.

This is even more evident in other instances of 'magical' actions I introduced at the beginning of this chapter. When I ask the door to please remain shut, arguably this is because I really want it to stay shut, and I imagine that if I ask her gently I might persuade her to do that. And so when I yell at the driver in another car who obviously can't hear me, this is because I really want to insult him, and I imagine that he can hear my insulting yells. And when I loudly root for the players of my favourite team that I am watching on TV, this is because I really want to cheer them on and I imagine that they can be cheered on by my loud rooting.

Of course, once again, sophisticated Humean explanations may be concocted for all these cases. One may say that I talk to the door because I desire to vent some of my irritation for its annoying broken handle and I believe that I can vent it by talking to the door. But, even granting that I do have a belief-desire pair like this, I don't think they are likely to be the states that most directly motivate me. Arguably, when I struggle with that broken handle my strongest desire is a desire to keep it shut once for all. This desire is indeed manifested also in some of my realistically purposeful actions, such as pushing the door hard with both my hands – which I *believe* to be a way to keep it shut. Besides (and probably also because such realistic actions do not seem to prove fully effective) such desire motivates also actions which are just imaginative ways to fulfil it. Given that what I take to be realistically effective ways to keep the door shut do not seem to work, I imagine some unrealistic ways to make that happen (*Perhaps, if I ask her gently…*) – and I then act upon such imaginings.

4.1. *The pervasiveness of superstitious thinking (and some conclusions about imagination's motivating power)*

Cases like the one just considered – where the very same desire motivates almost at the same time in conjunction with some belief and with some imagining – are far from uncommon.

When a few minutes ago the scary message that "Windows has stopped responding" appeared on my screen, my reaction (obviously driven by the desire not to lose my work) has been, almost simultaneously, to press CTRL+ALT+DEL and to implore 'him' not to abandon me right now, a few days before my deadline for submitting this book. When I go out climbing, desiring to be safe, I carefully tie-up my harness (which I believe to be the crucial safety measure) *and* I do that with my lucky golden karabiner (which I imagine to be the safest one). Just before the match, David Beckham's desire to play at his best motivates him to wear his brand-new lucky outfit *and* to do some helpful warm-up exercises. Our view and interactions with the world are pervaded by more or less 'magical', over-coherent elements, strictly intertwined with 'natural', realistic ones.

This ubiquity of magical thoughts and actions, as I noted before, is something on which all psychologists and anthropologists agree, and that they have stressed in various ways. So for example Nemeroff and Rozin write:

> We discard the notion of an evolutionary sequence from magic to religion to science, based primarily on our own evidence of the abundant presence of all three simultaneously in modern Western societies and in the thinking of individuals within these societies. (...) People comfortably employ multiple modes of thinking and action, blending scientific and natural approaches in a complementary fashion. (Nemeroff and Rozin 2001: 2)

And Guthrie (who, as we have seen, understands most magical thinking in terms of anthropomorphism) observes that:

> Faces and other human forms seem to pop out at us on all sides. Chance images in clouds, in landforms, and in ink blots present eyes, profiles, or whole figures. Voices murmur or whisper in wind and waves. We see the world not only as alive but also as humanlike. *Anthropomorphism pervades our thought and action.* (Guthrie 1995: 62)

Insofar as my account of superstitious actions and expressive behaviours is correct, then, we have a *very large* number of cases where imaginings motivate us to act as belief do, suggesting that the motivating power of imagination is far more extensive – and more similar to that of belief – than it is generally taken to be.

How extensive and how similar, precisely? As I said in the Introduction to this chapter, I think that these cases reveal imagination's motivating power to be actually *the same* of belief. But in order for this conclusion not to be hasty, some more argument is needed. Indeed, from the fact that in a number, *however large,* of cases, an agent who imagines that p is motivated to act as she would if she believed that p, it obviously does not follow that *in any possible case* an agent who imagines that p will be motivated to act as she would if she believed that p – which is what ought to be true if imaginings really have the same motivating power of beliefs. This latter claim needs independent support, based on a careful consideration of the conditions under which imaginings and belief motivate – which will be the business of the next chapter.

Before moving to that, however, I shall defend my account of superstitious and magical actions from a pretty radical challenge.

5. *Superstitious* aliefs?[58]

A radical challenge to the view that I have been defending in this chapter has been raised by Tamar Gendler in two seminal papers published in 2008 (reprinted in Gendler 2010). While agreeing that superstitious thoughts *cannot be beliefs,* Gendler warns us against jumping too easily to the conclusion that *therefore they must be imaginings.* In her view, neither belief nor imagination can play the relevant explanatory role here. Cases like those I have been discussing in this chapter require us to postulate the existence of a previously unrecognized mental state, that she calls *alief.* In this section I shall defend my view from Gendler's challenge.

5.1. *What is an* alief?

Gendler characterizes alief as a mental state with three associatively linked components: a representational component R ('the representation of some object or concept or situation or circumstance, perhaps propositionally, perhaps non-propositionally, perhaps conceptually, perhaps non-conceptually'); an affective component A ('the experience of some affective or emotional state'); and a behavioural component B ('the readying of some motor routine') (Gendler 2010: 263–4). The link between these three components consists in the fact that they are co-activated by some feature of the subject's environment, and this co-activation is difficult to break. While traditional objectual or propositional attitudes are

---

58   The material presented in this section is a result of joint work with Greg Currie. A
      version of it appears in Currie and Ichino (2012), followed by a reply from
      Gendler.

two-place relations between a subject and a simple representational content (naturally expressed as S believes that R), alief is a four-place relation between a subject and a threefold associatively linked content of the kind just described (S alieves R–A–B). The difference between alief and traditional cognitive attitudes is a radical one: alief is 'developmentally and conceptually antecedent' to such attitudes, and it is not definable in terms of them (See Gendler 2010: 262, 288).[59] Indeed, alief's three components do not constitute a mere cluster of different mental states; rather they form a unified representational-affective-behavioural state, that "there is no natural way of articulating" (Gendler 2010: 289). Nor, importantly, is the representational component of an alief a belief, or an imagining, or some other recognized state.

5.2. *'Poison' and 'Not Poison'*

To explain why, according to Gendler, a mental state of this sort is necessary to a proper understanding of superstitious actions, I shall focus on an example that she discusses at length. This is a case from a couple of psychological experiments I briefly mentioned before, conducted by Rozin and colleagues. In a first experiment subjects were invited to pour some sugar into two different bottles of water, and then to apply on one bottle the label 'sugar' and on the other the label 'Poison', making their own choice about which label to put on which bottle. Despite having poured the sugar themselves, and having applied the labels themselves, they turned out to be subsequently very reluctant to drink from the bottle marked 'Poison'. Call this the *Poison* scenario. In a follow-up study subjects were invited to do the same but using the two labels: 'Safe to consume' and 'Not Poison'. Interestingly, though the effects where a bit less pronounced than in the original study, the subjects again showed much more reluctance to drink from the Not poison bottles. Call this the *Not Poison* scenario.

This is a case for which I have granted a Sophisticate Humean explanation to be plausible. The explanation I suggested is something like this: seeing the label, a subject imagines the drink as poisoned, and this imagining has certain unpleasant emotional effects (as imaginings often do), which intensify the closer she gets to actually drinking the

---

59   Is *alief* itself supposed to be an attitude? Gendler denies that aliefs are attitudes (Gendler 2010: 263); but she says that she will introduce a new attitude called alief, and one section heading in her paper reads 'Alief and other attitudes' (Gendler 2010: 267).

stuff; naturally, she is therefore disinclined to drink it. Gendler, on the other hand, takes this to be a paradigmatic case of alief, the threefold content of which can be expressed (in an avowedly rough and ready way) as: 'Poison, Dangerous, Avoid!'.

Now, one may think that our two explanations are not incompatible. After all, we both agree to the salience of three elements in any plausible explanation of what is going on here: a state which represents the drink as poisoned, an affective state or states, a set of activated behavioural tendencies. And as I said, we do also agree, that the representation is not a belief: the subjects are convinced the drink is harmless. The point, however, is that in Gendler's view this representation cannot be an imagining, either. She provides two arguments for this.

Her first argument is (by her own admission) basically an appeal to intuitions. In a case like the one we are considering, she notes, explanations in terms of imagining are implausible because people are also unwilling (to a degree) to drink from bottles labelled 'Not poison'. Most subjects in the follow-up study, when faced with the choice of drinking from bottles labelled 'Not poison' or 'Safe to consume', opt for the latter. In Gendler's view, it is not likely that seeing a 'Not poison' label induces one to imagine that one actually is drinking poison:

> Can't we say that the source of subject's hesitation is that she first imagines that the bottle does contain poison and that she then somehow negates this, and that this enables her (...) to imagine the absence of poison? Perhaps this is indeed what happens. But how is this supposed to explain the subject's hesitancy to drink the liquid? Is the reason for her hesitancy supposed to be that she had been imagining that the bottle contained cyanide, though now she is not – and that what she imagined in the past (though fails to imagine now) somehow explains her action at present? Or that her current imagining that the bottle does not contain cyanide somehow contains within it (in not-fully-aufgehoben form) the antithetical imagining that the bottle does contain cyanide? And that somehow this negated semi-imagined content – content that she has, throughout the entire process, been fully consciously aware of explicitly disbelieving – sneaks into the control center for her motor routines and causes her to hesitate in front of the Kool-Aid? Really? Is this really what you think imagining is like? (Gendler 2010: 269–70)

However, we don't need to assume that subjects' avoidance behaviour is the product of some past but mysteriously still-active imagining, or that part of a negative imagining takes on a causal life of its own: in many situations it is entirely plausible that seeing a message of the form 'Not-p' provokes one to imagine p.[60] When Donne says that no man is an island, a spontaneous, appropriate and perhaps intended response is that we should imagine men as islands, though doubtless we go on to do other things with the metaphor. If a threatening Mafioso puts a label 'Not dead' on your loved one, that may very well be because it so easily prompts the contrary imagining. Notably, in the 'Not poison' case, the label also bore a skull and crossbones image preceded by the word 'Not'. An erotically charged image preceded by the word 'Not' is unlikely to provoke images of celibacy.

Similar sorts of worries lead me to reject Gendler's second argument – which she takes to be more general and substantive, but eventually, as I will show, turns out to be based on the same questionable intuitions just discussed (and on some conceptual confusion). "For those unconvinced by examples or lines of rhetorical questioning", Gendler offers the *argument from hyperopacity*.

5.3. *The argument from hyperopacity*

According to this argument, the representational component of alief is irreducibly different from imagination because it has the property of being hyperopaque, which imagination does not have.

> Alief contexts are what we might call hyperopaque: they do not permit *salva veritate* substitution even of expressions that the subject explicitly recognizes to be co-referential. Even if I believe that the phrases 'not poison' and 'safe to consume' pick out co-extensive classes of substances, even if I focus on that belief and hold it vividly before my mind, even if the synonymy of these two terms is crucial to my views about some other matter, still the aliefs activated by the two expressions may be wildly dissimilar. Imagination, by contrast, is not hyperopaque in this way. If I explicitly recognize that P and Q are synonymous, and I imagine P while focusing explicitly on the co-referentiality of P and Q, then in imagining P I imagine Q. Alief just isn't imagination. (Gendler 2010: 270)

There are two ambiguities in this argument. The first is due to an unacknowledged transition from 'co-referentiality' to 'synonymy'. Since the example given in the quotation, on which I want to focus, concerns the

---

60   Depending on cases, of course, it may also provoke imagining that Not-P. Generally speaking, what imaginings are prompted by what expressions is highly context-dependent. My point here is just that in the context of Rozin's experiment it is very plausible to suppose that 'Not poison' will provoke the imagining of poison. I discuss context dependence in connection with hyperopacity below: §5.3.

pair 'safe to consume'/'not poisonous', I will simply grant that this pair meets the condition of synonymy, and hence also the weaker condition of co-referentiality.[61] The second ambiguity is more significant: the definition of 'hyperopacity' changes as we go from the case of alief to that of imagination – a crucial change, since Gendler's claim is that there is a single property which alief has and imagination lacks. What is the change? Gendler specifies the hyperopacity that applies to alief as follows:

1)   Alief is hyperopaque insofar as, even if a subject vividly understands that two expressions P and Q are synonymous, the aliefs activated by P can be different from those activated by Q.

But the hyperopacity test applied to imagination is different:

2)   Imagination is not hyperopaque because, if a subject vividly understands that two expressions P and Q are synonymous, then her imagining that P will be the same as her imagining that Q.

Thus we have two distinct definitions:

H1) A state-type S is hyperopaque if it is possible that, when a subject vividly understands that two expressions P and Q are synonymous, a token of S activated by P is different from a token of S activated by Q.

H2) A state-type S is hyperopaque if it is possible that, when a subject vividly understands that two expressions P and Q are synonymous, her S-ing that P is distinct from her S-ing that Q.

As defined in H1, hyperopacity is a property that has to do with the causal power of expressions; in H2, it appears as a property concerning the identity conditions for mental states. These are quite different (and independent) properties: possession of the first, but not of the latter, is an empirical matter, depending on the contingent psychological effects of a given stimulus.

Should we understand Gendler as claiming that alief is hyperopaque in the sense of H1, while imagination is not? That claim would be false. There is every reason to think that imagination is hyperopaque in the sense of H1; indeed I don't know of a single, conventionally recognized mental state that isn't hyperopaque in this sense.

Take the *Not poison* scenario. I grant that this scenario provides an instance of H1: even though the subject recognizes the synonymy of

---

61   While granting this for the sake of the argument, I observe that 'Not poisonous' and 'Safe to consume' are not really synonyms, and not even co-referential. The expression 'Not poison' picks out a class of substances which includes substances that are 'safe to consume' (e.g. water), as well as substances that, even if not poisonous, are not 'safe to consume' (e.g. water with pieces of glass inside).

'not poison' and 'safe to consume', these two expressions cause her to act in two different ways, because they activate in her mind two different representations. The question then is: what kind of representations? My answer, already given, is that they are instances of imaginings. I have suggested that in the context of Rozin's experiment the label 'Not poison' activates an imagining of poison, while the label 'Safe to consume' does not. Thus imagination is hyperopaque in the sense of H1.

But so is, by the way, belief. Suppose Rozin's subjects are told that the experiment has been hijacked by a mad scientist who puts real poison in the bottle labelled 'Not poison'. Seeing that label will cause them to believe that the bottle is poisoned, while seeing the label 'Safe to consume' won't. Context can always interfere with the effects an expression has on the mind. Gendler has not given any reason to think that hyperopacity of type H1 distinguishes alief from imagination, or from anything else.

So there is now no barrier to thinking of imagination as the mental state that best explains *Not Poison*. And since the *Not Poison* scenario was brought on by Gendler as a way of casting doubt on the possibility that imagination explains the *Poison* scenario, neutralizing her argument about *Not Poison* allows me to explain *Poison* in terms of imagination as well.

What about hyperopacity as defined in H2? I can grant Gendler's claim that imagination is not hyperopaque in this sense, while alief is.[62] After all, I have never argued that alief and imagination are identical. Their distinctness is established by definition: alieving, in Gendler's view, is a four-place relation between a subject and a threefold content; imagining is a two-place relation between a subject and a single content. My interest here was in showing that imagination can account for cases like *Not Poison*, and hyperopacity in the sense of H2 is irrelevant to that question. What is relevant is H1, because the state involved in *Not Poison* needs to be hyperopaque in the sense of H1. And H1, far from being an exclusive property of alief, is a characteristic property of imagination, as well as of all other representational states I know of.

To conclude, I must note that Gendler's argument for *alief* is not based just on superstitious actions. She considers various examples of problematic behaviours of rather different kinds that in her view cannot be explained by appeal to 'traditional' folk-psychological states. Elsewhere, in a paper with Greg Currie, I have considered all her cases more systematically and argued that none of them require us to acknowledge the existence of aliefs, at least

---

62   More precisely, I grant that, if alief existed, it would be hyperopaque in the sense of H2.

as those states are officially characterized by her (although the alternative explanations we suggested are not always in terms of imaginings).[63]

But my interest in the present discussion was more specific: I meant to reject Gendler's claim that alief is necessary to explain my cases of superstitious actions, since imagination cannot do the job. I have argued that she does not provide good arguments for this view. I hope to have persuaded you of this. Gendler apparently is persuaded:

> Currie and Ichino are – I suspect – correct in their claim that my hyperopacity argument rests on an ambiguity. Alief is – of course – hyperopaque in their sense H1. But they have convinced me that a good deal more work is required for me to show that this distinguishes alief from imagination – or, for that matter, from any other mental state. (Gendler 2012: 807-808)

Conclusion

In this chapter I have considered four possible explanations for what I called 'superstitious'/'magical' actions. I have shown that Humean explanations in terms of belief-desire pairs are problematic: in the best case, they are implausible (Sophisticated Humean explanation); in the worst case, they presuppose an undesirable revision of our notion of belief, which misses out its epistemic dimension (Standard Humean explanation).

---

63   In fact, we suggest that most of Gendler's cases are better explained by lower-level representational states: generally of a perceptual kind, and sometimes even lower (though for some cases we consider the possibility of belief explanations). Our point is that while a few of these cases do plausibly require us to acknowledge representations at levels other than the personal one, none require us to acknowledge the existence of aliefs – at least as they are officially characterized by Gendler. Here it is worth noting a new argument for the existence of aliefs, recently put forward by Miri Albahari (2013). Albahari argues that aliefs (or, at least, some states with an associative, tripartite structure R-A-B very similar to aliefs) actually exist, though they do not have the pervasive explanatory role that Gendler gives them. Insofar as Albahari's argument is not based (just) on the exam of 'Gendler cases', but appeals also to independent empirical evidence (from Antonio Damasio's research), it might escape Currie and mine's criticisms. Indeed, Currie and I just argue that none of Gendler cases require us to recognize the existence of alief; we do not argue that there is no evidence whatsoever for the existence aliefs. I am actually inclined to think that our argument against the need to postulate a weird tripartite entity like Gendler's alief (rather than three distinct, though causally, related entities) may well apply also to Albahari's discussion. However, Albahari's interesting and rich paper is surely worth further consideration.

I have argued that the best explanation for superstitious/magical actions is in terms of imaginings, and that there is no need to introduce new cognitive categories like that of alief.

Far from being marginal and isolated, actions like these are very pervasive in our lives. This, I have suggested, reveals that imagination's motivating power is the same of belief. A proper defence of this suggestion, though, requires a closer consideration of the conditions under which imagination's and belief's motivating power is manifested – which I am going to articulate in the next chapter.

5.

THE POWERS OF IMAGINATION

In the last chapter I have argued that there are a large number of cases – cases I gathered under the broad labels of 'superstitious' and 'magical' actions – where the cognitive states that motivate us to act jointly with our conations seem to be totally insensitive to evidence and inferentially isolated from our whole system of beliefs. I have argued that, since at least some degree of sensitivity to evidence and inferential integration is necessary for belief, those cognitive states cannot be beliefs, and are better described as imaginings. I ended with the tentative suggestion that these cases reveal that imagination and belief have the same motivating power. In this chapter I will better defend this suggestion, developing a line of argument put forward by J. David Velleman (2000). After a recap of my discussion so far and of its place in the current debate on propositional imagination (§1), I shall discuss Velleman's argument for the thesis that imaginings and beliefs motivate action in the same ways (§2), showing that this thesis does not have the absurd consequences that it is generally taken to have (§3). I shall then point out some important differences between Velleman's view and my own, notably having to do with the different roles that we take imagination to play in our representation of – and interactions with – the real world (§4). Finally, I shall draw some general conclusions about the view of imagination and belief that I have been defending in this book, indicating possible developments for future research (§5).

1. *Where are we?*

Let's start with a brief recap of the big picture and our place in it. As I noted in Chapter 1, the basic reason that we have for thinking that mental states like belief, desire, imagination (or indeed any other mental state of that sort, functionally defined) actually exist is that postulating their existence helps us to explain a great number of things. Hence, any account of such states that aims for some psychological plausibility will be guided by considerations of explanatory power. Are those states helpful to explain our actions, reactions, and conscious experiences? And, if so, what is the most explanatorily helpful way to characterize their functional structure and their contents?

Being notably concerned with propositional imagination, I have been targeting this question at the relationships between imagination and belief, focussing on (the so-called) Hume's Problem of how to distinguish one from the other: what is the most explanatorily helpful way to draw the distinction between these two states?

My natural starting point to address this problem have been cases of daydreaming, engagement with fiction, pretence games, and 'modal thinking'. These are indeed what we can call the 'standard imaginative explananda': the phenomena of our human lives that most obviously require us to postulate an imaginative capacity *somehow* distinct from belief in order to be properly understood.

According to the dominant view in the contemporary debate, the relevant distinction here lies at the *functional* level. The cognitive states underlying our engagement with daydreams, fiction, or pretence, may have precisely the same contents as our beliefs, but differ from them in two key functional respects: (1) with respect to the cognitive inputs in response to which they are formed (they are not formed in response to real-world evidence as belief are), and (2) with respect to the behavioural outputs that they are able to produce (they do not motivate us to act as beliefs do). Call this the 'Standard View of imagination'.

As we have seen, some controversies concerning the motivational difference between imagination and belief arise within the Standard View in relation to cases of pretence, where imaginings are associated with characteristic action outputs. Advocates of the traditional 'Humean Theory of Motivation' point out that 'associated with' here does not mean 'causally responsible for': belief is the only cognitive state that (jointly with desire) can cause and rationalize action, and it does so also in cases of pretence, where the role of imaginings is merely indirect (see e.g. Nichols and Stich 2000). By contrast, advocates of the 'Imagination-as-Motivation Theory' contend that a proper understanding of pretence requires us to recognize that imagination has some autonomous motivating power that can be exerted with no mediation of beliefs (see e.g. Currie and Ravenscroft 2002).

In Chapter 3 I defended a versiochn of this latter view, arguing that pretenders are typically motivated by pairs of belief-like and desire-like imaginings. I have, however, also granted that this in itself does not prove that imagination has *the same* motivating power as belief. Indeed, beliefs typically motivate in conjunction with *real* desires; not with imaginative ones. And, perhaps more importantly, beliefs motivate action across many different contexts. If imaginings lead to action only in conjunction with imaginative desires and in the context of pretence, this would suggest that their motivating power is relevantly different from that of belief – if anything, much more limited.

This is something on which almost everyone seems to agree: whether episodes of pretence require us to credit imagination with direct motivating power or not, they do not in themselves require us to credit it with precisely the same motivating power of belief. So, they can at most constitute a challenge to the Humean View that motivating power is an *exclusive* prerogative of belief. But they do not ultimately challenge the Standard View, according to which belief has a distinctive motivating power that sets it apart from imagination.[1]

---

1 Nor, by the way, is the standard view challenged by another imaginative explanandum that has become quite standard in the contemporary debate on propositional imagination: the phenomenon of *mindreading*. Some of the most influential accounts in that debate, such as Nichols & Stich (2000) and Currie & Ravenscroft (2002), have been based on the idea that the same imaginative mechanisms that underlie pretence, play a key role in explaining our capacity to understand our own and other people's mental states. What imagination's role in mindreading precisely is and how it relates to its role in pretence is controversial, and surely considerations on this have important implications for the different accounts' architectural commitments. But not so much for their commitments concerning imagination's motivating power, since everyone agrees that the role of imagination in mind-reading, whatever it is, is an *off-line role*, which does not amount to generating behavioural outputs, but only to allowing mental predictions about other people's (or our own) behaviour.

In fact, here I should mention two *candidate* 'non-standard imaginative explananda' which have been discussed as such in the recent philosophical and psychological literature, and which do arguably constitute a challenge for the Standard View of imagination: namely, the phenomena of *self-deception* and *delusion*. For both these phenomena there have been advocates of non-doxastic accounts, defending explanations in terms of imaginings (see Gendler 2007 for self-deception; Currie and Ravenscroft 2002: Chapter 8 for delusions; see also Egan 2009's account of delusions as 'bimaginings'). Perhaps delusions may not be a big worry for a Standard Theorist: even if it turned out that they are best explained as imaginings (something on which I have doubts), the Standard View may still hold for the adult non-clinical population. That is, the Standard Theorist may (perhaps) still argue that in properly developed well-functioning subjects, imaginings do not motivate as beliefs do. But the case of self-deception is much more threatening, given the pervasiveness of this phenomenon in cognitively 'normal' population. For recent reviews and discussions of doxastic and non-doxastic accounts of self-deception and delusion, see contributions in Nottlemann (2013) – notably by Matthews (Chapter 5) and Bayne and Hattiangadi (Chapter 6).

My departure from the Standard View is due to the fact that, while I obviously agree that the 'standard explananda' just outlined must be accounted for in terms of imaginings, I do not think that they are the only ones. The role of imagination in our lives is not limited to cases of daydream, fiction, pretence, and modal reasoning; it is actually much larger than that. In the last chapter I argued that imaginings play the relevant explanatory role in a number of other cases: 'non-standard imaginative explananda' which I gathered under the labels of 'superstitious' and 'magical' actions. Far from being marginal and circumscribed, these actions are pervasive in all sorts of everyday contexts. If I am right that they are explained in terms of imaginings, this has important consequences for our account of imagination, revealing its motivating power to be the same of belief – as I shall argue in what follows.

2. Velleman and I[2]

The only philosopher I know who holds a view of imagination that is non-standard in the sense I just described is J. David Velleman. One of the basic claims for which he argues in his 2000 paper "On The Aim of Belief" is that imaginings and beliefs cannot be distinguished on the basis of their motivating powers. As I repeatedly said, the view of imagination that I have been defending here owes a lot to Velleman' view. It is now time to make this debt more explicit – and, hopefully, do something to pay it off, defending Velleman from (at least some of) his critics.

This, note, does not mean that I am going to endorse Velleman's view of imagination in full. As I shall point out, there are important aspects of that view that leave me unpersuaded. Still, what matters to me here is Velleman's thesis that imagination and belief have the same motivating powers. I think that this thesis is supported by the account of superstitious and magical actions that I defended in Chapter 4, and my main aim in this chapter is to show how it is so.

2.1. Velleman's argument

Surprisingly (and, I shall argue, somewhat unfortunately), Velleman's argument for the *non-standard* view that imagination and belief have the

---

2   The main argument defended in this section and the next is also discussed in
      Ichino (2019).

same motivating powers starts from the consideration of a *very standard* imaginative explanandum: pretence – and gives it considerable weight. The example discussed more at length in Velleman's paper is that of a child pretending that he is an elephant. This is due to the fact that, as we have seen in Chapter 3, Velleman doesn't seem to recognize the existence of desire-like imaginings, and takes pretence to be typically motivated by imaginings in conjunction with real desires (real desires of a special kind: what he calls 'wishes'). So, in his view, pretence actions are clear cases where imaginings motivate *precisely as beliefs do.*

I have already expressed my perplexities on this point: while endorsing most of Velleman's critical considerations against Humean accounts of pretence, I criticized the alternative account he defends, and argued that real desires (of any sort) are unlikely to play the relevant explanatory role in most cases of pretence play (see above, Chapter 3: § 4.3).

Luckily, however, I don't think that Velleman's conclusions about the motivating power of imagination crucially depend on his account of pretence. Velleman also discusses many cases of *non-pretence* actions that seem to elude desire-belief explanations and to require explanations in terms of desire-*imagining* pairs. These are the sorts of actions we are already familiar with from Chapter 4. His examples include actions like *talking to yourself* (when you imagine being in conversation with someone else); *expressive behaviours* (like my case of the sport fan who loudly encourages her team while watching a TV match); or *psychoanalytic cases* of actions where symbolic objects are treated as if they were what they imaginatively (and sub-consciously) stand for (like young Goethe throwing crockery out of the window as a phantasy of casting out his baby brother[3]).

Admittedly, Velleman's discussion of these cases is a bit quick – especially if compared with his thorough discussion of pretence. His arguments for the view that these actions are imagination-driven rely more often on appeals to intuitions than on full-fledged reasons against the plausibility of belief-desire explanations. Later on I shall say something more on this – and more in general on how Velleman's prevalent focus on pretence is problematic in the economy of his argument. But this is not too much of a worry for me here, since the idea that in these (and indeed other, more or less similar) cases the agents' imaginings motivate them to act in conjunction with their real desires is something I have already extensively argued for in Chapter 4. What I am notably concerned with here, as I said, is the next step of Velleman's argument: his move from

---

3   So, at least, Freud's explanation (which Velleman endorses) goes.

the consideration of all these cases where imaginings motivate, to the conclusion that imaginings have the same motivating power of belief – the same dispositional connection (via desire) to action:

> I have now introduced several categories of examples that feature motivation by imagining. *These examples show that imagining that p and believing that p are alike in disposing the subject to do what would satisfy his conations if p were true, other things being equal.* Admittedly, the examples have also shown that other things are rarely equal between cases of imagining and believing, and hence that the actual manifestations or these states are often different. But these differences do not undermine my thesis. After all, belief itself (…) can be characterized only in terms of its disposition to produce behaviour under various conditions, such as the presence of a relevant conation and the requisite motor skills, and the absence of conflicting motives and inhibitions. *The examples suggest that imaginings can be characterized as having the same conditional disposition as belief; the only differences have to do with the satisfaction of the associated conditions.* (Velleman 2000: 271-272, emphasis mine)

This argument needs a bit of unpacking – and, as I shall say, some better development. §2.2 will be devoted to that.

2.2. *Velleman unpacked and defended*

At the risk of being a bit pedantic, let's distinguish clearly the two claims that are at stake here:

(i)   There are a large number of cases where an agent who imagines that p is motivated to act in the same ways in which she would act if, all else being equal, she believed that p.

(ii)   In any possible case, an agent who imagines that p is motivated to act in the same ways in which she would act if, all else being equal, she believed that p.

My cases of superstitious/magical actions, and Velleman's analogous examples just seen, prove claim (i) to be true (insofar as the account we defended for them is right). That is, they are all cases where an agent's imagining that p motivates her to act in ways that would promote the satisfaction of her desires if p were true – which is the way in which beliefs typically motivate. But, of course, (i) does not entail (ii). And (ii) is what ought to be true if imaginings really had *the same motivating power* of beliefs.

Velleman's critics blame him for switching too easily from (i) to (ii).[4] According to Neil Van Leeuwen, for instance, "Velleman mistakenly generalizes from cases in which imagining that p and believing that p *happen* to yield similar behaviour to the conclusion that this holds for all cases". A conclusion which Van Leeuwen – in this respect fully aligned with the Standard View of imagination – considers "indefensible in virtue of its absurd consequences" (Van Leeuwen 2009: 232). Indeed – so the standard argument goes – even granting (if only for the sake of argument) that there are cases where imaginings motivate in conjunction with our desires, as beliefs do, there still remain many more cases where imaginings do *not* motivate in such ways – daydreams and responses to fiction being the most *obvious* examples.[5]

However, I do not think Velleman is the one who jumps to conclusions here. Although his argument requires some alterations and better development, it still provides compelling reasons for the view that imaginings have the same motivating power as beliefs. Conversely, the sorts of standard criticisms we have just seen tend to switch too easily from the consideration of cases where imaginings do not motivate to the conclusion that imagination's motivating power differs from that of belief – overlooking the fact that there are plenty of cases where beliefs do not motivate, either.

To see this point more clearly, consider again my standard example of daydreaming, where I imagine that I am the Duchess of Sussex on the day of my wedding. We all agree that, in cases like this, my imaginings do not motivate me to act: I do not wear an elegant white dress, I do not look for my chauffeur in order to be taken to Westminster Abbey, I do not pack my bags for the honeymoon... Indeed, I do not do anything but sit here, staring into space. However, it is one thing to agree on this; it is quite another thing to conclude that my imagining in this case does not motivate me to act *as I would if I believed what I imagine to be true*. This conclusion is not as obvious as it may *prima facie* seem to be.

---

4   More precisely, those critics who grant some version of (i) to be true: i.e. those critics who grant that in at least some of the cases that Velleman considers imaginings motivate as beliefs do. I-take Currie-and-Ravenscroft (2002) and Van Leeuwen (2009) to be critics of this sort.

5   As we have seen in Chapter-3 (§2), indeed, the idea that "when we consume fiction, daydream or fantasize, we do not typically produce actions that would be produced if we believed what we are imagining" is widely accepted as "a central *fact* about propositional imagination" (Nichols-2006: 6-7).

The fact is that it is not so obvious how I would act if I believed that I was the Duchess of Sussex on my wedding day. Actually, I think that if I really believed that, then I would probably try to escape before it was too late. The idea of marrying Prince Harry does not *really* sound appealing at all to me! And even granting that I was happy with this wedding... Would I wear a white dress? I probably would, if I wanted to conform to traditional practices and I believed that brides traditionally dress in white. Though I wouldn't if, instead, I wanted to surprise everyone with a bohemian style, or if I believed that brides traditionally dress in pink. Would I look for my chauffeur to be taken to Westminster Abbey? I probably would, if I believed that the ceremony will take place there. Though I wouldn't if, instead, I believed it to take place in a London registry office. And what if I got up in the morning with one of my awful migraines? In such a case, I may well have to remain in the darkness of my room for a while, hoping that it passes and it doesn't completely ruin my day as only migraines can do.

What these hypothetical scenarios reveal is a basic fact about the motivating power of beliefs, which I have already observed in previous chapters: whether beliefs motivate us to act and what sort of actions they motivate depends on a number of factors concerning our internal and external environment – factors which include, but are not exhausted by, the presence of relevant desires. In Chapter 3 I characterized belief's connection to action as a *dispositional* connection which is expected to manifest itself in the presence of the relevant desires, *if a number of other conditions are also satisfied* – while failures to satisfy such conditions can excuse lacks of behavioural manifestations without thereby compromising the holding of the disposition itself.

This is important to keep in mind when we compare belief's and imagination's motivating powers. It is true that the existence of cases where imaginings motivate in ways that would promote the satisfaction of our desires is not enough to conclude that imagination's motivating power is the same as belief's. But in order to support this conclusion we do not need to show that imaginings *always* motivate us to act in ways that would promote the satisfaction of our desires. We need to show that they motivate us to act in such ways *under the same conditions under which beliefs do so.*

This is indeed, I take it, what Velleman has in mind when he says that his examples "suggest that imaginings can be characterized as having the same conditional disposition as belief; the only differences have to do with the satisfaction of the associated conditions". Now, I have granted to his critics that he is a bit too quick in drawing this conclusion. Most of his discussion focuses on the cases where imaginings' motivating power is actually manifested, though to prove that their conditional disposition to action is precisely the same as belief he should have paid attention also to cases of lack of manifestation. More precisely, he should have shown that whenever an imagining that p does *not* motivate actions that would promote the satisfaction of the agent's desires, this lack of behavioural manifestation is excused by some condition C which (all else being equal) would also excuse the lack of behavioural manifestation of a belief that p.

While granting that Velleman doesn't, strictly speaking, prove this, however, I think that this is true – and my aim here is to develop Velleman's argument in such a way as to prove it. Of course, I can't possibly consider *every* possible case where imaginings do not motivate. But I will identify some basic conditions that in my view excuse all the cases of non-motivating imaginings pointed out by Velleman's opponents (i.e., notably, cases of daydreams and responses to fiction), as well as all other cases of non-motivating imaginings I can think of. Hence, I will conclude by shifting the onus of proof onto our opponents.

3. *Excusing conditions*

There are two sorts of factors that are most typically responsible for the lack of behavioural manifestation of our imaginings in paradigmatic cases of daydreams and fiction consumption: (1) factors concerning the meta-cognitions that typically accompany our imaginings in such cases: the beliefs and desires that, in such cases, we typically have *about* our imaginings; and, (2) factors concerning the kinds of propositional contents that our imaginings typically have in such cases, and the inferential networks into which they are integrated. I shall discuss these two sorts of factors in turn (in §§3.1, 3.2), and I shall argue that, all else being equal, these very same factors would also excuse the lack of behavioural manifestation of corresponding beliefs – i.e. of beliefs with the same contents.[6]

3.1. *Meta-cognitive factors: the 'Meta-cognition Condition'*

Why, when I daydream that I am the Duchess of Sussex on the day of my wedding, do I not act upon this imagining? Plausibly, that is because I

---

6   For the sake of simplicity, here I will focus on cases of daydream. I think it won't be hard for the reader to see how my arguments apply equally well to cases of fiction consumption. I will briefly show how it is so in footnote 13 below.

believe that it is *just* a daydream, and I do not see any point in acting upon it. I am sat at my desk in the office, it is already 7pm, and what I really want to do now is to stop daydreaming and procrastinating, in order to finish writing this section soon.

A situation like this is quite paradigmatic. Typically, when we have a daydream with content p, we are aware that p is something that we *merely* imagine and do not believe to be true; and – partly because of this – we desire to inhibit our motivation to act upon p (since we believe that the best chances to satisfy our desires rest on our representing reality accurately, and we want our actions to be realistically purposive). Simplifying a bit, let's then say that a standard case of daydreaming is one where the agent *imagines* that p, and:

(a) *Believes* (occurrently) that she does not really believe, but just imagines that p;

(b) *Desires* (occurrently) not to act upon her imagining that p.

These meta-beliefs and meta-desires concerning the agent's imagining are both factors that prevent the imagining itself from motivating.[7]

Arguably, either of these two meta-cognitive factors would also (all else being equal) prevent a *belief* that p from motivating. Now, admittedly, if we stick to the wedding case, the scenario we get if we keep everything the same as the daydream scenario, *apart from the fact that I believe, and not imagine, that I am the Duchess of Sussex*, is somewhat improbable. This would be a scenario where I believe that I am the Duchess of Sussex, though I have also for some reason come to believe that I don't believe but just imagine that, so I don't want to act upon this imagining, and I'm rather sat here in my office, wanting to finish my book... Yes: definitely improbable. Indeed, at least in cases of 'exotic' daydreams like this, the circumstances in which we imagine are not likely to be equal to the circumstances in which we would find ourselves if we believed what we imagine to be true.

But improbable does not mean impossible. What matters to my argument here is that you grant the following counterfactual claim: if that scenario occurred, the behavioural consequences of my belief that I am the Duchess of Sussex would not be different from the behavioural consequences of the corresponding daydream (i.e.: if that scenario occurred, I would fail to act upon my belief as I do fail to act upon my imagining in the daydream scenario). This seems very plausible. I think we can all agree that, all else being equal, if one believes that p but for some reason comes to believe that

---

7   In the scenario just sketched they do that jointly, but note that even just one of them taken alone may be enough.

she does not really believe that p, and/or comes to desire not to act upon p, then she won't act upon her belief that p.

As an example of the first condition – i.e. of a case where one believes that p, comes to believe that she does not believe that p, and hence fails to act upon p – think of a subject who believes that her partner is cheating on her, but somehow brings herself to believe that she doesn't *really* believe that (e.g. she tells herself that she is just paranoid, that she is excessively jealous, etc…). This subject will plausibly fail to act upon her first-order belief (the belief that HE IS CHEATING) in various ways. If you ask her about her romantic life, for instance, she may well sincerely tell you that it is coming up roses.[8]

Typical examples of the second condition – i.e. of cases where a lack of behavioural manifestation of a belief that p is 'excused' by the desire not to act upon p – are cases of pretence. The child who pretends that she is a cat and responds to your questions only by meowing, obviously does still believe that she is a child and that she can talk properly. But, for the duration of the game, she desires not to act upon these beliefs (and to act upon her imaginings, instead).

Eventually, then, it seems that we can formulate the following 'excusing condition' that holds both for belief's and imagination's lack of behavioural manifestation. *The meta-cognition condition:* both a belief that p and an imagining that p motivate the agent to act in ways that would promote the satisfaction of her desires if p were true, unless the agent: (1) believes that she doesn't really believe that p, or (2) desires not to act upon her representation of p. If either (1) or (2) are the case, this may excuse a lack of behavioural manifestation of the belief/imagining in question (without

---

8   This looks like a classic case of self-deception, which is a complex and controversial phenomenon. Without committing myself to any particular account of self-deception, I think that the description I sketched for the 'betrayed-partner' behaviour has psychological plausibility – i.e., that it is a plausible description of (some aspects of) what goes on in cases of this sort. If this doesn't persuade you, however, I think you can find your own example of a mistaken meta-belief that excuses a lack of behavioural manifestation of the related first-order belief (arguably, another example is provided by the psychological experiment I discussed in Chapter 2, § 4.5.1). And even if you cannot find any such examples, no problem – just skip to the next paragraph (and then to the next section). I am about discuss other excusing conditions for the lack of behavioural manifestation of paradigmatic imaginings. If you will agree with me that such conditions would also, all else being equal, excuse the lack of behavioural manifestation of beliefs with the same contents, this should be enough for me to establish my conclusion.

thereby compromising the holding of its behavioural disposition).[9] Since (1) and (2) are typically the case when we daydream, we can say that the lack of behavioural manifestation of our imaginings in such cases does not, in itself, reveal the difference between imagination's and belief's motivating powers that Velleman's opponents (and indeed all the standard imagination theorists) typically point out.

As I said, I think that there are also other factors that play a relevant role in preventing our imaginings (in cases of daydream, as well as in other cases) from motivating us: factors that do not (directly) concern the meta-cognitions we have about such imaginings, but have more to do with the propositional contents that such imaginings typically have, and the inferential network of other imaginings and representations into which they are integrated. I turn to these in the next section.

3.2. Contents and inferential network: the 'Know-how-to-do-that Condition'

A further reason why, when I daydream that I am the Duchess of Sussex on my wedding day, I do not act in ways that would promote the satisfaction of my desires, seems to be this: nothing in the content of my imagining actually tells me what I should do in order to act in such ways. Even if wanted to do that, I wouldn't know where to start.

A comparison with paradigmatic cases of belief-desire motivation will make this point clear. As we have seen, beliefs are (and ought to be) inferentially integrated with each other into a holistically coherent system, in a way in which imaginings are not. And the whole pattern of beliefs to which a belief that p belongs is crucial in determining what sort of actions, if any, p will motivate in conjunction with the relevant desires. In particular, in Chapter 3 we noted the key role of one specific type of beliefs that must be present in the system in order to allow the other beliefs to manifest their motivating potential: beliefs about what sort of actions we should perform in order to satisfy our desires – i.e. beliefs of the form "I

---

9   Note that in making this point I am not claiming that the meta-belief that I AM BELIEVING THAT P is necessary for my belief that p to have motivating force. This would be absurd, both developmentally (think of children who lack capacities for meta-cognition, but obviously act upon their beliefs) and conceptually (it would generate an infinite regress of meta-meta-meta-beliefs required to act). What I am suggesting is something different, and much more modest. Normally a belief that p has motivating power in itself, but we excuse lacks of manifestation of this power in case one has the mistaken meta-belief that she doesn't believe p.

can obtain ϕ if I perform action A" (where ϕ is something I desire). If the belief that TODAY IS MY WEDDING motivates any action at all, this is (also) because I have a number of wedding-related desires – e.g. the desire to dress properly, to be on time for the ceremony, etc. – *and* a number of *beliefs* about how to satisfy them – e.g. the belief that I can wear my white dress if I take it from the wardrobe, that I can be on time if I book a cab for 11am, etc. Without beliefs of this form, my belief that today is my wedding would fail to motivate me, even in the presence of relevant desires.

The point is that imaginings of this form are typically absent in paradigmatic cases of daydreaming. Daydreams are often little more than fleeting images: for a moment I imagine that I am the Duchess of Sussex, walking down the aisle – and that's all.[10] This propositional content is quite self-standing. I may, of course, elaborate on this, adding a number of other propositions. But the propositions I add are not typically the ones that would be needed to practically implement desire-satisfaction. This is, in a sense, a privilege of daydreaming: we can wear wonderful dresses without having to think about having to try them on beforehand, and enjoy wonderful parties without having to think about how to get there on time. And the fact that our patterns of imaginings when we daydream do not typically include imaginings whose contents specifically indicate how to satisfy our desires is then another reason why daydreams do not typically move us to act.

So we seem to have found another excusing condition that holds both for belief's and imagination's lack of behavioural manifestation. Call it the 'know-how-to-do-that condition': both a belief that p and an imagining that p motivate the agent to act in ways that would promote the satisfaction of her desires if: *either* p is a proposition of the form "I can obtain ϕ if I perform action A" (where ϕ is the content of one of the agent's relevant desires), *or* p is inferentially integrated into a network of believed/ imagined propositions which includes also propositions of that form.[11] If

---

10   With 'images' here I do not refer to visual imageries, but to scenarios that can be articulated in a propositional form. Although of course various kinds of imageries (visual, but also auditory, motor, olfactory etc.) can – and, arguably, typically do – accompany and 'enrich' the propositional contents of our daydreams. The ways in which such imageries are related to propositional imaginings is a fascinating topic, which however I should leave for another occasion (for classic discussions, see Williams 1973: Chapter 3; Peacocke 1985).

11   Importantly, "if" here should not be intended in the sense of a material conditional: the satisfaction of the 'know-how-to-do-that condition' is not in itself sufficient to guarantee behavioural manifestation, since – as we have seen - other excusing conditions may block it.

this 'know-how-to-do-that condition' is not satisfied, this can excuse a lack of behavioural manifestation of the belief/imagining in question, without thereby compromising the holding of its behavioural disposition.

This condition highlights the crucial role that the larger network of beliefs/imaginings to which a given belief or imagining belongs has in determining its behavioural manifestations. In particular, it highlights the fact that whether or not an imagining or a belief motivate, and what sorts of actions they motivate, crucially depends on the consequences that we (do or do not) draw from them.

This is important not only to understand why imaginings in cases of daydream *do not* motivate any action at all (while we would expect beliefs with the same contents, against the same background of desires, to motivate); but also to understand why in cases where imaginings *do* motivate, the ways in which they motivate look somehow *sui generis* (i.e. different from the ways in which we would expect beliefs with the same contents, against the same background of desires, to motivate).

Take, for example, some of the cases of motivating imaginings discussed in Chapter 4: superstitious imaginings. My superstitious grandma, who avoids travelling on Friday the 13th like the plague, does not warn me against travelling on that day; even though, I presume, she desires for me to be safe as she desires to be safe herself. If she really believed that travelling on Friday the 13th is dangerous, then we would expect her to warn me, too, against travelling. The reason why her superstitious imagining does not motivate her to do that, arguably, is that she does not draw from it the same consequences that she would draw from a belief with the same content.

Believing that TRAVELLING ON FRIDAY THE 13TH IS OBJECTIVELY DANGEROUS, she would also come to believe a number of propositions that obviously follow from the conjunction of this belief and the various other beliefs that she has about dangers, warnings, moral duties, etc... So, she would plausibly come to believe *not only* that travelling on Friday the 13th is dangerous *for her* (hence that *she* should avoid travelling that day), but also that travelling on Friday the 13th is dangerous *for me* (hence that *I* should avoid travelling that day as well, and that if I am not aware of this, then she should warn me). These are indeed obvious consequences that follow from the proposition that TRAVELLING ON FRIDAY 13TH IS DANGEROUS, and believing that proposition would normally commit an agent to believing such consequences.

Imagining that TRAVELLING ON FRIDAY 13TH IS DANGEROUS, on the other hand, does not commit my grandma to imagine all the obvious consequences of this proposition. As we have seen in Chapter 2, when we imagine a proposition we are much more free to *decide* what consequences to draw from it, and what consequences to ignore, instead.

The fact that my grandma's superstition is an imagining and not a belief, then, explains why she only draws from it the obvious consequences concerning her own danger, and does not draw from it the *equally obvious* consequences concerning my own danger. And this, in turn, explains why the *belief* that travelling on Friday 13th is dangerous would motivate my grandma both to avoid travelling herself *and* to warn me against doing that; while the *imagining* that travelling on Friday 13th is dangerous does *only* motivate her not to travel herself, but not to warn me against travelling.[12]

As it turns out, the fact that such an imagining and belief (having same contents, and operating on the same backgrounds of desires) motivate different actions is not due to their having intrinsically different motivating powers. It is rather due to the different inferential networks into which they are integrated. Once again, the critical difference between imagination and belief can be seen in their respective sensitivity to evidence (or vice versa to the will) and inferential integration (or lack thereof), rather than in their respective dispositional connections to action.

Cases like this latter one I discussed, anyway, are not typically considered by Velleman's (and my) opponents as counterexamples to the claim that imagination and belief have the same motivating power – for the simple reason that our opponents do not typically even consider superstitious actions to be imagination-driven. The standard counterexamples to the sameness of imagination and belief's motivating powers, as we have seen, are paradigmatic cases of daydream (and fiction consumption). Let's then return to them.

3.3. *My challenge*

I have identified two basic factors that seem to be responsible for the fact that in paradigmatic cases of daydreaming an imagining that p will typically fail to motivate actions that would promote the satisfaction of the agent's desires if p were true. First, the presence of 'inhibiting meta-cognitions': when I imagine that p in the context of a daydream I do also typically (occurrently) believe that I do not really believe, but just imagine that p, and I (occurrently) desire not to act upon my imagining. Second, the absence of imaginings about the sorts of actions I should perform in order to satisfy the relevant desires: daydreams do not typically include many

---

12   But don't worry: she will keep her fingers crossed for me whilst I travel!

propositions of the form "I can obtain ϕ if I perform action A". As we have seen, even just one of these two factors would be enough to also prevent a *belief* that p from motivating in the relevant ways (all else being equal).

What I argue is that these same factors are also responsible for the lack of behavioural manifestation of other paradigmatic cases of imaginings – such as imaginings in response to fiction – as well as of all other cases of imaginings I can think of.[13] I can, of course, think of cases where the lack of behavioural manifestation of imaginings is determined by some different factors (e.g. physical impairment). But these factors are always factors that, all else being equal, would also excuse lack of behavioural manifestation of corresponding beliefs. What I cannot think of, indeed, is a case in which an imagining that p fails to motivate and this lack of manifestation is *not* excused by the presence of a factor that would also excuse the lack of behavioural manifestation of a belief that p.

Can you think of a case like that? Here is my challenge to Velleman's and my opponents: find a case where an imagining does not motivate while, *all else being equal,* a belief with the same content would. I insist that no such case exists. As long as no one comes up with a counterexample, I can conclude that imagination and belief dispose us to act in the same ways, and do that under the same conditions; they may contingently differ with respect to the satisfaction of such conditions, but they do not differ in motivating power.

4. *Velleman and I – and the legacy of the Standard View*

"OK" – one may say at this point – "I can't find the counterexample you ask for, hence I must concede that imaginings dispose us to act in the same ways and under the same conditions as beliefs. However, I find plenty of cases where imaginings fail to satisfy these conditions, while beliefs with

---

13 I won't discuss such other cases in detail here, since I would basically just repeat the strategy employed for daydreaming cases. I think it is not hard to see how my arguments for daydreams apply, for example, to fiction. So, to come back to an example introduced in Chapter 2, a competent spectator of *Psycho* (who imagines that a young woman has been murdered in the shower) typically: (1) believes that she does not really believe, but just imagines, that a murder has taken place; (2) desires not to act upon this imagining; and (3) does not form imaginings about how to act in order to satisfy her story-related desires (e.g. imaginings like: in order to prevent that killer from killing other people, I should call the police). This is why she is not moved to inform the police that a murder has taken place.

the same contents meet them. So, the fact remains that beliefs play a much larger and important motivating role in our lives than imaginings do." Velleman grants this. Indeed, this is basically his position: imaginings have the same motivating *power* of beliefs, but they are much less likely to cause *actual* behaviour (Velleman 2000: 272). In his view, this is due notably due to the presence of (what I called) 'inhibiting meta-desires'. He sketches a developmental picture according to which imagination's motivating power is largely manifested during childhood, where pretence has a pervasive role in our lives; and then is progressively suppressed on the way to adulthood, when we acquire an "inhibition against the motivational force of unrealistic attitudes... [which] prevents us from manifesting the motivational force of wishes and imaginings, so that *we tend to act only on desires and beliefs*" (Velleman 2000: 263).

In this respect, Velleman seems still quite influenced by the 'Standard View' of imagination. Although, as we have seen, he recognizes that imagination motivates also a number of non-pretence actions (such as talking to oneself, or symbolic actions...), he takes these actions to be overall quite marginal and circumscribed in adult life. The basic behavioural manifestation of our imaginings remains as pretence, which has a rather limited space in properly developed cognitive systems.

As I said before, I take Velleman's focus on pretence to be misplaced. If anything, I take it to be somewhat in tension with his project to defend the *non-standard* view that imagination's motivating power is the same as belief's. I think this is indeed the primary reason why most critics reject Velleman's view. Many, myself included, do not even grant that pretence is a case where imagination motivates in conjunction with real desires as belief does. And even granting that, I can agree with Velleman's critics that *if imagination's motivating power were manifested only, or primarily, in pretence,* then the claim that this power is the same as belief's would not sound very plausible. Of course, there is nothing intrinsically objectionable in the view that the same disposition is manifested in systematically different ways. But on what grounds say this? Rather than postulating a power that is the same as belief's, but systematically inhibited, why not simply recognize a more limited power?

Van Leeuwen (2011), for example, argues that we should describe imagination's motivating power in terms of a disposition to act in ways that would promote the satisfaction of our desires were the imagined contents true, which is manifested *if the agent believes that she is in the context of pretence play (and wants to play)* (Van Leeuwen 2011: 227-229). Of course, Velleman here may reply that a characterization like this of imagination's motivating power does not allow for the other non-pretence manifestations of such power that he pointed out (e.g. expressive/symbolic behaviours) – which, even though circumscribed, must somehow be accounted for. But my point is that the reason why neither this nor any other attempts to differentiate imagination and belief's dispositional profiles seem to work is that the behavioural manifestations of our imaginings are not really that circumscribed: far from being limited to specific contexts (such as 'pretence' or 'symbolic ritual'), they are extremely pervasive and intertwined with beliefs' behavioural manifestations in most contexts of everyday life.

This is indeed what I have argued in Chapter 4, showing how our thinking is permeated by 'magical' elements that motivate actions in all sorts of circumstances (see again all the examples in Chapter 4: § 1). Whether we are driving our car, watching a TV match, climbing a mountain, or sitting for an important exam, our desires motivate us in conjunction with *both* beliefs *and* imaginings, producing behaviours that display at the same time realistic and 'magical' components. In my view, it is this pervasiveness of imagination's *actual* behavioural manifestations that constitutes the strongest reason in favour of the non-standard view that imagination's motivating *potential* is on a par with that of belief. So, it is this pervasiveness that Velleman would need to stress in order to defend his non-standard view from the attacks of his critics.

Velleman's problem, in the end, turns out to be this: that he tries to defend a non-standard characterization of imagination's functional profile without resolutely abandoning an overall quite standard view of the role that imagination actually plays in our cognitive life. That is, he tries to defend a non-standard characterization of imagination's functional profile without really abandoning the idea that imagination's actual explanatory role is basically limited to what I have called the 'standard imaginative explananda', among which pretence is the only one with a behavioural component.

What I have tried to show here, on the other hand, is that a non-standard characterization of imagination's functional profile can be successfully defended if we recognize – as we should – that the actual motivating role of imagination goes far beyond standard cases of children's pretence, and is manifested in a number of ways across the whole span of our life. It is not true that when we grow up imagination's motivating power is inhibited and its role is confined to daydream and fiction's consumption. In fully developed and well-functioning cognitive systems, imagination keeps competing with belief to influence the representation of the world and the interactions with it.

Conclusion (and a look ahead)

This book has been mainly concerned with the (so-called) Hume's problem of how to distinguish imagination from belief. On the basis of what I have argued in this chapter, I am finally in the position to clearly articulate my suggested solution for this problem. This will give me the opportunity to wrap up the account of imagination emerged in the discussion so far, and to draw some preliminary conclusions.

Distinguishing imagination from belief has not proven easy. On the account I have been defending, imagination and belief are alike in important respects. They have the same sorts of contents: namely, propositions. And their functional roles are much more similar than they may *prima facie* seem (and are generally taken) to be. Notably, such roles are the same with respect to behavioural, emotional and, to some extent at least, also cognitive *outputs*. The critical difference between imaginings and beliefs has to do with the cognitive *inputs* responsible for their formation, and – somewhat relatedly – with the ways in which they are (or are not) inferentially integrated with each other into a holistically coherent system.

Let's briefly review these various aspects of the functional roles of imagination and belief as I characterized them in my discussion.

Behavioural outputs. All else being equal, both imagining that p and believing that p dispose us to *act* in ways that would promote the satisfaction of our desires if p were true (as I argued in the present Chapter, building on the evidence from Chapter 4).

Emotional outputs. All else being equal, both imagining that p and believing that p dispose us to undergo *affective/emotional experiences* that would be appropriate if p were true – experiences which include a peculiar feeling of conviction about p (as I argued in Chapter 2[14]).

---

14   Here we can finally settle the question concerning the emotions vs. quasi-emotions debate, which I left open in Chapter 2: §3.1. As we saw there, philosophers like Walton have questioned whether the sorts of experiences produced by our imagining that p may really be the same – genuinely emotional – sorts of experiences produced by a belief that p, on the grounds of the idea that imagination-driven emotional states lack the motivating force of belief-driven emotional states. In considering this question, however, I also noted that strictly speaking the motivating force of emotional states piggybacks on the motivating force of the cognitive and conative states by which they are produced. Hence, since – as I argued – imaginings and beliefs have the same motivating force, we are entitled to say the same of the emotional outputs of imaginings and beliefs. Therefore, insofar as a difference in motivating force is the reason why advocates of 'quasi-emotions' argue that imagination-driven emotions are not, in fact, real emotions,

Cognitive outputs. All else being equal, both when we imagine that p and when we believe that p we are somehow disposed to draw theoretical inferences from p, thereby coming to imagine/believe various of p's consequences (as I argued, again, in Chapter 2).

This latter similarity concerning imagination's and belief's cognitive outputs, however, breaks down fairly soon. Although it is true that both beliefs and imaginings can be premises in our theoretical reasoning, the ways in which we draw inferences from a given proposition p are *not* the same irrespective of whether p is believed or imagined. Most notably, we seem to be (to some extents at least) free to decide what new imaginings we form from a given imagining that p, in ways in which we are not with a belief that p.

This leads us, finally, to the key functional difference between imaginings and beliefs, which (as we have seen in Chapter 3) has to do ultimately with the cognitive inputs in response to which they are formed and maintained – and with some related normative constraints.

Cognitive inputs (and inferential integration). Beliefs are formed and maintained in response to real-world evidence in ways in which imaginings are not. The formation of imaginings can be determined by our will, desires, intentions or, basically, by any sorts of evidence-insensitive factors. Among the kinds of evidence to which beliefs, but not imaginings, systematically respond, there is also what I called the 'inferential evidence' constituted by the whole system of the subject's pre-existing beliefs. This explains why beliefs are inferentially integrated with each other into a holistically coherent system, in a way in which imaginings are not. These differences at the level of cognitive inputs, as we have seen in Chapter 4, have also significant implications for the sorts of *normative constraints* that govern imaginings and beliefs, respectively. Beliefs are not only as a matter of fact sensitive to evidence to some degree; they are also governed by epistemic norms according to which they ought to be so sensitive – norms that do not apply to imaginings.[15]

---

we can reject their argument, and conclude that imagination-driven emotional experiences count as genuinely emotional.

15   Here it should be emphasized that, although the difference in cognitive inputs is the *only* critical one, it is a really *big* one. Belief's sensitivity to evidence is what makes it (more or less) reliably connected with reality: arguably something crucial for our survival in this world. And, as some authors have pointed out, this connection between beliefs and reality seems also to be what makes it possible for mental states in general, including imaginings, to have (wide) *content* (the suggestion here being, roughly, that beliefs can be *about* the world insofar as they are caused by real-world stimuli; while the other propositional attitudes 'inherit'

This is, briefly, the account of imagination and belief's functional architecture that I have been defending in this book. It suggests that to solve Hume's problem we should look at how imaginings and beliefs are formed – since, once they are formed, their powers upon our actions and reactions are basically the same.

Where does this account fall with respect to the typologies of mental states accounts that I discussed in Chapter 1? Does it presuppose a substantial revision of our folk-psychological notions of imagination and belief?

One may think that it obviously does. After all, this account departs quite a bit from the folk-psychological picture of imagination and belief that emerged in Chapter 3 from the analysis of our common uses of these terms.

On that folksy picture – which seems to be well captured by what I called the 'Standard View' of imagination – belief represents reality accurately, guiding our practical interactions with it; while imagination is reality insensitive and motivationally inert (or anyway motivationally very weak), and allows us to disengage from reality, escaping into fictional/daydreamed/hypothetical worlds. These imaginative escapes need not necessarily be just 'ends in themselves'; they may well be useful tools to get a better representation of reality (as when we imagine a possible world with a planet in which the liquid that people call 'water' is not H2O in order to clarify the essence natural kinds like water in our real world).[16] But what characterizes them is that imaginings *as such* remain perfectly isolated from our view of the world; they do not feature in our appraisal it, nor do they compete with belief to influence our practical interactions with it. If imaginings have any motivating power at all, it seems to be limited to children's pretence.

---

their contents from beliefs; on this see e.g. Currie and Ravenscroft 2002: 18-19; Van Leeuwen 2014: 704).

It is also worth noting that that the functional differences here at stake are actually two. First, a difference having to do with the inputs responsible for the formation of imaginings and beliefs. Second, a difference having to do with the relations that imaginings and beliefs have to each other. As it turns out, these differences are strictly related, and in this book I have often treated them together, as two aspects of one and the same thing – i.e. belief's sensitivity to evidence.

16 Note that those two possible functions of our imaginative escapes from reality – i.e. pure disengagement vs. epistemic tool for the formation of true/justified beliefs – are not in tension or alternative to each other. For example, our imaginative engagement with fictions is typically something that we undertake both for the sake of fun *and* with the hope of gaining important insights into the real world (as argued in Ichino and Currie (2017).

My account, on the other hand, credits imagination with much stronger motivating, cognitive and emotional powers; and with a much larger role in our lives. Imagination does not merely allow us to escape from reality into fictional worlds, but plays a key, direct role in our representation of – and practical engagement with – the real world itself. And indeed, many actions and reactions that folks commonly call 'beliefs' – such as superstitious (and, as we shall see in the next chapter, also religious) 'beliefs' – on my view turn out to be better understood in terms of imaginings.

In fact, I would like to add a word of caution here: my departure from folk-psychological intuitions may be less dramatic than it *prima facie* seems to be. For one thing, as I noted in Chapter 1, our common linguistic uses can be misleading in various ways. The fact that we use the general 'belief' in a broad way does not necessarily indicate that we do not make any distinctions among the various states that we gather under it. On the contrary, in Chapter 4 we have seen that at least some of us seem to draw an intuitive distinction between – e.g. – superstitious 'beliefs' and natural, scientific ones – treating them rather differently. A distinction which, by the way, on closer inspection may *also* emerge in our language: although admittedly sometimes we talk indistinguishably of 'scientific' and 'superstitious' *beliefs,* in other cases we do instead contrast 'beliefs' with 'mere superstitions'.[17]

The fact that we do not call such superstitious states 'superstitious imaginings' may simply be due to the fact that we tend to identify imagination with only *some* of its standard exercises – notably those having to do with playful or childish activities. Yet, we do somehow recognize that the superstitious states in question are like belief with respect to action guidance, although differently from belief they respond to the will, or to other 'hot' factors, rather than to real-world evidence. These considerations suggest that, after all, there may be room in our folk psychology for a mental state like the one that here I have called 'imagination'.

I don't want to place great weight on this point, though.[18] As I said in Chapter 1, whether there is anything in our folk-psychological picture of the mind that corresponds to what I have called imagination, and whether it actually deserves to be called like that, is a question that I will eventually leave up to the reader. I do think that the answer to this question is by and large positive: my account is revisionary, but just mildly so. However, if

---

17   In relation to this, see also next chapter's discussion of religious (vs. ordinary) uses of 'belief'.

18   "Squabbling about intuitions strikes me as vulgar..." (Fodor 1987: 10).

you are not comfortable with my use of 'imagination', you are welcome to provide your own label. What matters to me is that you grant the existence of a mental state which has the functional role I ascribed to imagination: that is, that you grant the existence of a cognitive state which is not formed in response to evidence, but can nonetheless drive actions (and reactions) in much the same ways in which belief does – and does so in a large range of circumstances.[19]

To conclude, let me note that imagination as I characterized it is a rather broad category. In this sense, too, it is not dissimilar from belief. As there are different sorts of evidential inputs in response to which beliefs can be formed (e.g. perceptual, testimonial, introspective inputs), corresponding to different sorts of beliefs, so too there are different sorts of non-evidential inputs in response to which imaginings can be formed, which correspond to different sorts of imaginings. In this book I have said little on this – and on the formation of imaginings more generally. But this is a fascinating (as well as intricate) issue – which arguably has important implications also for our understanding of imagination's normative dimensions and proper functions.

In the case of belief, I argued that the epistemic norms which apply to it depend on its having an epistemic function: i.e. on its being the product of mechanisms which have the function to represent reality accurately. What are the proper functions of the mechanisms which produce imaginative representations? Here I have been working mostly with the claim that imaginings *are not – nor ought to be –* formed in response to real-world evidence as beliefs are and ought to be. But how *are* imaginings formed, then? And are there any norms in accordance to which they *ought to be* formed?

---

19   Why does this matter? Why is it important to get clearer on the functional architecture of the mind? Why should we care whether a given cognition qualifies as a belief or imagining? A clear understanding of a given cognition's causal outputs and inputs is not only worthwhile in its own right; it is the basis for a proper assessment of its pragmatic and epistemic benefits/costs, on the one hand, and for the identification of effective ways to interact with it, on the other hand. And this, in turn, leads to a number of important implications. A consequence of my non-doxastic account of superstitious (an – as we shall see – religious) cognitions, for instance, is that we may enjoy their pragmatic benefits without worrying about their compromising agents' accurate representation of reality. Another is that to challenge such cognitions we won't appeal (only) to reasons. These considerations can inform psychological therapies as well as public policies (and, conversely, the success or failure of different interventions may tell us something about the mental mechanisms in play in different cases).

These questions open up an exciting research program, concerned with developing a more fine-grained taxonomy of different sorts of imaginings, of their proper functions (intended both causally and teleologically) and their related normative dimensions. Thus, for example we could have *aesthetic imaginings*, formed in response to fictional works of arts, which have fun and recreation as their most proper functions and 'responsiveness to what the author puts forward as true in the fiction' as a normative constraint to which they ought to obey. *Superstitious imaginings*, formed in response to cultural transmission, with the proper function of promoting social cohesion, and 'fidelity to tradition' as a proper normative constraint. And so on and so forth, with *daydream imaginings* (perhaps the most unconstrained?), *pretence imaginings, magical imaginings, ideological imaginings, conspiracist imaginings...*

This book has emphasized the similarities between these forms of imaginings, as opposed to doxastic states. But it is important also to explore the differences between them – and between them and various other forms of imaginings that we may discover to be operating in our complex cognitive systems. This is a big project, that goes beyond the scope of the present discussion. But I shall conclude the book with something in its spirit – devoting the last chapter to a specific kind of imaginings which play a crucial role in human life and culture since very ancient times: religious imaginings.

6.
RELIGIOUS (SO-CALLED) BELIEFS AND IMAGINATION

In the previous chapters I have argued that imagination plays a larger role in our cognitive life than it has traditionally been taken to play. This role goes far beyond the domains of daydreams, fiction, pretence and modal thinking, encompassing also all the thoughts and actions that I have gathered in the broad categories of 'magic' and 'superstition'. I am inclined to think that imagination's role is actually even larger than that: many other thoughts and actions that are commonly understood in terms of belief may turn out to be better explained as imaginings, instead. In this chapter I shall argue that this is the case with so-called 'religious beliefs' (or, at least, with many instances of them).

I see that my claims may look less plausible for religion than for superstition. Hopefully my arguments in chapter 4 managed to persuade you that most superstitious people do not really believe, but just imagine, that travelling on Friday the 13th is dangerous. But if I tell you that most religious people do not really believe, and just imagine, that God exists, I'm not so sure you will still agree. Religious beliefs, you will say, are different, far more serious things: why deny that people really hold them? I don't deny that religious 'beliefs' differ from superstitions in important ways – which is why I am treating them separately; let alone I deny that religion is a serious thing – quite the opposite. But I argue that the relevant differences here are not at the level of the attitude: like superstitions, religious attitudes are best understood as kinds of imaginings. In §1 I specify what precisely I refer to by the label *religious beliefs*, and what types of religious 'beliefs' I am mostly concerned with. In §2 I review some key features of belief and consider why religious attitudes are commonly taken to display such features. In § 3 I argue that, on closer inspection, religious attitudes do not display such features, and are rather better understood as kinds of imaginings. In §4 I develop and defend this view, considering two possible ways to interpret religious people's sincere avowals, and two corresponding forms in which religious imaginings typically come. I then conclude with the suggestion that religious propositions are more apt to be imagined than to be believed.[1]

1. So-called religious 'beliefs'

My aim here is to gain a better understanding of those kinds of mental states that people commonly avow and ascribe to each other as "religious beliefs". I take it that what identifies these states as such is their peculiar content: the non-controversial feature shared by all religious (so-called) beliefs is indeed that of having a *religious* content. My notion of 'religious content' is fairly broad: it includes any propositional content concerning entities or situations that are, not just metaphorically or symbolically, somehow transcendent, not fully explainable in natural terms, and purely spiritual – provided that the content in question is part of a set of contents (i.e. of propositions) at least one of which makes reference to some sort of God/Gods.[2] The kind of attitude by which such a content is entertained, on the other hand, seems much more questionable, and anyway variable. Philosophers, psychologists and anthropologists interested in different aspects of religion typically assume that it is an attitude of belief – and

---

1   This view has important implications for our understanding of the rationality of religious cognition, which will emerge along my discussion. Note that, on the other hand, my view has no (straightforward) implications for the ontological question of God's existence. What I discuss are people's attitudes towards God's existence, not God's existence itself. My thesis that so-called religious beliefs are in fact imaginings does not exclude the possibility that the propositional contents of such imaginings are true.

2   Typically, but not necessarily, the God/Gods of an established religious tradition. This is a rather broad characterization of religious contents; but the reference to God/Gods is enough to set religious 'beliefs' apart from other sorts of supernatural thoughts like superstitions. On this view, indeed, generic 'beliefs' in hidden supernatural forces/entities such as ghosts or spirits do not in themselves count as 'religious' unless they are linked to other 'beliefs' concerning some kind of god (e.g., unless ghosts are considered to be the souls of the departed who have not been welcome by God in paradise). Nor on the other hand, would count as 'religious' a belief concerning just the ideals of love and altruism expressed by Jesus in the Gospel, with no essential commitment to transcendent truths (e.g. Jesus is God's son), even if of course such a belief might be strictly related to a system of proper religious ones. In sum, here I am characterizing religious 'beliefs' as attitudes (of whatever kind) towards propositions that: (i) refer to something supernatural/transcendent and (ii) belong to a set of propositions at least one of which refers to some sort of god. 'Beliefs' in ghosts fail to meet (ii); beliefs in immanent ideals such as love and altruism fail to meet (i).

what I am going to do here is to question this common assumption.[3] I do not say that religious propositional contents *cannot* be genuinely believed, nor that as a matter of fact they are *never* believed; but just that in many cases where we take them to be believed, they actually are imagined.

The cases I am going to discuss concern primarily religious attitudes of members of our contemporary Western society, normally educated, sensitive, and intelligent. I will consider notably Christian people, whose fundamental religious 'beliefs' are related to the idea that there is one God who created the Universe and everything in it, and that Jesus of Nazareth is his son, who died and was resurrected for us. This Christian God is conceived as an immaterial omnipotent being with important psychological properties – such as omniscience and infinite goodness. Actually, I do think that most of my claims could be extended to other religions, epochs and cultures, as the cognitive underpinnings of religion are likely to display some nearly universal features. But I won't commit myself to this broader view here, since the empirical evidence I have considered so far is mostly restricted to the contemporary, Western, Christian religious 'believers' I mentioned.[4]

---

3   To be fair, in the philosophy of religion there are extensive debates on the nature of faith and the mental attitudes it involves. Many agree that it is not reducible to propositional belief, but involves also affective and conative components (cf. Bishop 2010 for a review of the relevant literature). More in general, few would argue that an exhaustive description of the inner life of religious people can be traced back to propositional belief. Still, most authors agree that among the mental states of religious people there are *also* authentic propositional beliefs – i.e. that most religious people really believe propositions such as GOD EXISTS. A notable exception to this widespread agreement is constituted by recent works by Neil Van Leeuwen (2014, 2017). Van Leeuwen's view and mine are similar with respect to the negative claim that religious attitudes are *not* genuine beliefs. But we make different positive suggestions about how to best characterize such attitudes in non-doxastic terms. I appeal to imagination; Van Leeuwen argues that we need to recognize a distinctive cognitive category that he calls 'religious credence'. For a more extensive discussion of Van Leeuwen's position, see Ichino (2020 and in preparation). For further references and an overview of the debate, see Ichino et. al (2016). For an exchange between Van Leeuwen and myself on these issues, see this thread on the *Imperfect Cognitions Blog:* http://imperfectcognitions.blogspot.co.uk/2015/01/imagination-is-not-just-for-fakers.html.

4   I will refer in particular to studies in psychology and cognitive anthropology. I will also draw on analysis of ordinary language in religious contexts (including Catholic Catechism and literature from theological studies and the philosophy of religion). Empirical research in the cognitive sciences of religion has been growing fast in the last decades, and lots of relevant cross-cultural data are now available, which open interesting new scenarios of research.

Unless otherwise specified, what I say should then be intended as restricted to them– even when, for the ease of exposition, I will make apparently unqualified claims about religious people/attitudes. Again for ease of exposition, I will sometimes use the expression "religious *beliefs*" – omitting to specify that they are just *supposed* beliefs. Henceforth, the expression "religious *beliefs*" should be intended as label indicating those propositional attitudes (whatever they are) towards the kind of religious contents I described, which are commonly avowed by (or ascribed to) religious people.

2. *Doxastic reasons*

Here are three important reasons why religious attitudes look so much as authentic beliefs, or anyway much closer to authentic beliefs than superstitions.

1) Sensitivity to evidence. Religious 'beliefs' are not indifferent to evidence as superstitions seem to be. Religious people justify their 'beliefs' by appeal to evidence from at least two sources. First, a (kind of) testimonial evidence from the sacred tradition: such things as sacred texts, catechism, or also documents on lives and miracles of saints are often pointed out as tangible signs of God's existence. Second, religious people often appeal to a (quasi-) perceptual evidence from peculiar spiritual experiences: many religious people take their 'beliefs' to be supported by special experiences they have lived through, such as the overwhelming feeling of God's disembodied presence, a mystic communion with other souls, or even spiritual encounters with the person of Jesus Christ (see Kierkegaard 1844). Both these kinds of evidence are hard to find in support of superstitions.

2) Holistic coherence. Religious 'beliefs' display a kind of holistic coherence that cannot be equally seen in superstitions. Not only religious 'beliefs' form a pretty wide internally coherent system; but they also seem to be quite well-integrated with subjects' other earthly beliefs, at least insofar as they attempt to make sense of such other beliefs, framing them into a globally coherent picture of the world. If a superstition like that concerning Friday the 13th is at odds with some basic physic laws that any normally educated person recognizes as valid (i.e. space/time homogeneity), the religious 'belief' that our world has been created by an intelligent God might be taken to account for everything that happens in this world, physical laws included.

In the previous chapters I have argued that sensitivity to evidence and holistic coherence are key features of belief – not only necessary, but also sufficient to set it apart from imagination. Insofar as that is true, (1) and (2) look as powerful – if not conclusive – reasons to qualify religious attitudes as beliefs. There is also a third reason to do that, having to do with a feature of belief which – even if not constitutive in the sense just specified – plays a crucial role in our practices of belief ascription: typically, a subject who believes that p does also believe that she believes that p and is disposed to manifest that belief in her sincere avowals.

3) Sincere avowals. This seems to be the most straightforward reason why we credit religious people with authentic beliefs: they earnestly avow such beliefs. While, as we have seen in Chapter 4, superstitious people are often reluctant to admit their superstitious thoughts (in public, but even to themselves), religious people are eager to avow their 'beliefs'. Religious 'beliefs' are expressed much more frequently and with greater conviction than superstitions; actually, more frequently and vehemently than any other ordinary belief. In ordinary talk, we often omit explicit expressions of belief towards our own assertions. In religious contexts, on the contrary, people tend to make their attitude of 'belief' explicit, and with a particular emphasis: assertions like "*I believe* that God is listening to me" are (quite emphatically) uttered much more often than corresponding assertions as "God is listening to me". And the public profession of the *Credo* ('I believe') is indeed an essential part of Catholic mass.

Since we generally have no reason to take such public avowals to be insincere – and given the reasons presented in (1) and (2) above – it seems after all quite reasonable to credit religious people with authentic religious beliefs.[5] However, I will argue that, in spite of the apparent reasonableness, we shouldn't do that.

3. *Anti-doxastic reasons*

While surely agreeing that reasons (1)-(3) just discussed point out important differences between religious 'beliefs' and superstitions, I argue that these differences do not lie at the level of the attitude as they are purported to do: reasons (1)-(3) are *not* good reasons to think that religious attitudes, differently from superstitious attitudes, are genuine beliefs. Vice versa, on closer inspection, the features of the religious attitude that

---

5   There are arguably other reasons why religious beliefs look so much as authentic beliefs (e.g. reasons having to do with the strong support they get from well-established traditions). Here I have selected these ones because they are the most critical for an assessment of their doxastic status.

these three reasons highlight turn out to be much better understood if we qualify this attitude as imagining. In what follows I shall defend this view, overturning (1)-(3) in *three opposite anti-doxastic reasons.*

1*) Religious 'beliefs' are not really sensitive to evidence as they *prima facie* seem to be. For a propositional attitude to be sensitive to evidence, the subject to which we ascribe that attitude must display some degree of openness to revise or reject the relevant proposition – even if her revisions' criteria are far from perfectly rational. Religious 'beliefs' do not seem to display even a minimal degree of such sensitivity. They are related to evidence just in the sense that religious people appeal to some evidence to justify them; but the evidence which is appealed to seems to be available only to corroborate, and never to revise/falsify, religious propositions. Appealing to evidence is not the same as being sensitive to it.

This applies to both the kinds of evidence mentioned above: evidence from the Sacred tradition, as well as evidence from inner experiences. Sacred texts are not really read with the critical (even minimally critical) eye with which people read other non-fictional texts. There doesn't seem to be any piece of independent evidence that could persuade a religious reader to reject the biblical claim that God created human kind in his image. And something similar is true, *mutatis mutandis*, for to the evidence from inner experience. In fact, here it is not even clear how precisely the evidential relation between the content of such experiences and the propositions describing God is supposed to work. How is it that the (presumably non-conceptual) content of such idiosyncratic experiences supports propositions concerning the existence of an eternal omnipotent God, rather than, say, propositions concerning a temporal and finitely powerful being? (Rey 2009: 10 raises a similar question) And anyway it seems clear that, however it works, this is always a relation of corroboration/confirmation: the experiences in question provide evidence that strengthens, and (almost) never weakens or discards, the relevant religious attitudes. Conversions based on mystic experiences go typically in one and the same direction: from atheism to religion; while, apparently the fading of inner feelings is not among the reasons that people mention to explain their abandonment of previous religious 'beliefs'.

Empirical studies on religious disaffiliation show that subjects typically provide a rather different sorts of reasons – appealing to factors such as maturation ("When I grew up and started making decisions of my own, I stopped going to Church"), practical contingencies ("I moved to a different community and never got involved in a new church"), or personal conflicts with other members of the Church – most often with a religious leader (see Roozen 1980; Albrecht and Bahr 1983; Sauvayre 2011). These are not really the sort of evidence-sensitive factors that seem to be required for belief formation/maintenance/extinguishment. Note that the distinction I am making here between *sensitivity* and *appeals* to evidence is not just a matter of degree. Of course, sensitivity to evidence does come in degrees. And the rich empirical literature on *confirmation bias* strongly suggests that the sensitivity of most ordinary beliefs is much lower than one would expect from a perfectly rational subject. But my point is not that religious attitudes' sensitivity to evidence is *too low* – even lower than the already low average – in order for them to count as beliefs. What I am suggesting is that generally their relation to evidence is of a rather different kind, *which parallels very closely that of paradigmatic instances of imaginings.* The religious attitude towards a proposition like god is good and his love endures forever (*Psalm* 100) is not 'very resistant to counterevidence', but seems to depend on factors other than evidence. Notably, it seems to be in important respects subject to the will: the commitment to the idea of a loving God is often described as 'a matter of choice', a conscious decision (or a 'bet'): something springing primarily from inner motivation.

Not that religious 'beliefs' are always the outcome of an intentional deliberation (people sometimes say that after certain experiences – such as an unexpected recovery – they couldn't help but believe in God). But nor do imagining, which can similarly 'come to our mind' without our previous decision, and even against our will. What matters is that, once imaginings and religious 'beliefs' are present to our mind, we can, as it were, decide what to do with them.

And, importantly, there does not seem to be anything wrong with that. Like imaginings, religious attitudes do not seem to be regulated by the same normative constraints that govern belief. While the tendency to confirmation biases is obviously a fault of ordinary beliefs, the firmness and steadiness of religious 'beliefs' can be – and often is – seen as a virtue.[6]

---

6   Just think of Karl Barth's celebration of the *decision of faith* (Barth 1964: Chapter 2), or of the Christian motto *Credo quia absurdum* ("I believe because it is absurd"). Failures of recognizing these normative differences between religious and ordinary *beliefs* lead to positions such as those of so-called "Brights", according to which religious people do not have a rational view of the world, and base their reasoning on bad science or logical fallacies (http://www.the-brights. net/ ; see e.g. Dawkins 2006; Dennett 2003). Similar positions in my view misunderstand some basic aspects of the phenomenon religion.

2*) The supposed *holistic coherence* of religious 'beliefs' is also highly dubious. We can often detect incoherencies *internal* to individual sets of religious 'beliefs' (e.g.: the same subject believing that God is omnipotent *and* that God cannot prevent natural disasters). Most importantly, there seem to be many *external* incoherencies between religious and natural beliefs. Many religious views seem to contradict widely accepted scientific views, as well as other beliefs that play crucial roles in our view of the world.[7] To be clear, the problem here is not that religious people hold beliefs that a careful analysis reveals to be inconsistent: admittedly, this happens quite frequently also in the sets of our ordinary beliefs.[8] In fact, it is not even obvious whether the religious and scientific 'beliefs' in question actually *are* inconsistent: the question whether there might be ways to reconcile them is a hard and highly controversial one, that goes far beyond the scope of my discussion here.[9] What matters here is the fact that, *rightly or wrongly,* religious people themselves do often see and openly recognize tensions among their religious and natural beliefs; but do not drop any of the views from which such tensions arise, nor indeed seem to feel a pressure to do that.

Think for example of common views about death and afterlife, where religious and natural explanations pull in opposite directions. A number of studies in psychology and cognitive anthropology confirm that religious people hold 'in parallel' two opposite views of death: the 'natural view' that death implies the total cessation of any physical *and mental* process, and the 'supernatural view' that death is a transition after which our disembodied minds/souls continue a conscious existence. The natural view is generally acquired first (a proper understanding of the idea of an afterlife emerges around six/seven years old); but it is not subsequently abandoned. The newly acquired supernatural view does not displace the natural view, nor influence it in any respect; it simply coexist alongside it. Religious and natural reasoning on this topic do not interact (Astuti and Harris 2008; Harris 2012: Chapter 9[10]).

---

7   E.g. 'beliefs' in the 'creation from nothing' vs. beliefs in physical principles of conservation; 'belief' that humans are designed by God vs. belief that humans are the product of natural selection.

8   As I noted in Chapter 3, psychological literature on human reasoning shows how prone we are to systematic mistakes in deductive and probabilistic thinking (see above, Chapter 3: §1.1).

9   On this, see the current live between Plantinga and Dennett; Plantinga argues that many alleged contradictions between religion and science (e.g. creationism vs. evolutionism) are not really such (Dennett and Plantinga 2011).

10   See notably Astuti and Harris' studies on Spanish Catholic and Mexican Vezo communities.

The same seems to happen with all religious ideas, since the first moment when they are acquired. Children's developing beliefs about various kinds of natural causal relations (e.g. relations between their mind and other minds or between the mind and the physical world) are not affected by their simultaneous acquirement of religious ideas about supernatural relations (e.g. relations between and God and humanity, or God and angels). Around three/four years old, when children become aware of the fact that other minds and the physical world cannot be modified by thought alone, those educated in religious families are also introduced to the idea of silent inner prayer. Even though the power of silent prayer presupposes mechanisms that run against the natural mechanisms of mental-mental or mental-physical causation that children are mastering, their developing understanding of those natural relations is not compromised. Children do not make deductions from the idea that inner mental prayers can be heard and answered: for example, they do not come to think that, since prayer can be effective, so it is possible that also silent wishes on falling stars are effective. On the contrary, their confidence in the efficacy of wishes quickly decreases between four and six years, and by the age of six very few children display it; while 'belief' in the efficacy of prayer follows the opposite trend, and at the age of six about all children who have received a religious education declare that prayers can be answered (See Wolley 2000; Harris and Koenig 2006).

Psychologists explain this and other similar findings with the very same notion of 'quarantining' by which they characterize the imaginative attitude: the idea is that, similarly to what they do with 'imaginary beliefs' about fictional stories, children segregate their religious 'beliefs', preventing them from influencing their understanding of real world's mechanisms. One question here is how children come to understand that they should keep this 'quarantined attitude' towards religious beliefs, notwithstanding that, differently from fictional stories, religious matters are presented utterly seriously, just as real beliefs. This leads me to my next point, concerning religious people's sincere avowals of belief.

3*) Reason (3) presented above makes appeal to what we can call a 'principle of first-person authority', which credits people with a reliable knowledge of themselves, and consider their self-reports as 'true by default': i.e. true until proof to the contrary. If acceptance should be our default attitude towards people's self-reports, surely it should be our attitude towards their religious self-reports, which are expressed with a particular emphasis and conviction. So, we should credit religious people with genuine religious beliefs. This was, roughly, the point of reason (3) above.

But it is not so obvious that applying the principle of first-person authority to religious believers' avowals leads to the conclusion that their religious attitudes are genuine beliefs. That principle does not prescribe unconditional acceptance of people's self-reports; it prescribes, as I have just noted, acceptance *until proof to the contrary*. And, arguably, reasons (1*) and (2*) just discussed do constitute proofs to the contrary in the case of religious people: religious people's emphatic avowals are controverted by the insensitivity to evidence and inferential isolation of their supposed 'beliefs'.

Actually, the characteristic emphasis with which religious beliefs are avowed – and indeed the very fact that they are avowed more often and eagerly than beliefs on other mundane matters, may even provide further proof *against* their doxastic status. This is indeed one of the hypotheses that have been suggested to explain how children come to quarantine the religious 'beliefs' that they acquire from adult's testimony. Considering testimonies about entities that they cannot experience by first-hand observation, children use what psychologists call the 'presupposition metric' (see e.g. Harris 2012: Chapter 8): depending on whether the existence of such entities is unreflectively presupposed or vice versa ostentatiously affirmed, they draw different conclusions about the sort of attitude that their informants bear towards the entities in question.

Compare for example the testimonies that children hear about invisible entities like germs and oxygen with those they hear about invisible religious entities like God. Children will typically learn about germs or oxygen from adults' remarks that take the existence of these entities for granted, without making it explicit. They will often hear remarks as: "Wash your hands, which are full of germs!", or "Anyone needs oxygen to breathe"; but very rarely explicit assertions such as: "There really exist germ, and they can hurt us", or "I believe in oxygen". On the other hand, children will often hear such explicit assertions about God (for example, each time they go to church services), as well as about fictional characters like Santa Claus: "I believe in God!"; "Trust me: Santa really exist!". Hence, children will come to the conclusion that God's existence is not considered by adults in the same way in which oxygen's existence is considered. And they will do the same, keeping God and Santa Claus apart from their real-world beliefs.[11]

---

11   A related possibility that psychologists point out is that children use a 'consensus metric', registering the degree of expressed consensus concerning the existence of the invisible entities they are told about. Since the consensus about God's existence is not at all universal, they are more circumspect in taking this existence for true

Arguably, there are also other linguistic differences that children's sensitive antennae might capture. There are some striking differences between our uses of "belief" in religious and ordinary contexts, which seem to reveal substantial differences in the underlying mental attitudes. While in ordinary contexts "I believe" weakens our assertions, in religious contexts it typically has an opposite, intensifying role. Compare: "I believe they never met before" vs. "I believe that God will listen to my prayers!". In the former case, "I believe" expresses an attitude which is open to corrections ("as far as I know, they never met... But I might be wrong"); in the latter, it expresses a strong conviction, based on self-sufficient inner trust which doesn't need further confirmation ("I think so... And that's all!").

Another obvious difference between religious and ordinary talk of "belief" (which corresponds, somewhat, to the one just mentioned) has to do with the use of "believe in" vs. "believe that". Actually, we do happen to use "believe in" also in non-religious contexts – e.g. for encouragements such as: "you can do that, I *believe in* you!". However, this is precisely because in similar cases – as in most cases of religious avowals – we do not use "believe" to express our opinion on how we deem things actually to be, but rather to express something different, which can be an exhortation, an assurance, a hope, a wishful hypothesis; but *not* really an evidence-grounded judgement.

As it turns out, then, sincere avowals of religious 'beliefs' are not only in themselves *insufficient* to credit people with genuine religious beliefs, such avowals may even provide positive reasons not to do so, suggesting that we ascribe a different sort of attitude instead. My reasons (1*) and (2*), in turn, suggest that this attitude has much in common with paradigmatic instances of imaginings. In the next section I shall better develop and defend this suggestion.

and drawing inferences from that. It is also possible that children notice the inconsistencies between the religious and the earthly testimonies they are given and, realizing that the circle of ordinary beliefs where the earthly testimonies come from is much bigger than the circle of religious 'beliefs' where religious testimonies come from, they make a difference between them, treating the religious 'beliefs' more as particular stories than as real, universal truths. These seem all plausible hypotheses that can explain, or concur to explain, how children come to quarantine their religious beliefs from all their other beliefs. See Harris and Koenig (2006); Harris (2012): Chapter 8; Harris and Corriveau (2014).

4. *Religious imaginings*

The picture that has emerged from my considerations so far reveals some striking functional similarities between the religious attitude and imagination. In particular, similarities concerning the cognitive inputs in response to which religious attitudes and imaginings are typically formed, and concerning the sort of inferential relations that they typically have with each other and with the whole system of religious subjects' beliefs. Religious attitudes display the same sort of sensitivity (or insensitivity, or selective sensitivity) to such factors as will, inner feelings, and inferential reasons that imaginings typically display.

Here I haven't said much about religious attitudes' characteristic phenomenology; nor about the various (ritual and non-ritual) actions that such attitudes typically motivate. But though these are surely important and interesting dimensions of the religious attitude, I do not take them to be critical to assess its doxastic/non-doxastic status – since on my account beliefs and imaginings do not critically differ neither in emotional nor in behavioural outputs.

However, there is an output factor that raises some problems for my suggestion that religious attitudes are imaginings: the characteristic verbal actions motivated by religious 'beliefs', which I discussed in (3*) above. As I have portrayed it, the case of religious 'believers' is a case where people avow something that in fact they do not really believe, but just imagine. In order for my suggestion to be plausible, I should explain *why* religious people make such avowals.

To begin, I would like to emphasize the fact that so far I have been assuming that religious avowals are *sincere*. This is not an assumption I really want to question; at least, not for the vast majority of cases. Of course, there *may* be some cases of hypocrisy – like those described in Dan Dennett and Linda La Scola's book *Caught in the Pulpit. Leaving Belief Behind*. The book tells a number of stories of "men and women who entered the pulpit with the best intentions, and have come to recognize that they no longer hold the beliefs they parishioners think they do"; yet "still have a congregation awaiting for them each Sabbath, trusting them to speak the truth from the pulpit" (Dennett and La Scola 2013: 1).

In fact, the authors themselves admit that the dimension of this phenomenon is far from clear. And anyway, no matters how widespread hypocrisy may be among clerics, I would not say that it is the norm, and even not that it is particularly frequent, among common secular 'believers'. If I can see some reasons – such as social pressure or financial worries – why a priest with an established position in her community may be moved to make *in*sincere avowals of religious belief, I do not think these are reasons that plausibly hold for the majority of the members in such community.[12]

4.1. *Two forms of religious imaginings*

Ruling out the hypothesis that they are insincere, I would then suggest that religious people's avowals of beliefs can be explained in two different ways, which correspond to two different meanings we may attribute to such avowals. On the one hand, we could take them literally, as genuine expressions of authentic beliefs, thus assuming that religious people have faulty self-knowledge (that is: we could explain religious beliefs avowals in terms of *meta-cognitive mistakes*). On the other hand, we could think that religious beliefs' avowals are uttered with the intention of communicating something different from their literal meaning; if so, they would not necessarily come from a fault in self-knowledge, and indeed what I argue is that in similar cases they would be conscious expressions of (a kind of) imaginative attitude. These two different explanations correspond to two forms in which religious imaginings typically come. Let's briefly consider both of them.[13]

4.1.1. *Meta-cognitive mistakes: religious 'beliefs' as unrecognized imaginings*

It seems plausible that, at least in some cases, religious people's avowals of beliefs are precisely what they seem to be: sincere assertions of genuine beliefs. That is, with their avowals, sometimes religious people really intend to communicate their beliefs about God, in the same way in which they intend

---

12 Nor, indeed, I think Dennett and La Scola would suggest that hypocrisy is the norm. After all, as we have seen, they say that their unbelieving-clergies have "a congregation awaiting for them each Sabbath, trusting them to speak the truth from the pulpit". The disagreement between these authors and I has to do with how we understand the religious attitude of the typical members of such congregations. Dennett and La Scola take such attitudes to be false, irrational beliefs (although, interestingly, note that in this passage they talk in terms of trust!). I have argued that they are better understood as imaginings. But I should still explain why, then, such attitudes are avowed as beliefs.

13 Here I limit myself to put these forward as *plausible hypotheses* to explain many instances of religious people's avowal of belief. Arguably, they are both empirically testable in various ways; though admittedly here I do not provide much empirical evidence in their favour.

to communicate their beliefs about other things when they avow to believe those things. Since we have seen that there are more compelling reasons to think that religious people do not really believe, but merely imagine, the contents of their avowals, then we should conclude that such avowals are due to a fault in self-knowledge: a mistaken beliefs about their own beliefs.

Roughly, what may happen in such cases is that some other powerful mental state – such as fear of death, or a desire for meaning, or even just a desire for social homologation – blurs religious people's view of their minds, and in particular shut out their awareness that God's existence is purely imagined, while leading them *to believe that they really believe* in it. Importantly, notice that these cases are different from Dennett's cases of hypocrisy: here the relevant non-doxastic factors (such as emotions, or social pressure) that are causally responsible for beliefs' avowal are not clearly recognized as such by religious 'believers'. This arguably involves some irrationality on their part; but no insincerity (and by the way, as I noticed in previous chapters, that is a sort of irrationality not uncommon in cognitively normal population).

Anyway, I do not think this is the best explanation for most cases of religious beliefs avowals.

4.1.2. *Non-literal speaking: religious 'beliefs' as trusting imaginings*

I do not think that religious people's avowals of beliefs generally come from a mistaken view of their own minds. On the contrary, religious people are generally aware of the peculiarity of their attitudes towards God's existence and other religious (supposed) facts. They see that they do not take such facts in the same way they take many other facts in their ordinary lives, since 'believing' in God is something they somehow decide to do, while other ordinary, earthly beliefs are things that, so to say, force themselves in their minds. Hence, they also realize that they cannot properly *believe* that God exists, but they can at most imagine it, trying to give to this imagining the serious form of an hypothesis through which to read the world.

The point, then, is to explain why religious people, even being aware that their attitude is not really belief, do persist in calling it "belief", rather than choosing a more precise term. Here we should recall first of all that a basic feature of belief is the fact to be 'negation incomplete': there are propositions that a subject neither believes nor disbelieves (see above, Chapter 4: §3.2). The fact that religious 'believers' do not really believe that God exists, does not imply that they believe that God does *not* exist. Lacking a definite belief on whether God exists or not, religious 'believers' have something like an inclination (perhaps due to some related spiritual experience), or a preference (perhaps due to need of meaning/metaphysical answers, or even just to a calculus à la Pascal) for the view that He/She exists.[14] Their penchant for this view makes religious people very willing to enjoy (at least some of) the imaginings which represent it, and to give to these imaginings a great role in their lives, since this represents the best possible approximation to the experience they would have if that view were indeed true. Thus, they imagine that God exists and that they believe so, i.e. they make-believe that God exists.

In many cases, in order to make-believe at best that p is the case, one should behave as much as possible as if she believed that p (see Walton 1990: Part IV); hence she should also avow to believe so. That is why religious people do often avow to *believe* that God exists: if, on the contrary, they avowed to (merely) *imagine* that God exists, this would damage their participation in the quasi-experience of God existence. But in doing this they do not merely pretend to avow an attitude of belief; by means of such a little pretence they also seriously avow a different attitude. They avow an attitude of *faith*, which, in turn, could be seen as a decision to give space in their lives to an imagining: an imagining that is not taken as mere fiction, but rather as *serious and fruitful hypothesis by which looking at – and making sense of – the world*.

As I said, I am inclined to think that this latter, more mindful, form in which religious imaginings may come is more common than the first, 'unrecognized' form I described. Though it is of course possible for the latter to harden into the first.

4.2. *Religious contents and imaginative contents*

To conclude, further reasons in favour of the view that so-called religious beliefs are best seen as imaginings come from the consideration of the kinds of contents that they typically display.

This may sound surprising. Conforming to the dominant view in the contemporary debate, indeed, in Chapter 2 I have argued that propositional

---

14 George Rey argues that most religious people definitely believe that God does not exist, and are self-deceived. I find this implausible. As I have it, religious people always believe that it is possible, or even probable, that God exists. These beliefs, even if logically consistent with the belief that God exists, are not 'pragmatically consistent' with it: generally, if I believe that x is probably true I do not at the same time believe that x is true. On the other hand, the belief that x is probable fits well with the imagining that x is the case.

imagination and belief have the same sort of contents, and only differ in functional roles. If there is no feature pertaining just to content that can distinguish imaginings from beliefs, of course I cannot plausibly appeal to some feature pertaining to the content of so-called religious beliefs in order to argue that they are, instead, imaginings. And indeed in §1 above I explicitly recognized that, though I take religious contents to be most often imagined, I allow that the very same contents can also be believed. Without denying any of this, however, I am going to argue that there are some kinds of propositional contents that are *much more likely* to be imagined than to be believed; and that religious beliefs do often have contents of those kinds.

Imaginative contents often display some peculiar features that we do not typically find in belief's contents. One is a high degree of 'narrativity'.[15] Narrativity is a property that representations can possess to various degrees. Typically, highly narrative representations are *stories,* which represent particular events connected by temporal and causal relations, where intentional agents usually play a prominent role. If we can draw an intuitive distinction between *stories* and – for example – *theories,* this is at least partly because theories represent just general, abstract principles, which are often causally, but not chronologically, related to each other. This difference can be described by saying that theories are not narrative in kind (or that they display a very low degree of narrativity).

Now, narrativity in itself does not characterize only imaginative contents. In our lives we deal also with many non-fictional narratives. But imaginative contents are quite univocally characterized by narrativity at least when narrativity occurs in conjunction with two other features: incoherence and incompleteness.

Narrative imaginative contents are often incoherent: fictions typically involve contradictions of various kinds. Think for example of the story where 5 and 7 do and do not equal 12; or of time-travel stories where the same event occurs and does not occur at a time *t*. We can easily imagine similar contradictions, while at the same time recognizing them as such. Indeed, we are perfectly able to enjoy similar stories. On the contrary, believing them, if we recognize them as such, is something we are not able to do.

Besides, imaginative contents, especially (but not only) when they are narrative in kind, are often intrinsically incomplete, undetermined in their details. When we imagine the story of Hamlet, the detail about what Hamlet had for breakfast on the day of his death is undetermined, and questions about

---

15   I take this notion of narrativity and its characterization from Currie and Jureidini (2004) and Currie (2010).

this detail seem inappropriate (or anyway impossible to answer). In the case of beliefs' contents, on the contrary, incompleteness does not seem to be intrinsic: all lacking details seem to be, at least in principle, possible to fill out.[16]

Even if we do not consider any of the previous features to be in itself exclusive of imaginative contents, I think we can grant that the conjunction of these three features is very common in some kinds of imaginative contents (e.g. those of imaginings in response to fictional stories); whilst it can hardly, if ever, be found in the contents of beliefs (for a similar claim, see Gendler 2010: §5). My point is that these features of high narrativity, inconsistence, and intrinsic incompleteness that typically characterize imaginative contents are characteristic features of religious beliefs' contents as well.

The high narrativity of religious beliefs' contents is quite evident. Sacred texts – at least in the Judeo-Christian tradition – generally communicate 'religious truths' by means of stories.[17] Indeed, the Bible is 'the narration par excellence', which goes from the Genesis of Universe to its Apocalypse. And, within this story, Jesus, too, speaks in parables to his disciples. Consequently, common religious beliefs do not concern general, abstract truths, but stories where these general truths are framed in particular, contextualized episodes. While most theologians argue that God is a completely distinct reality, separated from us by an ontological gap and only indirectly knowable, common 'believers', by contrast, tend to tell stories where God is seen as 'a character like all the others': a highly anthropomorphic being, part of our human chronological history, who interacts with us in all sorts of particular circumstances. Various psychological and anthropological studies found that, even when people avow abstract theological beliefs on God's properties, if they are faced with particular tasks where they are required to describe God or to answer questions about God, they typically fall back on more concrete, narrative representations of him/her and of his/her actions (See Barrett and Keil 1996; Barrett 1998; Boyer 2001, Chapter 4).

---

16 In fact, what I am calling 'intrinsic incompleteness' is not strictly speaking a feature of propositional contents themselves. It seems rather to be a feature of 'fictional truth' (as opposed to 'truth' tout court). I see that more work here is required to better articulate this point; and more generally to better clarify the (somewhat parallel?) relations between imagination and fictionality, on the one hand, and belief and truth, on the other. This is one respect in which, as I said, my considerations in this Section are still rather tentative.

17 From this point of view, as far as I know Koran is quite different. If that is true, this would be an interesting difference, which would be definitely worth considering; but I do not do that here.

Moreover, as I noted in § 3 above, religious beliefs' contents, like imaginative contents, are often characterized by internal incoherencies (e.g. God is omnipotent, but he cannot avoid natural disasters). Finally, they also display intrinsic incompleteness. As Georges Rey observes, religious contents are "oddly detail-resistant" (Rey 2009: 17). Some details concerning creation, for example, seem to be inherently undetermined: questions as "In which language did God say: 'Let there be light'?" sound as odd as questions like "What did Hamlet have for breakfast?".

All these structural similarities – both at the level of the attitude and of the content – support the view that so-called religious beliefs are, in fact, better seen as kinds of imaginings: *stories* that religious people allow to play a great role in their lives, but that, nonetheless, remain accurately quarantined from their ordinary beliefs and can be 'endorsed' or not depending on people's will.

Conclusion

In this chapter I have argued that so-called religious beliefs (or, at least, many instances of them) are actually not beliefs, but imaginings. Having rejected some reasons why they look like authentic beliefs, I have argued that they share many more functions with paradigmatic imaginings, pointing out also some striking similarities between religious and imaginative contents. This view does not have the undesirable consequences that it may *prima facie* seem to have: it does not force us to say that most religious 'believers' are hypocrites, nor even that they have faulty self-knowledge. On the contrary, it helps us to make more rational sense of religious avowals of 'belief', and to better understand the peculiar normative dimension of religious attitudes.

REFERENCES

Albahari, Miri (2014), "Alief or belief? A contextual approach to belief ascription", *Philosophical Studies*, 167, 3: 701-720.

Albrecht, Stan L. and Bahr, Howard M. (1983), "Patterns of Religious Disaffiliation: A Study of Lifelong Mormons, Mormon Converts, and Former Mormons", *Journal for the Scientific Study of Religion*, 22, 4: 366-379.

American Psychiatric Association (2013), "Obsessive-Compulsive and Related Disorders", in *Diagnostic and Statistical Manual of Mental Disorders* (5th ed.).

Anscombe, Elizabeth M. (1957), *Intention*, Basil Blackwell, Oxford.

Armstrong, David M. (1973), *Belief, Truth and Knowledge*, Cambridge University Press.

Astuti, Rita and Harris, Paul L.(2008), "Understanding mortality and the life of the ancestors in rural Madagascar", *Cognitive Science*, 3, 4: 713-740.

Barrett, Justin (1998), "Cognitive Constraints on Hindu Concepts of the Divine", *Journal for the Scientific Study of Religion*, 37, 4: 608-619.

Barrett, Justin, and Keil, Frank (1996), "Conceptualizing a non-natural Entity. Anthropomorphism in God Concepts", *Cognitive Psychology*, 31: 220-247.

Barrett, Justin and Rickert, Rebekah (2003), "Anthropomorphism or Preparedness? Exploring Children's God Concepts", *Review of Religious Research*, 44, 3: 300-312.

Barth, Karl (1964), *God Here and Now*, Routledge & Kegan Paul.

Bayne, Tim and Pacherie, Elisabeth (2005), "In Defence of the Doxastic Conception of Delusions", *Mind & Language*, 20, 2: 163–188.

Bayne, Tim and Hattiangadi, Anandi (2013), "Belief and its Bedfellows", in Nottelmann, Nikolaj (2013) (eds.), *New Essays on Belief. Constitution, Content* and *Structure*, Palgrave Macmillan, UK: 124-144.

Bortolotti, Lisa (2010), *Delusions and Other Irrational Beliefs*, Oxford University Press, Oxford.

Boyer, Pascal (2001), *Religion Explained,* Vintage Books, London.

Bishop, John, "Faith", *The Stanford Encyclopedia of Philosophy* (Fall 2010 Edition), Edward N. Zalta (ed.), URL = <http://plato.stanford.edu/archives/fall2010/entries/faith/>

Braithwaite, Richard B. (1933), "The Nature of Believing", *Proceedings of the Aristotelian Society, New Series,* 33: 129-146.

Bratman, Michael (1992), "Practical Reasoning and Acceptance in a Context", *Mind,* 101: 1-16.

Brugger, Peter and Viaud-Delmon, Isabelle ((2010), "Superstitiousness in Obsessive-Compulsive Disorders", *), "Superstitiousness in obsessive-compulsive disorder"* Dialogues in Clinical Neuroscience, 12 (2), pp. 250–254.

Byrne, Ruth M. J. (2005), *The rational imagination. How People Creates Alternatives to Reality,* The MIT Press, Cambridge, MA.

Carruthers, Peter (2010), "Introspection: Divided and Partly Eliminated," *Philosophy and Phenomenological Research,* 80: 76-111.

Churchland, Paul M. (1981), "Eliminative Materialism and the Propositional Attitudes," *Journal of Philosophy,* 78: 67–90.

Cohen, L. Jonathan (1989), "Belief and Acceptance", *Mind,* 98: 367-389.

Cohen, A. (1962), *"An experiment on small rewards for discrepant compliance* and attitude change", in Brehm, J. and *Cohen, A.* (Eds.), *Explorations in cognitive dissonance,* Wiley.

Currie, Gregory (1990), *The Nature of Fiction,* Cambridge University Press, Cambridge.

Currie, Gregory (1995), *Image and Mind: Film, Philosophy and Cognitive Science,* Cambridge University Press, New York.

Currie, Gregory (1995a), "Imagination and Simulation: Aesthetics meets Cognitive Science", in Davies, Martin and Stone, Tony (eds.), *Mental Simulation,* Blackwell: 151-169.

Currie, Gregory (1997), "The Paradox of Caring: Fiction and the Philosophy of Mind", in Hjort, M., and Laver, S. (eds.), *Emotion and the Arts,* Oxford University Press, Oxford: 63-77.

Currie, Gregory (1998), "Pretence and Pretending", *Mind & Language,* 13: 33-55 (reprinted in Currie 2004: 191-209).

Currie, G. (2002), "Desire in Imagination", in Gendler, Tamar and Hawthorne, John (eds.), *Conceivability and Possibility,* Oxford University Press: 201-222.

Currie, Gregory (2004), *Arts and Minds,* Oxford University Press, New York.

Currie, Gregory, and Ravenscroft, Ian (2002), *Recreative Minds: Imagination in Philosophy and Psychology*, Oxford University Press, Oxford.

Currie, Gregory and Jureidini, Jon (2004), "Narrative and Coherence", *Mind & Language*, 19, 4: 409-427.

Currie, Gregory (2010), "Tragedy", *Analysis*, 70, 4: 632-638.

Currie, Gregory and Ichino, Anna (2012): "Aliefs don't Exist, though Some of their Relatives Do", *Analysis*, 72 (4): 788-798.

Currie, Gregory and Ichino, Anna (2013), "Imagination and Make-Believe", Gaut, Berys (eds.), *The Routledge Companion to Aesthetics*, 3rd Edition: 320-329.

Currie, Gregory and Ichino, Anna (2015), "Truth and Trust in Fiction" (*Under Review*).

Damasio, Antonio R. (1994), *Descartes's Error. Emotion, Reason, and the Human Brain*, Avon Books, New York.

Davidson, Donald (1963), "Actions, Reasons and Causes", *Journal of Philosophy*, 60: 685–700.

Davidson, Donald (1980), *Essays on Actions and Events*, Oxford University Press, Oxford.

Dawkins, Richard, (2006) *The God Delusion*, Black Swan Edition, London.

Dennett, Daniel (2006), *Breaking the Spell*, Penguin Books, UK.

Dennett, Daniel and Plantinga, Alvin (2011), *Science and Religion. Are they compatible?*, Oxford University Press, Oxford.

Dennett, Daniel and La Scola, Linda (2013), *Caught in the Pulpit. Leaving Belief Behind*, Pitchstone Publishing, Durham, North Carolina, USA.

Doggett, Tyler, and Egan, Andy (2007), "Wanting Things You Don't Want: The Case for an Imaginative Analogue of Desire", *Philosophers' Imprint*, 7, 9: 1-17.

Egan, Andy (2008), "Imagination, Delusion and Self-deception", in Bayne, Tim and Fernandez, Jordi (eds.), *Delusion and Self-Deception: Affective Influences on Belief-formation*, Psychology Press: 263–280.

Einstein, Danielle and Menzies, Ross (2004), "The Presence of Magical Thinking in Obsessive Compulsive Disorder", *Behaviour Research and Therapy*, 42, 5: 539–549.

Fodor, Jerry (1987), *Psychosemantics. The Problem of Meaning in the Philosophy of Mind*, MIT Press, Cambridge, MA.

Frazer, James G. (1922), *The Golden Bough*, Macmillan, London.

Friedman, Ori and Leslie, Alan (2007), "The conceptual underpinnings of pretense: Pretending is not 'behaving-as-if'", *Cognition*, 105: 103-124.

Friend, Stacie (2003), *"How I really feel about JFK"*, in: Kieran, Matthew, and Lopes, Dominc McIver, (eds.) *Imagination, Philosophy and the Arts,* Routledge, London: 35-53.

Funkhouser, Eric and Spaulding, Shannon (2009), "Imagination and Other Scripts", *Philosophical Studies,* 143: 291-314.

Gendler, Tamar (2000), "The Puzzle of Imaginative Resistance", *The Journal of Philosophy,* 97, 2: 55-81.

Gendler, Tamar (2003), "On the Relation between Pretense and Belief", in Kieran, Matthew, and Lopes, Dominc McIver, (eds.) *Imagination, Philosophy and the Arts,* Routledge, London: 125-141.

Gendler, Tamar (2006), "Imaginative Contagion", *Metaphilosophy,* 37, 2: 182-203.

Gendler, Tamar (2007), "Self-Deception as Pretence", *Philosophical Perspectives,* 21: 231-258.

Gendler, Tamar (2008), "Alief and Belief", *The Journal of Philosophy,* 105: 643-663.

Gendler, Tamar (2008a), "Alief in Action (and Reaction)", in *Mind & Language,* 23, 5: 552-585.

Gendler, Tamar (2010), *Intuition, Imagination and Philosophical Methodology,* Oxford University Press, New York.

Gendler, Tamar (2012), "Between Reason and Reflex: Response to Commentators", *Analysis,* 72, 4: 799-811.

Gendler, Tamar and Kovakovich, Karson (2006), "Genuine Rational Fictional Emotions", in Kieran, Matthew (eds.) *Contemporary Debates in Aesthetics and the Philosophy of Art,* Blackwell, New York: 241-253.

Gmelch, George (1978), "Baseball Magic", *Human Nature,* 1, 8: 32-40.

Goldman, Alvin (2006), *Simulating Minds: The Philosophy, Psychology and Neuroscience of Mindreading,* Oxford University Press, New York.

Goldman, Alvin (1989), "Interpretation Psychologized," *Mind & Language,* 4: 161–185.

Gordon, Robert (1986), "Folk-psychology as Simulation", *Mind & Language,* 1: 158-171.

Guthrie, Stuart E. (1993), *Faces in the Clouds: A New Theory of Religion,* Oxford University Press, New York.

Haidt, Jonathan (2012), *The Righteous Mind. Why Good People Are Divided from Politics and Religion,* Penguin Books, UK.

Harris, Paul L. (2000), *The Work of the Imagination,* Blackwell, Oxford.

Harris, Paul L. (2012), *Trusting What You Are Told. How Children Learn from Others,* Harvard University Press, Cambridge MA.

Harris, Paul L. and Corriveau, Kathleen (2014), "Learning from Testimony about Religion and Science", in Robinson, E. and Einav, S. (eds.), *Trust and Skepticism: Children's Selective Learning From Testimony*, Psychology Press, Hove, East Sussex, UK.

Hauser, Mark (2000), *Wild Minds: What Animals Really Think*, Henry Holt and Company, New York.

Harris, Paul and Koenig, Melissa (2006), "Trust in Testimony: How Children Learn about Science and Religion", *Child Development*, 77: 505-524.

Hood, Bruce (2012), *Supersense. From Superstition to Religion – the Brain Science of Belief*, Constable, London.

Humberstone, I.L. (1992), "Direction of Fit", *Mind*, New Series, 101, 401: 59-83.

Hume, David (1777/1993), *An Enquiry Concerning Human Understanding*, E. Steinberg (ed.), , Hackett Publishing Company Indianapolis/ Cambridge.

Hume, David (1739-40), *A Treatise on Human Nature*.

Huppert, Jonathan D. and Roth, Deborah, A. (2003), "Treating obsessive-compulsive disorder with Exposure and Response prevention", *The Behaviour Analyst Today*, 4: 66-70.

Hursthouse, Rosalind (1991), "Arational Actions", *The Journal of Philosophy*, 88, 2: 57-68.

Huston, Matthew (2012), *The Seven Laws of Magical Thinking. How Irrationality Makes you Happy, Healthy and Sane*, Oneworld Publications, London.

Ichino, Anna, Miyazono, Kengo and Liao, Shen-yi (2016): "Imagination and Belief", in Duncan Pritchard (eds.), *Oxford Bibliographies in Philosophy Series*, Oxford University Press.

Ichino, Anna and Currie, Gregory (2017): "Truth and Trust in Fiction", in Ema Sullivan-Bissett, Helen Bradley, and Paul Noordhof (eds.) *Art and Belief*, Oxford University Press: 63-82.

Ichino, Anna (2018), "Superstitious Confabulations", *Topoi*, 4: 1-15.

Ichino, Anna (2019), "Imagination and Belief in Action", *Philosophia*, 47: 1517-1534.

Ichino, Anna (Manuscript, in preparation), "Religious Imaginings".

Ichino, Anna (2020), *Credo in un solo Dio… O me lo immagino? I meccanismi cognitivi sottesi al pensiero religioso*, Raffaello Cortina Editore, Milano.

Izard, Carroll (1991), *Psychology of Emotion*, Plenum Press, New York.

Kahneman, Daniel (2011), *Thinking Fast and Slow,* Penguin Books, London.

Kahneman, Daniel, and Tversky, Amos (1982), *Judgment Under Uncertainty: Heuristics and Biases,* Cambridge University Press, New York.

Kieran, Matthew and Lopes, Dominic (eds.) (2003), *Imagination, Philosophy, and the Arts,* Routledge, London.

Kierkegaard, Søren (1844), *Philosophical Fragments or a Fragment of Philosophy by Johannes Climacus,* available online at: http://polts.com/Research_files/Source%20Material/Kierkegaard/Philosophical%20Fragments.pdf

Kind, Amy (2011), "The Puzzle of Imaginative Desire", *Australasian Journal of Philosophy,* 89: 421-439.

Kind, Amy (2016), (Eds.) *The Routledge Handbook of the Philosophy of Imagination,* Routledge.

Lang, Peter (1984), "Cognition and Emotion: Concept and Action", in Izard, C. Kagan, J. and Zajonc, R. (eds.), *Emotions, Cognition and Behaviour,* Cambridge University Press, Cambridge: 192-226.

Langland-Hassan, Peter (2012), "Pretense, Imagination and Belief: the Single Attitude Theory", *Philosophical Studies,* 159: 155-179.

Leslie, Alan (1987), "Pretense and Representation: The Origins of 'Theory of Mind'", in *Psychological Review,* 94: 412-426.

Leslie, Alan (1994), "Pretending and believing: Issues in the theory of ToMM", *Cognition,* 50: 211–238.

Leslie, Alan (2002), "Pretense and representation revisited", in N.L. Stein, P.J. Bauer, and M. Rabinowitz (eds.), *Representation, memory and development. Essays in honor of Jean Mandler,* Mahwah, NJ, Lawrence Erlbaum: 103-114.

Lewis, David, (1972), "Psychophysical and Theoretical Identifications," *Australasian Journal of Philosophy,* 50: 249–58.

Lewis, David (1978), "Truth in Fiction", *American Philosophical Quarterly,* 15: 37–46. (Reprinted in Lewis, David, *Philosophical Papers* (Vol. 1), Oxford University Press, 1983: 261–275)

Lewis, David (1994), "Reduction of Mind", in Guttenplan, Samuel (ed.), *A Companion to Philosophy of Mind,* Blackwell, Oxford: 412–31.

Liao, Shen-yi and Doggett, Tyler (2014), "The Imagination Box", *Journal of Philosophy,* 111, 5: 259-275.

Lyons, William (1980), *Emotions,* Cambridge University Press, Cambridge.

Lillard, Angeline S. (2002), "Pretend Play and Cognitive Development", in Goswami, U. (ed.), *Handbook of Cognitive Development*, Blackwell, London.

Lindeman, Marjaana, and Aarnio, Kia (2007), "Superstitious, magical, and paranormal beliefs: An integrative model", *Journal of Research in Personality*, 41: 731-744.

Linder, Darwyn, Cooper, Joel and Jones, Edward (1965), "Decision freedom as a determinant of the role of incentive magnitude in attitude change", *Journal of Personality and Social Psychology*, 6: 245-254.

Matravers, Derek (1997), "The Paradox of Fiction: The Report Versus the Perceptual Model", in Hjort, M., and Laver, S. (eds), *Emotion and the Arts*, Oxford University Press, Oxford: 78-92.

Matravers, Derek (2010), "Why we Should Give Up on the Imagination", *Midwest Studies in Philosophy*, 34, 1: 190–199.

McGrew, John and McFall, Richard (1990), "A Scientific Inquiry into the Validity of Astrology", *Journal of Scientific Exploration*, 4, 1: 75-83.

Moran, Richard, (1994), "The Expression of Feeling in Imagination", *The Philosophical Review*, 103, 1: 75-106.

Nemeroff, Carol and Rozin, Paul (2002), "The Makings of the Magical Mind", in Rosengren, Karl, Harris, Paul L., and Johnson, Carl, (eds.) (2000): 1-34.

Nichols, Shaun (2004), "Imagining and Believing: the Promise of a Single Code", *Journal of Aesthetics and Art Criticism*, Special issue on Art, Mind, and Cognitive Science, 62: 129-139.

Nichols, Shaun (2006), "Just the Imagination: Why Imagining Doesn't Behave Like Believing", *Mind & Language,* 21: 459-474.

Nichols, Shaun (eds.) (2006), *The Architecture of the Imagination: New Essays on Pretence, Possibility, and Fiction*, Oxford University Press, Oxford.

Nichols, Shaun, and Stich, Stephen (2000), "A Cognitive Theory of Pretense", *Cognition*, 74: 115-147.

Nisbett, Richard E., and Wilson, Timothy (1977), "On Saying More than We Can Know", *Psychological Review,* 84, 3: 231-259.

Noordhof, Paul (2001), "Believe what you want", *Proceedings of the Aristotelian Society,* 101: 247-265.

Nottelmann, Nikolaj (2013) (eds.), *New Essays on Belief. Constitution, Content* and *Structure,* Palgrave Macmillan, UK.

O'Brien, Lucy (2004), "Imagination and the Motivational View of Belief", *Analysis,* 65, 1: 55-62.

Owens, David J. (2003), "Does Belief Have an Aim?", *Philosophical Studies*, 115, 3: 283–305.

Peacocke, Christopher (1985), "Imagination, Experience, and Possibility", in Foster J. and Robinson, H. (eds.), *Essays on Berkeley: A Tercentennial Celebration*, Oxford University Press.

Perner, Joseph (1991), *Understanding the Representational Mind*, MIT Press, Cambridge MA.

Polger, Thomas W. (2006), *Natural Minds*, MIT Press, Cambridge, MA.

Radford, Colin (1975), "How Can We Be Moved by the Fate of Anna Karenina? *Proceedings of the Aristotelian Society*, Supplementary Volumes, 49: 67-93.

Ramsey, Frank P. (1926) "Truth and Probability", in Ramsey, Frank, *The Foundations of Mathematics and other Logical Essays*, edited by R.B. Braithwaite, London: Kegan, Paul, Trench, Trubner & Co: 156-198.

Ramsey, William, Stich, Stephen, and Garon, Joseph (1990), "Connectionism, Eliminativism and the Future of Folk Psychology", *Philosophical Perspectives*, 4: 499–533.

Ravenscroft, Ian (2005), *Philosophy of Mind. A Beginner's Guide*, Oxford University Press.

Rey, George (1988), "Towards a Computational Account of Akrasia and Self-deception", in *Perspectives on Self-deception*, University California Press, Berkeley: 265-296.

Rey, George (2009), "Meta-Atheism: Religious Avowals as Self-deceptions", long version on-line (an expansion of the version appeared in Martin, R., and Kolak, D. (eds.) (2006), *The Experience of Philosophy*, Oxford University Press).

Risen (2016), "Believing what we don't believe: acquiescing to superstitions & other powerful intuitions. Psychological Review 4:182–207.

Romdenh-Romluc, Komarine (2013), "Habit and attention", in Moran, D. and Jensen, J. (eds.) *The Phenomenology of Embodied Subjectivity*, Springer: 3-19.

Roozen, David A. (1980), "Church Dropouts: Changing Patterns of Disengagement and Re-Entry", *Review of Religious Research*, 21, 4: *Supplement: The Unchurched American: A Second Look:* 427-450.

Rosengren, Karl, Harris, Paul L., and Johnson, Carl, (eds.) (2000), *Imagining the Impossible*, Cambridge University Press, Cambridge MA.

Rozin, Paul, Millman, Linda, and Nemeroff, Carol (1986), "Operation of the laws of sympathetic magic in disgust and other domains", *Journal of Personality and Social Psychology*, 50, 4: 703-712.

Ryle, Gilber (1949), *The Concept of Mind*, Hutchinsons University Library, London.

Sauvayre, Romy (2011), "Le changement de croyances extremes: du cadre cognitif aux conflits de valeurs", *European Journal of Social Sciences*, 49: 61-82.

Schellenberg, Susanna (2013), "Belief and desire in Imagination and Immersion", *Journal of Philosophy*, 110, 9: 497-517.

Schroeder, Timothy and Matheson, Carl (2006), "Imagination and Emotion", in Nichols, Shaun (2006) (ed.): 19-40.

Schwitzgebel, Eric (2001), "In-between believing", in *Philosophical Quarterly*, 51: 76-82.

Schwitzgebel, Eric (2002), "A Phenomenal, Dispositional Account of Belief», *Nous*, 36: 249-275.

Schwitzgebel, Eric, "Belief", *The Stanford Encyclopedia of Philosophy* (Summer 2015 Edition), Edward N. Zalta (ed.), forthcoming URL = <http://plato.stanford.edu/archives/sum2015/entries/belief/>.

Schwitzgebel, Eric (2010), "Acting Contrary to Our Professed Beliefs, or the Gulf Between Occurrent Judgment and Dispositional Belief", *Pacific Philosophical Quarterly*, 91: 531-553.

Schwitzgebel, E. (2013), "A Dispositional Approach to Attitudes: Thinking Outside of the Belief Box" in Nottelmann, Nikolaj (2013) (eds.), *New Essays on Belief. Constitution, Content* and *Structure*, Palgrave Macmillan, UK: 75-99.

Searle, John (1983), *Intentionality: An Essay in the Philosophy of Mind*, Cambridge University Press, Cambridge.

Shah, Nishi and Velleman, J. David (2005), "Doxastic Deliberation", in *Philosophical Review*, 114, 4: 497-534.

Sinhababu, Neil (2012), "Distinguishing belief and imagination", *Pacific Philosophical Quarterly*, 94: 152–165.

Sinhababu, Neil (2016), "Imagination and Belief", in Kind, Amy (Eds.) *The Routledge Handbook of the Philosophy of Imagination*, Routledge.

Smith, Michael (1987), "The Humean Theory of Motivation", *Mind*, New Series, 96, 381: 36-61.

Smith, Michael (1994), *The Moral Problem*, Blackwell Publishing, USA.

Sperber, Dan (1996), *Explaining Culture*, Blackwell Publishing, Oxford.

Stalnaker, Robert (1980), *Inquiry*, MIT Press, Cambridge MA.

Steglich–Petersen, Asbjørn (2006), "No Norm Needed: On the Aim of Belief", *The Philosophical Quarterly*, 56, 225: 499–516.

Stich, Stephen (1991), "Do True Believers Exist?," *Aristotelian Society Supplement*, 65: 229–44.

Stich, Stephen(1996), *Deconstructing the Mind*, Oxford University Press, New York.

Stich, Stephen and Ravenscroft, Ian (1993), "What *is* Folk Psychology?" *Cognition*, 50: 447–68.

Sullivan-Bissett, Ema (2014), *Belief, Truth, and Biological Function*, Doctoral Dissertation, University of York.

Tagliafico, Daniela (2011), *Pretense. A Relativist Account*, Mimesis – Filosofie analitiche Labont.

Taylor, Shelley E. and Brown, Jonathan (1988), "Illusion and Well-Being: A Social Psychological Perspective on Mental Health", *Psychological Bulletin*, 103, 2: 193-210.

Todd R. K. and Bradley J. R. (2004), "The Self-serving Bias and Beliefs about Rationality", Economic *Inquiry*, Vol. 42, Issue 2, pp. 237–246.

Van Leeuwen, Neil (2009) "The Motivational Role of Belief", *Philosophical Papers*, 38, 2: 219-246.

Van Leeuwen, Neil (2011) "Imagination is where the Action is", *Journal of Philosophy*, 108, 2: 55-77.

Van Leeuwen, Neil (2014), "Religious Credence is Not Factual Belief", *Cognition*, 133, 3: 698-715.

Van Leeuwen, Neil (2017), "Do Religious Beliefs Respond to Evidence?", *Philosophical Explorations,* 20: 52-72.

Velleman, J. David, (2000), *The Possibility of Practical Reason*, Clarendon Press, Oxford.

Vrana, Scott.R. and Lang Peter.J. (1984), "Fear, imagery and the startle-probe reflex", *Journal of Abnormal Psychology*, 99: 179-195.

Vyse, Stuart (2014), *Believing in Magic. The Psychology of Superstition (Updated Edition),* Oxford University Press, Oxford.

Walton, Kendall L. (1978), "Fearing Fictions", *Journal of Philosophy*, 75,1: 5-27.

Walton, Kendall L. (1990), *Mimesis as Make-Believe. On the Foundations of Representational Arts,* Harvard University Press, Cambridge, MA.

Weinberg, Jonathan and Meskin, Aaron (2006), "Puzzling Over the Imagination: Philosophical Problems, Architectural Solutions," in Nichols (2006) (eds.): 175-202.

Williams, Bernard (1973), *Problems of the Self,* Cambridge University Press, Cambridge.

Wittgenstein, Ludwig (1967), "Remarks on Frazer's Golden Bough", *Synthese*, 17: 233-253.

Wood, Michael, Douglas, Karen and Sutton, Robbie (2012), "Dead and alive: Belief in Contradictory Conspiracy Theories", *Social Psychological and Personality Science,* 3: 767-773.

Wood, Michael, and Douglas, Karen (2013), "What about Building 7? A Social Psychological Study of Online Discussion of 9/11 Conspiracy Theories", *Frontiers In Psychology*, 4: 1-9.

Wolley, Jaqueline (2000), "The development of beliefs about direct mental-physical causality in imagination, magic and religion", in Rosengren, Karl, Harris, Paul L., and Johnson, Carl, (eds.) (2000): 99-129.

Wolley, Jaqueline. and Phelps, K. (2001), "The development of children's beliefs about prayer", *Journal of Cognition and Culture,* 1, 2: 139-167.

MIMESIS GROUP
www.mimesis-group.com

MIMESIS INTERNATIONAL
www.mimesisinternational.com
info@mimesisinternational.com

MIMESIS EDIZIONI
www.mimesisedizioni.it
mimesis@mimesisedizioni.it

ÉDITIONS MIMÉSIS
www.editionsmimesis.fr
info@editionsmimesis.fr

MIMESIS COMMUNICATION
www.mim-c.net

MIMESIS EU
www.mim-eu.com

Printed by
Geca Industrie Grafiche – San Giuliano Milanese (MI)
April 2020